The Economics of Illegal Immigration

The Economics of Illegal Immigration

By Chisato Yoshida and Alan D. Woodland

First published 2005 by
PALGRAVE MACMILLAN
Houndmills, Basingstoke, Hampshire RG21 6XS and
175 Fifth Avenue, New York, N.Y. 10010
Companies and representatives throughout the world

PALGRAVE MACMILLAN is the global academic imprint of the Palgrave Macmillan division of St. Martin's Press, LLC and of Palgrave Macmillan Ltd. Macmillan® is a registered trademark in the United States, United Kingdom and other countries. Palgrave is a registered trademark in the European Union and other countries.

ISBN-13: 978–1–4039–2075–1 hardback
ISBN-10: 1–4039–2075–3 hardback

This book is printed on paper suitable for recycling and made from fully managed and sustained forest sources.

A catalogue record for this book is available from the British Library.

Library of Congress Cataloging-in-Publication Data

Yoshida, Chisato.
  The economics of illegal immigration / by Chisato Yoshida and Alan D. Woodland.
    p. cm.
  Includes bibliographical references and index.
  ISBN 1–4039–2075–3 (cloth)
    1. Emigration and immigration–Economic aspects. 2. Illegal aliens–Economic aspects. 3. Alien labor. I. Woodland, A. D. II. Title.
  JV6217.Y667 2005
  331.6′21724–dc22   2005045257

10   9   8   7   6   5   4   3   2   1
14   13   12   11   10   09   08   07   06   05

Printed and bound in Great Britain by
Antony Rowe Ltd, Chippenham and Eastbourne

Contents

Foreword

The recent globalization of national economies has led to a rapid increase in the international mobility of goods, capital, information and labor. We observe many labor movements from less developed countries, such as those in Southeast Asia and South-America, to developed countries, such as those in Europe, North America and Japan. These international labor movements are often motivated by the large wage differentials between these countries.

This international labor mobility leads to serious problems associated with illegal employment of foreign migrants in labor-importing countries, which are usually the developed countries. Foreign migrants often work illegally as unskilled workers in the host country's firms by *legally* entering the host country with a short-term sightseeing or training visa, and then illegally over-staying their time in the host country.

In addition, there are many illegal foreign workers in developed countries who have *illegally* migrated to the host country and work illegally in the host country's firms. For example, there has been a recent increase in the number of illegal Mexican migrants to the United States (US). These illegal Mexican migrants are called "wet backs" in the US. Their name derives from the anecdote that their backs get wet when they illegally migrate from Mexico to the US by swimming across the river Rio Grande at the border between the two countries (Borjas (1990)).

The governments of developed countries deal with the problem of illegal foreign workers mainly by using the following two enforcement tools: border patrol and internal enforcement. Border patrol involves the prevention of attempted illegal migration at the border. Internal enforcement involves catching foreign workers who are working illegally in domestic firms, a process sometimes called employer sanctions.

Ethier (1986a) broke new ground by analyzing the effects of border and internal enforcement policies in a one-country model using a crime-theoretic analysis (Becker (1968)). In his model, Ethier examined how a small country could use domestic border control and internal enforcement policies to achieve domestic policy objectives regarding illegal immigration and income distribution.

Bond and Chen (1987) extended the Ethier model by constructing a standard, two-country, one-good, two-factor model. In their paper, they analyzed the effect of interior inspections by the host country's government on the host country's welfare. They showed that imposition of the enforcement policy by the labor-importing country's government might or might not improve the host country's welfare.

However, Bond and Chen (1987) did not examine the effects of the enforcement policy on the welfare of the foreign (labor-exporting) country or on global welfare, which, in a two-country model, is composed of the sum of the welfare of the host country and the welfare of the foreign country. Moreover, they did not examine any welfare effects in the presence of international capital mobility.

These earlier studies of illegal immigration analyzed only the effects of the host country's enforcement policies on the host country's welfare. In this book, we use the model developed by Bond and Chen (1987) to examine the effects of enforcement on the welfare of both the host country and the foreign country, as well as examining the effects of enforcement on global welfare.

We also extend the Bond and Chen model using a Cobb-Douglas production function. We examine the costs and benefits of the internal enforcement policy, regardless of whether or not the necessary conditions obtained from Bond and Chen (1987) can be implemented. We consider the case where capital is immobile between countries, as well as the case in which capital is allowed to be mobile between the two countries. We explore whether or not we can feasibly meet the necessary conditions for the optimal enforcement level to be positive.

Bucci and Tenorio (1996) already introduced a government budget constraint into a one-small-country model on illegal immigration, and examined the effects of financing the internal enforcement on the host country's welfare. We extend their model by introducing a budget constraint on the host country's government, following the Bucci and Tenorio model. Put another way, we incorporate this finance constraint imposed on the enforcement into the above model.

This book is divided into three parts. Using the Bond and Chen model, the first part analyzes the welfare effects of border and internal enforcement, as outlined above. We consider whether an internal enforcement policy by the host country's government can be *a Pareto-improving policy* in the sense of increasing both countries' welfare simultaneously. In short, we assess the policy in terms of global welfare. The second part extends the Bond and Chen model utilizing a Cobb-Douglas production function. We investigate whether or not there is an optimal level of the internal enforcement in view of the host country's welfare. We discovered the optimal level of the enforcement. Hence, we know how an immigration bureau in the labor-receiving country can optimally put the immigration policy into effect. The main aim of the book is to offer necessary information for the immigration authority to optimally carry out the internal enforcement.

As supplements, in Chapters 8, 9 and 10 in the third part, we add analyses of the welfare effects of a profit-sharing scheme. In the Chapters 8 and 9, we use the standard (two-country, one good, two-factor) model as introduced in Part I, and examine whether or not the profit-sharing scheme by the host country's government is justified from the viewpoint of global welfare. We also focus on large-scale unemployment within an urban area in a less developed country (LDC). Chapter 10 develops a generalized Harris and Todaro (1970) model in which a profit-sharing scheme is put into force in the urban sector, and explores the effects of the policy on the urban unemployment and the LDC's welfare.

This book was initiated while Yoshida visited the University of Sydney, Sydney, Australia during the period June 2000 – May 2001. Yoshida gratefully acknowledges the hospitality of the University of Sydney during his visit, and financial support provided by a Grant-in-Aid for Scientific Research (No.16530120) and the Japan Economic Research Foundation. Woodland gratefully acknowledges the financial support of the Australian Research Council.

List of Tables

List of Figure and Maps

Figure

Maps

1
Introduction

1.1 Introduction

The Schengen Agreement, named after the Luxembourg village where it was signed, was enacted in 1985 and assured the *free circulation of goods and persons* within the European Economic Community, now the European Union (EU). The Dublin Convention of 1990 supplemented the Schengen Agreement. It clarified which EU country is responsible for handling requests for asylum and refugee status, and was also designed to curtail people from "shopping around" in Europe for the best refugee "deal" (Vianna (1996), Birchard (1997)).

The Schengen Agreement yielded the benefit that most Europeans are in a "swift morsel". The agreement became effective in March 1995 but took a year to be fully executed and currently applies to the Benelux trio, Germany, France, Spain and Portugal. Most other EU countries also wish to be party to the agreement as soon as the paperwork allows.[1] Italy, for example, has signed the Schengen Agreement but cannot put it into force until its borders are less porous to *illegal immigrants*. Norway and Iceland, both outside the EU but sharing a passport union with insiders Denmark, Sweden and Finland, have also asked to join the agreement. Inside Schengen-land, travelers do not need to show their passports when crossing a national border (Perlmutter (1996), The Economist (24 August, 1996), European Report (28 July, 1999), The Economist (14 August, 1999), Zhan (1999)).

International crime, terrorism, drugs and *illegal immigration*, however, have reduced some of the early enthusiasm for the agreement. The new lack of restrictions induces qualms also. France, for instance, still regularly checks passage on its northern frontier with Belgium owing to concerns regarding drugs coming from the Netherlands. Border police

1

check passengers arriving at German airports from "sensitive" areas exterior to the EU twice: once as they get off their flight and a second time inside the terminal, since Schengenites have required that the exclusion of internal frontier controls be compensated by stricter inspection of tourists arriving from outside the signatory states (The Economist (24 August, 1996), European Report (28 July, 1999)).

As shown in European Report (28 July, 1999), The Economist (24 August, 1996), it is known that:

> Random police securities on tourists away from frontiers have augmented witness the gendarmes at tollgates on French expressways. Such securities are made easier by the fact that Schengen countries obligate their citizens to carry identity cards. A computerized system allows police forces to interchange information on the movement of criminals, terrorists and *illegal immigrants*. The names of people refused a visa by one country are circulated to the others, lest they apply somewhere else. The agreement provides for the revocation of securities on individuals at internal borders, with accompanying measures to guarantee the security of the citizens of signatory states. This includes checks at external borders, visas and restrictions on the freedom of movement of third-country citizens, measures to combat *illegal immigration*, police cooperation, mutual assistance in criminal matters, measures to combat drugs, and an information exchange system, SIS, notably on people refused entry.

The North American Free Trade Agreement (NAFTA) between the US, Canada and Mexico was ratified on 12 August, 1992. It provides a plan for free trade within these three North American countries, which over fifteen years will gradually eliminate tariffs and stimulate trade and investment. In terms of total population, this agreement created the world's largest common market, with 390 million people (Gianaris (1998)). NAFTA was put into effect in 1994. The agreement was expected to accelerate capital exports from the US to Mexico and therefore to expedite economic growth in Mexico (Yoshida (1999)).

The establishment of assembly plants known as *maquiladoras*, located mainly in cities near Mexico's northern border, began in 1965 under the Border Industrialization Program (BIP) established by Mexico's government. Under the BIP the Mexican federal government enacted a plan to permit wholly owned subsidiaries of foreign companies to operate in Mexico (Arreola and Curtis (1993)). Joining firms were given reductions in the duties charged for assembled products under items 806.30 and

807.00 of the Tariff Schedule of the US, whereby only value-added taxes based principally on cheap labor and small overheads were apportioned to materials that were exported and then imported back into the US (Arreola and Curtis (1993), Gianaris (1998), Thelen (1999)).

Since the 1970s, maquiladoras have become an industry that is important on any scale. Most plants are direct subsidiaries of US corporations, and some are locally owned subcontractors.[2] Many Japanese and Korean firms have also made inroads into the area by establishing their own assembly plants. Typical maquiladora industries are electrical parts and electronics, auto parts, and clothing manufacturers. In maquiladoras, parts and items are assembled by low-wage Mexicans, usually using fairly simple manual or machine processes. The inputs are purchased outside Mexico, and the final goods are exported and consumed outside Mexico (Thelen (1999)). The purpose of maquiladoras is to obtain inexpensive assembly (Heyman (1991)). It has indeed given US and Canadian industries more competition, by utilizing low-wage Mexican labor, advanced US technology and rich Canadian resources.

Mexico has experienced a jump in exports with NAFTA's trade liberalization. We know from Global Finance (November 1996) that the maquiladora program has also brought prosperity to Mexico:

> The country's export boom has not evaporated, says Hector Chavez, an economist in the Mexico City office of Santander Investment. It has decelerated. Exports this year should hit record highs. Chavez argues that the peso's value has not affected exports, but that it has stimulated imports. Indeed, this year imports have grown 21 percent in the first nine months, to $64 billion, with the bulk of the influx feeding the maquiladora facilities on the US border. At the same time, exports have remained strong, climbing 19 percent after last year's surge, hitting a record $69.7 billion in the first nine months of 1996. One big contributor to exports is Pemex, which, with higher crude prices, has racked up some $7.6 billion in international sales this year.

> We estimate that this year's trade surplus will be $6.6 billion, slightly below last year's, says Chavez. It also looks like a fair number of companies are now reaching near-full capacity as they maintain their export market shares and are increasing production for the preferred higher-margin domestic market. Next year could be an expansion year for some.

Economic growth in Mexico due to the free-trade policy was expected to reduce illegal immigration from Mexico to the US. However, there has still been an increase in the number of illegal Mexicans migrating to the US. Markusen and Zahnisher (1999) used empirically plausible and relevant trade models to demonstrate that NAFTA is unlikely to induce Mexicans to cease migration to the US, since the wages of unskilled Mexican workers are likely to remain low compared with their potential wages as legal or illegal immigrants to the US. Illegal Mexican migrants are often called "wet backs" in the US, a name derived from the anecdote that their backs get wet when swimming across the Rio Grande, the border between the two countries, when illegally migrating from Mexico to the US (Borjas (1990)).

While the US-Canada border is longer, it is Mexico's border with the US that is the true frontier – a no man's land of desert, mountains and scrappy urban settlements. Today many of the migrants who once clustered at the border hoping to cross illegally into the US have found what has long been an anomaly: a Mexican job. For the able-bodied, there is often work to be had. However, wages remain about one-eighth of those paid across the mountains or desert to the north. Yet even as NAFTA has, in a commercial sense, made the frontier be-tween the two countries more permeable than ever, the US Border Pa-trol has reinforced its efforts to ensure that *only Mexico's products and not its people – find their way into the United States.* In urban areas like Tijuana, gray steel walls now bisect the horizon – an American version of the Great Wall of China. In more distant locations, border agents use sophisticated technology developed for the military – from infrared night-vision goggles to motion sensors embedded in the ground – to detect would-be immigrants. For many of those who do manage to find a way into the US, life is, at best, only marginally better. Wages are higher, but *illegal immigrants* live in perpetual fear of detection and banishment. To minimize their need to move about, the migrants who reap crops in Southern California build primitive huts near the fields where they work. Lacking cooking or sanitary facilities and, in many cases, even fresh water, these immigrants regularly suffer malnutrition and other health problems. They buy their food from vendors who drive trucks to their hideouts. These same vendors arrange to send the immigrants' meager savings to their families in Mexico. Clearly, the real border that separates impoverished Mexicans from their wealthier neighbors in the US is not a line etched in the desert sand – it is the invisible but impenetrable gulf that separates those whose basic daily needs are met without much thought or effort from those for whom daily existence remains a constant struggle to survive (Salgado (1998)).[3]

Although the huge numbers of illegal aliens from Mexico are supposed to increase unemployment among US workers, Dorantes and Huang (1997) showed that immigrants from Mexico are complements to US workers in the aggregate production process. This implies that job replacement in US labor markets caused by large inflows of Mexican immigrants will be minimal (cf. Harper (1995)). Winegarden and Khor (1993), using an econometric model of income inequality in US native-born households, showed that the growing presence of deportable immigrants has increased income inequality in the native-born population, though the impact has been small. Bean, Frisbie, Tells and Lowell (1992) and Greenwood and Hunt (1995) had similar findings. Furthermore, Bean, Lowell and Taylor (1988) examined the impact of illegal Mexican aliens on the incomes of other workers in the Southwest US. They concluded that the inflow of illegal Mexican migrant workers caused the earnings of other groups to increase slightly, but that the effects on legal immigrants were small and negative. This means that jobs held by illegal Mexican immigrants complement those of other workers (Borjas (1986a)).

Considering the market unifications within the EU and North America, detailed above, it is clear that while free movement of goods within markets is permitted, this does not necessarily hold true for labor. The disparities that exist in both wages and employment opportunities between rich and poor countries inside the common markets have, however, caused a mass influx of the poorer countries' residents into the wealthier countries.

The *legal* flow of foreign migrants has recently faced restriction by the immigration authorities of host countries, which has caused illegal immigration from the poorer, less developed countries to the wealthier, developed countries. Illegal immigration is usually considered a problem of the host or labor importing country. An illegal immigrant is often defined as a person dwelling in a country with no official residence permit (Staring (2000)).

In response to the rapid increase in illegal immigration, the US Congress passed the Simpson-Rodino law, known as the Immigration Reform and Control Act (IRCA), in 1986. IRCA provisions provided three fundamental components to reduce illegal immigration to the US: (1) employer sanctions for knowingly hiring undocumented aliens (illegal immigrants and legal migrants lacking work authorization); (2) an amnesty program for long-time resident illegal immigrants; (3) increased resources for border patrol (Gimpel and Edwards Jr. (1999)).

Numerous studies have examined the effects of intensified IRCA on the US labor market. We know that tougher immigration controls generally cause the wages of US unskilled workers to increase and those of US skilled workers and the rental prices of US capital to decrease (Bond and Chen (1987), Djajic (1997), Yoshida (2000b)). These phenomena occur mainly because we usually assume that in the US labor market, foreign (Mexican) illegal workers are substitutes for US unskilled workers, whereas illegal workers are complements to US skilled workers. However, Phillips and Massey (1999) concluded that IRCA appears to have helped create an underground labor market in the US, and is unlikely to have deterred illegal migration from Mexico to the US. We can only surmise that IRCA has reduced the wages of both illegal Mexicans and unskilled Americans who compete in the US unskilled labor market. Moreover, IRCA's legalization program promoted the participation of authorized immigrants in the US unskilled labor market, which seems to have contributed to depressing the wages of unskilled workers. Studies on the impact of IRCA have not yet identified the reasons for this change.

We present some important topics related to the impact of illegal immigration on host countries, especially the US and member states of the EU, which have always faced the problem of massive illegal immigration from neighboring countries. Section 1.2 overviews the definition of illegal immigration. Section 1.3 introduces the changes in US immigration laws and policies after 1980. In Section 1.4, we present immigration policy in EU. In Section 1.5, we survey the literature on the effects of illegal immigration or immigration law on US society. In Section 1.6, we outline theoretical analyses in relation to the effects of undocumented aliens or immigration controls on the US or EU economy. In the final section, we briefly illustrate sequent chapters.

1.2 Illegal immigration: An overview

Since the 1980's there has been an increasing number of incentives for international migration, with still greater incentives expected in the future.[4] In many poor countries population growth exceeds the pace of employment creation. Internal disturbances caused by political, ethnic and religious frictions reduce many residents to refugee status, who then take shelter in safer and more prosperous countries. The extreme per-capita income gap between developed and less developed countries also induces large-scale migration. In addition, technological improvements in transportation and communications between countries that have created global goods and services markets and have urged tax avoidance and evasion reduce the costs of international migration, thereby encouraging international labor flows. These factors have caused undocumented illegal immigration from poor countries to wealthier, developed countries (see Kudrle (2003)).

However, the aforementioned external and internal factors stimulating migration are not sufficient to explain recent migration flows. Baldacci, Inglese and Strozza (1999) pointed out some other factors:

(a) illegal immigration is highly correlated with total immigration;
(b) in new immigrant-receiving countries, like Italy since the end of the 1970s, the informal sector of the economy has been swiftly developed;
(c) labor market segmentation within a local area and at a production level can engender imbalances between demand and supply for labor, which differ among regions.

The US government classifies illegal entrants under two categories. The first category includes persons who enter the country without any kind of legal visa (called "EWIs" since they "enter without inspection"). The second category includes persons who enter with legal visas (tourists and students, for example), but who then stay beyond the permitted time limit (called "visa overstayers" or "visa-abusers"). Most EWIs in the US are from Mexico, and most visa overstayers are from non-Mexican countries (see Bean, Edmonston and Passel (1990)). First-time Mexican migrants into the US often obtain assistance from US-based relatives and friends, and/or buy services from a "coyote" (a professional people-smuggler) in finding housing and employment (Cornelius (1989)).

Undocumented workers in the US are usually divided into three categories: "settlers", "sojourners" and "commuters". Settlers are those migrants who intend to stay permanently in the host country. Sojourners are those who intend to return to their country of origin after a prolonged stay. Commuters are those who do not actually live in the country, but rather cross the border between the host country and their native country to work illegally during the daytime in the host country (see Bean, Edmonston and Passel (1990)).

It is generally accepted, assuming that apprehensions are proportional to crossings, that the number of apprehensions by the US Border Patrol on the US-Mexico border is highly sensitive to the prevailing economic conditions in both countries. Fewer illegal aliens are apprehended when the Mexican economy is relatively robust. When the wage level in Mexico rises or the unemployment rate in Mexico drops, the number of apprehensions drops, as fewer Mexicans attempt to enter the US illegally.[5] On the other hand, the number of apprehensions of illegal Mexican immigrants by the US Border Patrol is higher in the month following a large devaluation of the peso, when the Mexican real wage drops, or when average weekly hours worked in US non-agricultural industries rise (Hanson and Spilimbergo (1996)). When the US economy improves, the number of apprehensions rises, implying that increases in the US wage level and decreases in the US unemployment rate cause the number of deportable aliens apprehended to increase. Furthermore, more illegal workers are apprehended when conditions in the US agriculture sector improve relative to those in Mexico, because the flow of farm workers depends upon the relative prosperity of the agricultural sector in the two countries.[6] Moreover, Hanson and Spilimbergo (1999) have stated: Mexican attempted illegal immigration into the US is highly sensitive to transitions in Mexican wages, which is derived from the fact that the elasticity of border apprehensions with regard to Mexican real wage is -0.64 to -0.86. The elasticity of border captures in regard to border interdiction is positive, and hence there may be increasing returns to scale in border patrol. We observe from those contributions on illegal immigration between US and Mexico that a reduction in a disparity in wage between the two economies forces undocumented immigration to reduce (see Hanson and Spilimbergo (p.1354-1355, (1999)).

It is difficult to obtain a precise estimate of the levels of current and anticipated immigration due to the above-mentioned factors. Host countries have been reluctant to receive all such immigrants.[7] Unauthorized migration to industrialized countries has rapidly increased, owing to a combination of restrictive immigration policies and expanding migratory pressures.[8] For example, the number of undocumented immigrants in the US was an estimated 3,158,000 in June 1986, of which 2,195,000 were from Mexico (see Woodrow (1990)). As of 1993, the total population of undocumented aliens residing in the US was an estimated 3,400,000, a slight increase on the 1986 figures (see Espenshade (1994)). The population of undocumented immigrants residing in the US in October 1996 was about 5.0 million, with a range of about 4.6 to 5.4 million. Of this group, 2.7 million or 54 percent were from Mexico (US Immigration and Naturalization Service (hereafter INS) (1997)). The estimated 7 million unauthorized immigrants who were living in the United States in 2000 constituted 2.5 percent of the total US population of just over 281 million (see Table 1.1).[9]

Table 1.1 Estimates of the unauthorized resident population in the top 15 countries of origin and states of residence: January 1990 and 2000 (thousands) (Source: US Department of Homeland Security (2003))

Country of origin	Population 2000	Population 1990	State of residence	Population 2000	Population 1990
All countries	7000	3500	All states	7000	3500
Mexico	4808	2040	California	2209	1476
El Salvador	189	298	Texas	1041	438
Guatemala	144	118	New York	489	357
Colombia	141	51	Illinois	432	194
Honduras*	138	42	Florida	337	239
China	115	70	Arizona	283	88
Ecuador	108	37	Georgia	228	34
Dominican Republic	91	46	New Jersey	221	95
Philippines	85	70	North Carolina	206	26
Brazil	77	20	Colorado	144	31
Haiti	76	67	Washington	136	39
India	70	28	Virginia	103	48
Peru	61	27	Nevada	101	27
Korea	55	24	Oregon	90	26
Canada	47	25	Massachusetts	87	53
Other	795	537	Other	892	328

* The estimate for 2000 includes 105,000 Hondurans who were granted temporary protected status in December 1998.

The number of illegal residents living in US in January 2000 was twice that in 1990. There were about 4.5 million unlawful residents in five states with the largest irregular resident populations in January 2000 – California, Texas, New York, Illinois and Florida. California had an illegal resident population of about 2.2 million or nearly 32 percent of the total in January 2000. The state of Texas had the second largest number of illegal residents in US – more than one million. Table 1.1 shows top 15 states with respect to illegal resident populations within US.

Table 1.1 also presents estimated populations of illegal residents by country of origin. Mexico has been the greatest source country of illegal immigration to US in the 1900s. The estimated number of illegal resident inhabitants was about 2.0 million in January 1990, while that rose to 4.8 million in January 2000. Mexico amounted to roughly 69 percent of the whole of illegal resident population in January 2000. The top 15 countries of source accounted for 89 percent of the whole.

The INS reported that the number of apprehensions in the US interior was 88,752 during 1996 (US INS (1997)). This implies that illegal aliens already established in the US faced a one to two percent probability of being arrested. It is certain that employer sanctions have not been as effective as the US Congress expected when these sanctions were enacted in 1986. Simpson (1998) claimed that he believed 'the problem lies not with the statute, but with the administration and enforcement of the law'. He also suggested that the INS place a much higher priority on the enforcement of employer sanctions, that the US Labor Department have a role in the identification and charging of violators, and that US prosecutors levy heavy penalties, especially upon employers who are repeat offenders.

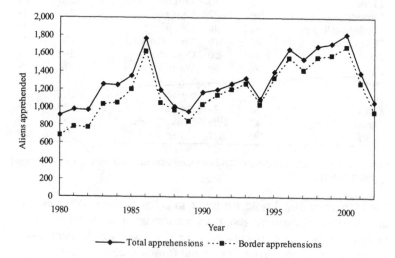

Figure 1.1   Illegal aliens apprehended, 1980-2002 (in thousands)

(Source: US Department of Homeland Security (2003))

We indicate time series data of total and border apprehensions of illegal immigration in Figure 1.1. Border apprehensions in the southwest in fiscal year 1986 were the highest in the 1980s. The apprehensions then decreased in consecutive years in no time after enactment of the IRCA of 1986. This law changed the status of unauthorized residents to be legal, laid down sanctions against employers who hire irregular aliens, and approved a rise in the budget of border patrol (cf. Section 1.3 US immigration laws & policies). The number of apprehensions declined to 852,506 in 1989 and then began increasing. Some major INS operations have the purpose of which is to deploy agents nearby the frontier to deter illegal entry. Operation Hold-the-Line was first executed in El Paso in September 1993, and consequently Operation Gatekeeper was initiated in San Diego in October 1994. The latter operation caused the number of apprehensions in El Centro, CA and Tucson, AZ, the sectors east of San Diego to increase. Both Tucson and El Centro had then fewer apprehensions between 2000 and 2002 than San Diego and El Paso. Apprehensions in McAllen exceeded those in El Paso following Operation Hold-the-Line in 1994, and thereby the INS newly began Operation Rio Grande in McAllen in August 1997. As a result, El Paso is again a leading sector in the number of apprehensions along the Texas-Mexico boundary.[10] It is well known that Mexican would-be illegal migrants find it easy to illegally cross the border between US and Mexico every mid-night when US border agents change shift. They will hereafter continue to illegally migrate into US in order to earn a salary about five times as much as that they do in Mexico and support their family dwelling in their native country, Mexico. Once the migrants safely cross the border, the immigration bureau may experience difficulty in finding them in the US. This evidence may be reliable, since Figure 1.1 shows that the probability of the detection of the unauthorized migrants within US each year after 1990 is approximately 2-3 % on average.

We turn to some relevant topics on illegal immigration in European countries. It is known from the estimation of the European Commission that there are nearly 3 million undocumented immigrants in the 15-nation EU. Many migrants are usually washed up on Spanish and Italian beaches, delivered by gangs on rachitic boats. A Moroccan immigrants' rights group in Spain, ATIME, estimated in 2002 that about 4,000 people had drowned since 1997 in the Strait of Gibraltar and in the Atlantic between Africa and the Canary Islands (BBC News (28 January, 2003)).

Europeans' attention has been paid to immigration, most notably the incident in June 2001 in which 58 Chinese died while attempting to cross the English Channel and get into England inside an airtight lorry container (CNN News (8 February, 2001)). Once the illegal migrants enter a destination country, they are seldom found by police or an immigration department. For example, BBC News (27 February, 2003) broadcast the following incident:

A search has begun for four suspected illegal immigrants on the run in the south west of Scotland. Police said the suspects are not thought to pose a danger to the public. The three men and a women are thought to be of Romanian or other Eastern European origin. They fled into woodland in the early hours of Thursday morning after their car was stopped by police. The suspected illegal immigrants made off after their car was pulled over on the A75 euro route near Newton Stewart, Dumfries and Galloway. Officers on foot and dog handlers have been scouring the countryside but so far without success. Police have refused to confirm reports that the four arrived in the region off a ferry from Northern Ireland. An appeal has being made to the public to report anyone sightings of the suspects.

The illegal migrants who have succeeded in getting into a host country usually work in the industries of service, construction et cetera. As shown on the BBC News (26 February, 2003), 28 irregular workers who are car-wash staff were arrested after immigration officials raided two car washes in Leeds, UK. Immigration Service has announced four of these workers are facing deportation, and a further 15 workers detained had applications for asylum pending. We know from the *Sydney Morning Herald* (10 March, 2003) that there are a lot of asylum seekers in Britain whose number is a record 110,000 in the past year. Referring to the newspaper, the plans of the government of the UK are described as follows:

New plans to curb the inflow of economic migrants require that all asylum seekers arriving in Britain be sent to Albania, the poorest country in Europe. Under the scheme, Albania will house the refugees in specially built detention centres while their claims are processed. Although the Home Office hopes to build the camps in conjunction with other European Union nations, ministers are determined to press ahead alone, if they have to. The plan could also help to stem the tide of asylum seekers and illegal immigrants into Britain from Albania, which is now notorious for organised criminals dealing in drugs and people-smuggling. There were officially 1065 asylum cases from Albania in 2001, but many more are thought to have gone undetected as Albanians often pretend to be from other eastern European countries on arrival.

Before and during the war in Iraq, a lot of Iraqis have escaped to outlying countries. However, Denmark, Norway, Sweden and Britain have frozen decisions on Iraqi asylum claims, and in the United States tough new security measures – named "Operation Liberty Shield" – allows for the detention of asylum seekers from Iraq and at least 33 other countries, human rights group Amnesty International said (CNN News (29 March, 2003)).

The Iraq war has caused a swift increase in asylum seekers who enter the UK from Iraq. However, the government of UK has not agreed to the claims of Iraqis seeking asylum in the UK until the situation in the Gulf becomes clearer (BBC News (24 March, 2003)). Earlier in 2003, Prime Minister Tony Blair said the numbers of people arriving in the UK to claim asylum should halve by September of this year. Moreover, this British plan to deport asylum seekers to special centres outside Europe has received "substantial support" from EU ministers, Home Secretary David Blunkett said (BBC News (28 March, 2003)).

In Japan, the Legal Affairs Bureau confirmed that the number of illegal aliens in Japan in January 2002 was 224,067. In 2001 the Ministry of Justice announced that the number of foreign workers employed in Japan, including foreign workers of Japanese descent and part-time workers on foreign student visas, was 735,960. It is generally accepted that it is difficult to estimate the number of clandestine foreign workers in Japan. These figures are quite important. Illegal foreign residents in Japan may encourage further illegal immigration, both by assisting and encouraging illegal immigration and illegal job acquisition, and by sheltering newcomers. Furthermore, current illegal residents can share information and skills with would-be illegal migrants, to help them to reduce the likelihood of exposure by government enforcement schemes.

Illegal foreign workers usually get jobs under working conditions that are hard, grubby, and risky, and which do not comply with labor legislation. They cannot belong to unions and cannot access social security or legal protection.[11] The inflow of unauthorized foreign labor implies an increase in the supply of labor in the host country, and therefore the wages of the host country's low-skilled workers decrease in the long run (see Greenwood, Hunt and Kohli (1997)). These workers take jobs at wage levels that host country workers will not accept. This implies that they may displace unskilled native-born workers in the short run, causing serious national unemployment problems (see Greenwood, Hunt and Kohli (1997)).[12] Some analysts argue that in the absence of illegal workers many low-wage industries in the US that hire such workers would be forced to shut down and/or relocate abroad, due to the high domestic labor costs of legal workers. Consequently, the employment opportunities for legal domestic workers would be reduced (cf. Sehgal and Vialet (1980) and Piore (1986)). The effect of immigration on the host country's workers remains a controversial issue.

Unauthorized illegal foreign workers make up the bottom of the social pyramid. They often find employment in the construction industry and in service industries, for example, in hotel work, gardening, nursery work, maintenance, dishwashing, cooking, bussing tables, gas stations, car-wash work, and the entertainment and amusement trades, including bars, restaurants, and mahjong parlors (cf. Chavez (1992)).[13]

The underground economy inhabited by clandestine foreign workers has expanded in developed countries. There are several reasons for this. Firstly, employers can avoid paying withholding taxes by hiring illegal labor.[14] Secondly, employers can impose piece-rate payment upon illegal workers since there are no trade unions or labor legislation to protect them.[15] As mentioned above, illegal workers find employment in low-wage or high-risk labor-intensive industries. This implies that those sectors cannot make the best use of scale economies and the demand for employment fluctuates. It is easy to understand in such circumstances why several major service industries are willing to hire illegal foreign workers.[16]

1.3 US immigration laws & policies

We illustrate the changes to US immigration laws enacted by the US Congress after 1980, explaining their background and rationale. The US Congress passed Immigration Reform and Control Act (IRCA) in 1986, which was touted as the be-all remedy for illegal immigration. The aim of this law was to reduce undocumented migration from Mexico through the use of four tools: (1) penalties against employers who knowingly hired unlawful immigrants, i.e., employer sanctions; (2) additional expenditure on the US Border Patrol to prevent possible migrants from illegally crossing the frontier between the US and Mexico; (3) amnesty for current undocumented immigrants, authorizing them to receive permanent residence in the US after January 1, 1982 (the Legally Authorized Worker program); and (4) a special legalization program offered to undocumented agricultural workers (known as the Special Agricultural Worker program, SAW) to conciliate growers in Texas and California and earn their support (US Congress (1986), Calavita (1998), Durand, Massey and Parrado (1999), Phillips and Massey (1999)).

O'Meara (1999) has observed:

> The concern for illegal migrants does not make a great deal of sense, given the opportunities available for legal immigration. The United States allows more legal immigration than all other countries in the world combined, but still suffers a minimum of one million illegal aliens residing and working in the United States during any given year.

Representative Lamar Smith of Texas, chairman of the Judiciary Sub-committee on Immigration and Claims, is intimately aware of the problem.

With the problem of illegal immigration having been addressed by IRCA, the attention of policy makers turned to reforming policies regarding legal immigration. The US Congress passed the Immigration Act of 1990, which increased occupation-based admissions from 54,000 to 140,000 a year. It also placed a ceiling of 10,000 on unskilled workers within these occupation-based admissions, and imposed an education requirement on a lottery program increasing admissions from countries "adversely affected" by the Immigration and Nationality Act Amendments of 1965. These and other reforms were not sufficient, however, to alter the essentially family-based nature of US immigration (Lowell (1996)).

We know the following facts from Calavita (1998). The debate on recent immigration reforms forced Congress to incorporate three fundamental factors into the Act. First is a reflection of restructuring within the US economy, such as the decline in the proportion of the workforce in the manufacturing sector and the increase in the proportion in the service sector. Related to this shift is the concern that the US workforce can supply neither the highly skilled technicians and professionals required in the new service sector, nor the large number of entry-level workers that this sector depends upon. Second, while in the past the majority of legal immigrants to the US have settled in urban areas in the Northwest corridor, it is precisely these locations that have been hardest hit by the shift to a service-oriented economy, and by the loss of manufacturing jobs in these locations as global competition has sent such employers overseas in search of cheaper labor. Third, there has been a steady decline in US fertility rates, such that immigration now accounts for a substantial portion (30 percent) of population growth in the US and provides over 33 percent of new workforce entrants. Within the context of these factors, the Congressional debate focused on how to provide workers for the US economy to enhance its global competitiveness, without jeopardizing the interests of US workers by displacement, wage depression, or debilitating bargaining positions.

Briggs (1991) pointed out some modifications of, and problems with, the Immigration Act of 1990:

Labor shortage in the service sector should be viewed as an opportunity to educate youth, re-train adults, eliminate discriminatory barriers, and introduce voluntary relocation programs to assist would-be workers to move from labor-surplus to labor-shortage areas. The national priority must always be to prepare citizen workers for jobs in the expanding employment areas of the US economy, e.g., the service sector. To respond to labor shortages by immediately using immigration policy to fill jobs in an economy that is not at full employment is analogous to proposing to take a shortcut through quicksand. Immigrants can fill the jobs, but the social costs to the nation are a loss of opportunities for citizens, with all of the attendant social and human costs.

In a dynamic industrialized economy, such as that of the US, employment shortages for qualified workers should be expected to occur from time to time. These shortages cannot always be overcome simply by raising wages. In most cases the shortages can be expected to occur in situations that require extensive educational and training preparation. In the long run, the nation's human resource strategy should also be to prepare citizens for these jobs. Hence, the actual number of work-related visas granted each year should be flexible, and that number should include the option of being anywhere from zero to the politically set ceiling (e.g., 140,000 under the new law). As presently designed, the new law – with its fixed annual infusion of work-related immigrants – can be expected to dampen market pressures that are desperately needed to improve the nation's human resource development system.

In 1996, 10 years after the enactment of IRCA, Congress took giant steps to try to correct its flaws. The Illegal Immigration Reform and Immigrant Responsibility Act of 1996, or IIRIRA, contained a provision that repealed Section 245(i) of the 1994 law allowing an alien to "adjust status" (obtain permanent resident status) in the US without leaving the country by paying a $1,000 fee.[17] Allen Kay, a spokesman for Smith, told *Insight* that "for the first time measures were adopted to penalize aliens for their illegal stay in the US. They had to stay outside the US between three and 10 years, depending on the length of time they were here illegally. The thought behind it was that no employer is going to wait that long for an employee to return" (O'Meara (1999)).

US INS has so far carried out those immigration law shown above. However, on 1 March, 2003, INS enforcement and service functions and responsibilities shifted to the Department of Homeland Security (DHS).

1.4 Immigration policy in EU

The EU council adopted a comprehensive scheme to combat illegal immigration and trafficking of human beings in EU on 28 February 2002.[18] Consequently the EU council has also selected a plan for the management of the external borders of the Member States of EU on 13 June 2002, following a Commission Communication towards an integrated management of the external borders of the Member States of the EU of 7 May 2002.

This legislation reinforces the following six areas for action:[19]

1. Visa policy
   Possibilities for the exchange of information among Member States on issued visas have to be assessed. To that end, the Commission is undertaking a feasibility study on the creation of a European visa information system.
2. Infrastructure for information exchange, cooperation and coordination
   Towards enhancement of cooperation and coordination of Member States' law-enforcement agencies, a permanent technical support facility could be established to assist in information gathering, analysis and dissemination, to coordinate operational co-operation and to manage common databases for migration management.
3. Border management
   Towards the creation of a European border guard, first steps are taken to facilitate this process, namely with the organisation of a number of pilot projects for the close operational co-operation of border guard services of Member States.
4. Police co-operation
   Police cooperation must be strengthened with the advanced involvement of Europol.
5. Aliens law and criminal law
   The concept of adequate and comparable sanctions against promoters of illegal immigration should be further upgraded and harmonised. This includes, in particular, severe punishment of criminal activities. The seizure of illegally obtained financial advantages has also been identified as a key factor.
6. Return and readmission policy
   Return policy must be further built up with a focus on internal co-ordination such as the creation of common standards and the initiation of common measures.

Those schemes were carried out before long as a common EU immigration policy. EU nations are afflicted with an influx of illegal immigrants due to the Afghanistan and Iraqi wars, disputes in Africa and a large disparity in income between the EU nations and the other countries – North African and east European countries. The government of Holland has accepted 400,000 refugee seekers for the past ten years. However, the right-wing party, which aims to remove refugee seekers, has expanded their seats in the House of Holland in a general election in 2002. The Lower Chamber in Holland enacted a law that causes 26,000 refugee seekers from Asia and Africa to return to their mother countries on 17 February 2004 (Asahi Shimbun (18 February, 2004)). Owing to a severe objection by the Conservative Party, Germany has long delayed adopting a new immigration policy that involves simplification on immigration procedures, for example, the "Green Card System", the purpose of which is to annually receive 20,000 migrants from India and Russia who specialize in IT (information and technology) technologies (Nihon Keizai Shimbun (27 February, 2004)). Germany may be compelled to reject this policy, since migrants from lower wage countries find it easier to obtain jobs than Germans. Hence, we expect that the EU council will intensify those immigration plans discussed above.

1.5 The economic effects of immigration

There has been much research concerning the effect of immigration on the wages of the host-country's workers. In the US, for example, it might be expected that US workers would object to the inflow of migrants from foreign low-wage countries if they brought about a decrease in the wages of native workers. Hence, it is meaningful to analyze the effects of immigration on the wages of the labor-importing country's workforce.

Bean, Lowell and Taylor (1988) estimated the effect of undocumented Mexican workers in labor markets across the southwestern United States upon the earnings of the following six labor-force groups: (a) undocumented workers, (b) legal immigrants, (c) American-born males of Mexican origin, (d) black males, (e) white males of non-Mexican origin, and (f) females. The (statistically significant) effects of illegal Mexican immigrants were found to be negative upon white males' wages (substitution effect) and positive (complementary effect) upon females' wages. The effects of legal Mexican immigrants upon native-born Mexican males and black males were positive. The magnitudes of the effect are hard to interpret, but the authors refer to them as not very sizable. The concern that undocumented immigration may be depressing the earnings of native-born workers does not appear to be borne out by these results.

Altonji and Card (1991) estimated the effect of an inflow of immigrants on the unskilled labor pool of a city. They found that the average city in their sample experienced a 1.4 percent increase in population during the 1970s due to immigration. They estimated that this translated into an average reduction in the wages of unskilled native workers of between 0.4 and 1.7 percent. Clearly, this does not point to immigration as a major explanation of the increase in income inequality seen in the US during the 1970s and 1980s. The study that gives most weight to immigration as an explanation for the rising inequality of wages is that by Borjas (1994), in which one-third of the wage ratio of post-college graduates to high school drop-outs is explained by the arrival of less-skilled immigrants to the United States. This result is dependent on the particular ratio on which he focuses.

Borjas, Freeman and Katz (1992) showed that foreign workers entering the country increased the labor supply of high school graduates in 1988 by only 6 percent. Thus, it is logical to believe that the negative effect on wages will be more severe at lower levels of education, thereby increasing the inequality of earnings. They showed that a one-percentage point increase in the proportion of immigrants reduces the absolute wage of dropouts by no more than 1.2 percent.

Sorensen, Bean, Ku and Zimmerman (1992) examined the effects of immigration on earnings, using the technique mentioned earlier in connection with their study of hours worked. Their basic finding was that 'immigration has a very small effect on native earnings'. The elasticity (with respect to the proportion of foreign-born) was +.03, -.07 and -.04 for native white males, black males and Hispanic males respectively.

Borjas and Ramey (1993) looked at relative wages in a panel of 44 Standard Metropolitan Statistical Areas (SMSAs) in the US from 1977-1991, using data from the Current Population Survey. They estimated that a one percent increment in the number of foreign-born workers yielded a six percent decline in the wages of high-school dropouts relative to college graduates.

The general equilibrium model of Cline (1997) also allowed for immigration to affect the ratio of wages of skilled to unskilled workers. He estimated that the increase in unskilled immigrant labor from 2.8 million workers in 1973 to 6.9 million in 1993 accounted for a two percentage-point rise in the skilled/unskilled wage ratio during that time, slightly more than ten percent of the overall increase. He attributed his finding of a larger effect of immigration on the fact that his model encompasses the entire US economy, not just that of its largest cities.

As mentioned above, Phillips and Massey (1999) concluded that IRCA seems to have helped to create an underground labor market in the US, since it is unlikely to have deterred illegal immigration from Mexico to the US. We can only assume that IRCA has reduced the wages of both illegal Mexican immigrants and unskilled native Americans who compete in the US low-skilled labor market.

When considering the impacts of immigrants on wages in a host country, Venturini (1999) gives useful suggestions, examining whether non-regular foreigners and native workers are competitive or not. She has explained that the irregular foreign workers are far less competitive than home workers, from which they are complementary in a non-traded services sector. She has also concluded that this happens because a lot of the young unemployed are secondary school-leavers who are reluctant to work in a same manner as the foreigners, and hence do not compete with them in the same labor market.

1.6 Theoretical analyses of illegal immigration

The disparities between developed and developing countries in terms of wages and opportunities for employment have caused a mass influx of foreign aliens into developed countries, which recently have tended to restrict immigration. These government restrictions, combined with migratory pressures from poorer to richer countries, result in illegal immigration from these poorer, less developed countries to wealthier, developed countries. Hence, illegal immigration is considered the problem of the developed or host country (Ethier (1986a, b), Bond and Chen (1987)).

There are two economic reasons for developed countries to curtail the inflow of migrants. It is possible that developed countries may increase their domestic welfare by limiting the inflow of migrants. These countries impose income taxes on domestic workers. The inflow of illegal labor causes a reduction in the wages of domestic workers and a reduction of total taxes collected, due to the taxation of lower disposable incomes, unless there is a corresponding increase in the tax rate.[20] Therefore, domestic workers in host countries are hurt twice by the influx of immigrants – first by the lowering of disposable incomes and then by the reduction of the tax base used to finance the provision of government services.

By using a standard neo-classical model of factor movements, a two-country (host country and foreign country), one good, two-factor (labor and capital) model, we can demonstrate that it is never optimal, in terms of national income, to control immigration. The reason is that the equalization of factor prices induced by factor movements between countries causes an improvement in national income.

Ethier (1986a) pioneered the one, small-country model of illegal immigration.[21] Bond and Chen (1987) extended the Ethier model by constructing a two-country model of illegal immigration. They assumed that the host country's domestic firms could discern between legal domestic workers and illegal foreign workers. The host country's government enacts an enforcement scheme to catch and expose firms that employ illegal foreign workers, and these firms pay fines to the domestic government.[22] Domestic, risk-neutral firms hire illegal foreign labor at a level such that the wage of legal domestic workers is equal to the foreign worker's wage plus the expected penalty. In equilibrium, unauthorized foreign workers receive a lower wage than native workers.[23] Bond and Chen demonstrated that the introduction of internal enforcement may improve the host country's income if the host country is large enough for the enforcement policy to affect the foreign country's wage, and if the marginal cost of enforcement is sufficiently low.

All workers in the host country receive the same wage when domestic firms cannot distinguish between legal domestic workers and illegal foreign workers.[24] Domestic firms determine the employment level of workers when the wages of legal domestic workers are equal to the wages of illegal foreign workers plus the product of the share of illegal labor in the domestic labor force and the expected fine. Bond and Chen (1987) showed that enforcement is less likely to be a desirable policy in terms of the country's income in the no-discernment case, where firms are unable to distinguish between legal and illegal migrants, than in the discernment case.

Another reason for limiting the inflow of foreign workers is the income distribution effects of immigration. Under perfectly flexible wages and full employment the inflow of illegal foreign workers harms domestic workers, for whom they are close substitutes, because the wages of the host country's workers decrease. Thus, it is favorable to domestic workers for their government to enact restrictive immigration schemes.

The tools available to the host country's government to limit the inflow of foreign labor include border patrol and the detection of domestic firms hiring illegal foreign workers (Ethier (1986a)). Ethier (1986a) showed that an intensification of border enforcement must decrease national welfare, and hence is costly in terms of the country's income.

The US border patrol spent $362 million on its activities in 1993 (see Hess (1994)). Much of the cost was in salaries and wages for 3,990 border-patrol agents. An estimated $12.2 million was allocated for machinery and equipment needed for enforcement, such as helicopters, all-terrain vehicles, infra-red sensing devices, and special lighting (US Office of Management and Budget (1993)). The efforts of the border patrol using these resources resulted in 1,282,000 apprehensions in 1993 (Warren (1994)). The risk of being apprehended on any given attempt to enter the US unlawfully is about 30 percent, a risk that is greater than the one to two percent arrest probability within the US (Espenshade (1994), Hanson and Spilimbergo (1996)).[25] Massey and Singer (1995) estimated the probability of apprehension among Mexican migrants attempting to illegally cross into the US over the period 1965-1989 at an average of around 33 percent, with a range of 20 percent to 40 percent.[26]

In order to restrict this massive undocumented migration, the Clinton Administration increased budgetary allocations to the INS and to the US Border Patrol at the cost of interior enforcement (Espenshade and Acevedo (1995)).[27] However, would-be illegal migrants try to re-enter the US on a subsequent occasion despite prior apprehensions (see Chiswick (1986b)). Furthermore, we know that illegal migrants may confer positive externalities on each other, since an increase in attempted illegal border crossings results in lower apprehension probabilities given fixed enforcement resources (Espenshade and Acevedo (1995)).

Efforts by immigration authorities to curb the inflow of illegal migrants to the US by enforcing IRCA have not stopped the inflow (Woodrow and Passel (1990)). Bean, Espenshade, White and Dymowski (1990) and Espenshade (1990) estimated that IRCA might have lessened the flow of undocumented migrants into the US by as much as 40 to 50 percent in the two years after the law was enacted. In contrast to these estimates, it was suggested by Bustamante (1990), Cornelius (1990), Massey, Donato and Liang (1990), Woodrow and Passel (1990) and Donato, Durand and Massey (1992) that IRCA has had little effect in checking the influx of deportable aliens from Mexico to the US. We confirm that in spite of the recent US immigration reform, the number of Mexicans attempting to migrate illegally into the US is still quite massive. It is inevitable that a more restrictive US Border Patrol is needed. However, since the INS can impose few financial penalties on apprehended aliens, border patrol activities remain costly in terms of their financial burden on the US.

Governments need to search for less expensive means of controlling the influx of illegal aliens. As mentioned in Bond and Chen (1987), inspection of domestic firms can be less costly than border enforcement. Ethier (1986a) showed that the host country can cut down the cost of a restrictive immigration policy by using a combination of border and internal measures, rather than using either policy exclusively.[28]

We briefly summarize other research on illegal immigration.[29] Using a two-country model introduced by Ramaswami (1968) with internationally mobile capital and illegal immigration, Djajic (1987) showed that some policies restricting illegal immigration may benefit a host country's unskilled workers while harming other domestic factors of production, such as skilled workers and capital.[30]

Hill and Pearce (1987) introduced a model that determined which industries were more likely to be observed by immigration authorities, and then considered the impacts of restrictive immigration policies.

Dell'Aringa and Neri (1987) analyzed the effect of illegal workers on the Italian labor market using a single good, two-sector economy, in which the sectors consisted of an official economy and an underground economy. Assuming that capital was mobile between the two sectors and that both sectors produced the same good, they showed that illegal migrant workers are only hired in the informal sector.

Todaro and Maruszko (1987) constructed a two-country model invoking the Todaro (1969), and Harris and Todaro (1970) models of internal migration in developing countries. Todaro and Maruszko assumed that the illegal labor flow depends upon the income that an illegal alien expects to gain in the host country relative to that expected in his native country, and then analyzed the effects on the host country's economy of tightening border patrol and internal enforcement. They concluded that a higher capture rate and stricter employer sanctions lead to a reduction in both the illegal migration rate and the level of unemployment in the host country.

Chiswick (1988a) invoked a three-factor model of the immigrant-receiving country introduced by Chiswick (1982). He showed that the addition of illegal foreign workers to a host country's labor force leads to a decline in the wages of low-skilled native workers and an increase in the wages of high-skilled native workers and an increase in the return to (physical) capital.

Nguyen (1989, 1991) developed a multi-sector model of a parallel economy composed of legal and illegal aliens. In his model the government controls the markets of both types of labor using two tools: wage controls on legal labor through minimum wage legislation, and quantity controls on illegal aliens by restrictive immigration policies. Nguyen concluded that: (1) amnesty for undocumented workers would raise the unemployment of legal workers, whereas a restrictive immigration policy would lower it, and (2) tougher employer sanctions under constant minimum wages might not be an effective measure to reduce the number of unauthorized workers.

Carter (1993) incorporated efficiency wages into the Heckscher-Ohlin model of illegal immigration. He concluded that when illegal immigration cannot be restricted, the welfare of the high-wage country improves by utilizing a capital-outflow policy, and that this decreases illegal immigration and hence increases the number of higher wage jobs for the host country's domestic workers.

Faini and Venturini (1993) have designed how the migration decision is achieved. They indicated that determinants of the migration decision are the wage differential, real GDP (gross domestic product) per capita in a source country of illegal immigration, employment growth in receiving countries, lagged dependent variable, unemployment rate in the sending country, unemployment rate in a host country and share of non-agriculture employment.

Gonzalez (1994) postulated a generalized Harris and Todaro (1970) model, in which capital is internally immobile and the economy is divided into union and non-union sectors, with undocumented migrants employed only in the latter.[31] Gonzalez examined the welfare effects of border and internal enforcement, and showed that tightening immigration controls does not necessarily worsen national income in the presence of a union.

Campos and Lien (1995), using a push-pull theory, described that 'a narrow preoccupation with tougher immigration laws is wasteful and may be marginally effective', since the push-pull forces causing immigration are not weakened by stricter immigration policies.

Steineck (1995) discussed the characteristics of illegal immigrants in the EU. He concluded that the effectiveness and efficiency of restrictive immigration polices by EU countries make illegal immigration less attractive, by enforcing employer sanctions on employers hiring illegal aliens and by opening doors to legal immigrants.

Djajic (1997) developed a three-sector model composed of a formal economy having two sectors producing two internationally traded goods and an informal or underground sector producing one non-traded good. Djajic examined the effects of tougher employer sanctions and amnesty, i.e., legalization of the status of illegal aliens, on the host country's economy. He concluded that in the short run, hiring more illegal foreign workers within the underground economy increases the welfare of skilled domestic labor. On the other hand, it has a negative or a positive effect on the income of unskilled native workers, depending upon whether unskilled natives compete with foreign illegal immigrants for low-skilled jobs in the underground economy. He also showed that in the long run, all domestic labor might benefit from the inflow of illegal aliens, since the entry of illegal foreign labor makes larger rents possible.

Bandyopadhyay and Bandyopadhyay (1998) introduced a general equilibrium model of illegal immigration, where the labor-exporting country has three sectors (agriculture, manufacture, and high tech) and the host country is assumed to have a one-good sector. They concluded that when capital is immobile between the two countries, trade liberalization of the high-tech sector reduces illegal immigration. The reason is that capital in the high-tech sector is absorbed in the manufacturing sector, which induces the labor/capital ratio in the latter sector to decrease, thereby raising the wages of unskilled labor employed in the agricultural or manufacturing sector. This depresses the incentives for unskilled workers to emigrate to the host country. They suggested that under restricted capital mobility, the host country should negotiate reductions in obstacles to capital mobility, because capital imports promote a capital shift from the high-tech sector to the manufacturing sector, which increases the wages of unskilled labor in the labor-exporting country.

Carter (1999) developed an efficiency wage/dual labor market model of illegal immigration. The Carter model is a standard (two-country, one-good, two-factor) model of international factor mobility. The single good of the host country is produced using three factors: capital, native workers and illegal immigrants. There are two types of jobs: primary and secondary. Illegal aliens are employed in secondary jobs, in which employers can easily monitor work effort, while native workers choose the high-wage primary jobs. However, Carter posed an important problem: more illegal immigrants may begin to occupy primary jobs as the number of aliens in the host country grows, causing severe competition between natives and migrants. He stated that 'deporting illegals working in high-wage jobs is superior to deporting those with low-wage jobs or preventing entry by the migrants in the first place'.

Gatsios, Hatzipanayotou and Michael (1999) constructed a general equilibrium model in which both countries have identical consumers producing many privately traded goods and one public consumption good. The government of each country finances the production of the public good through income taxes and then provides it to consumers free of charge. They demonstrated that exogenous intentional migration might reduce wages in the labor exporting country, raise wages in the host country, and worsen welfare in both countries.[32]

Razin and Sadka (1999) constructed an overlapping-generations model with (legal) immigration, where each generation lives for two periods.

They showed that in their dynamic context, the net burden that low-skilled migration imposes on the native-born population could be a net gain, by redistributing income from young migrants to elderly natives who rely on a pension system. In an ever-lasting economy, migrants make a positive contribution to the existing old and possibly to all other generations as well.

Hillman and Weiss (1999) introduced a competitive open economy model of illegal immigration, consisting of a traded goods and a non-traded goods sector. They maintained that as long as the median voter is identified as a mobile worker hired outside the sector where illegal immigrants are permitted to work, there is no majority support for amnesty. However, they also demonstrated that there is majority support for illegal immigration and for growth in the size of the illegal immigrant population. Furthermore, they expected that 'the illegally present population becomes too large and strains the limit of credibility of immigration that is illegal yet permissible, which gives rise to amnesty proposals (that are usually not put to popular vote)'.[33]

Levine (1999) developed a Harris-and-Todaro-type, two-bloc, one-good model of East-West illegal migration within European countries, in which labor markets in both blocs are imperfect. He analyzed the effects of restrictive immigration control by a mythical all-European planner who seeks to maximize total GDP (Gross Domestic Product) net of migration costs. For large differences in GDP per head in the two regions, he showed that the socially optimal level of migration is generally far less than that under laissez-faire. He also concluded that under a combination of high wage flexibility in the West, low flexibility in the East and an inefficient technology for controlling immigration, laissez-faire migration is small and no immigration controls are necessary – if anything, subsidies may be necessary to encourage migration.

In a recent paper, Gaytan-Fregoso and Lahiri (2000) have developed a new model in which the decision to migrate is made by families rather than individuals, but with *no risk* for illegal immigrants to be apprehended by border patrol. They concluded that an increase in foreign aid causes the level of unlawful immigration to increase. Gaytan-Fregoso and Lahiri (2001) have also extended their two-country model to analyze a connection between commodity trade and illegal immigration, substituting the trade between the countries for it. They stated that a trade reform, that is, a tariff reduction between America and Mexico, reduces illegal immigration from the latter.

Agiomirgianakis and Zervoyianni (2001) have introduced an open economy with heterogeous labor and which imports foreign irregular unskilled workers. They showed that when skilled native wage setters and policymakers in the economy act as Nash players, illegal immigration causes the position of the entire native labor force, which involves both skilled and unskilled workers, to be better off. On the other hand, they concluded that when the native skilled workers and the policymakers perform cooperatively, illegal immigration might make the entire native workforce worse off.

Epstein (2003) has modeled the facts that legal immigrants employ illegal immigrants for various services, such as housecleaning, teaching, daycare, cooking and providing religious services, and illegal immigrants may also themselves hire other illegal immigrants. He has found that an increase in the tax on legal immigrants' income lessens the level of illegal migrants they can employ, thus promoting assimilation.

Although general fiscal issues are discussed in these studies, none explicitly considers the effects of immigration reform on government finances. Since reforms such as the US IRCA of 1986 prescribe increased enforcement and employer fines, their enactment will affect the government budget. Bucci and Tenorio (1996) analyzed the effects of using alternative financing instruments on the host country's income when an immigration reform, such as the introduction of employer sanctions, is undertaken. Their analysis utilized a one, small country illegal immigration model, and incorporated a government budget constraint similar to Ethier's.

As mentioned in the Introduction, the chief limitation of these analyses of illegal immigration is that they only examine restrictive immigration policies in terms of their effect on the host country. In addition, we find no research on optimal enforcement levels of employer sanctions from the viewpoint of the host country's income. In short, there do not appear to be any studies that explain (1) how those interdiction policies influence the host country's welfare as well as the source country's welfare, and (2) how the enforcement should be optimally put in force in view of the host country's income, making use of some micro-economic methods.

Illegal immigration is an issue to not only a labor importing country but also a labor exporting country, since the individual enforcement affects both economies. This may bring about the key to how to assess the enforcement, which is to estimate it from the viewpoint of the global income consisting of a host and a foreign country incomes combined. Hence, the first main subject of this book is to assess border patrol or interior enforcement from the viewpoint of the global income. Each country is interdependent, since there are two-way factor movements, i.e., labor and capital flows between the countries. A scheme to keep a factor movement from freely moving between the areas may have influence on a country that carries out the plan as well as another country. Therefore, if the policy causes both economies to be better off, then we should regard the design as a desirable one from the viewpoint of the global welfare. We will propose one way to estimate a policy that a country enforces through this task, that is, the first objective.

We have not found any previous works that have overtly derived an optimal level of enforcement of interior interdictions, using a general two-country model. Ethier (1986a, b) has explained why the labor-importing country should have an interdiction policy. Ethier suggested that the country encompass three policy objectives. The first is to exploit market power with respect to mobile workers; that is, to maximize the national income. The second is to manage the internal distribution of income between skilled and unskilled workers in the host country. The third objective is to control the level of immigration in the country for some social reasons. We consider the first target, the maximization of the national income. If there is a level of interior enforcement that maximizes the host country's welfare, then we can derive the optimal level of enforcement from the model. We provide the second main subject of the book to accomplish this task.

This book brings into focus two important issues that have not yet been examined. The first is to assess border patrol and internal inspection by the host country's government from the point of view of global welfare. The second is to discover an optimal level of interior enforcement in terms of the host country's welfare.

1.7 Outline

Part I consists of four chapters. Chapter 2 develops the Bond and Chen (1987) model of undocumented illegal immigration, when capital is immobile between the labor importing (host) country and the labor-exporting country. We complement their analysis by examining the impact of tougher internal inspection on the labor-exporting or foreign country's welfare and on global welfare, the latter being composed of the combined income of the two countries.

Chapter 3 re-examines the Bond and Chen model when capital is mobile between countries. We then reconsider the effects of stricter employer sanctions on domestic welfare, foreign welfare, and global welfare.

Chapter 4 extends Ethier's (1986) one, small-country model of illegal immigration by constructing a standard (two-country, one-good, two-factor) model. It also examines the effects of border patrol on the welfare of the host country, the foreign country, and the two countries combined (i.e., global welfare), both in the presence and in the absence of capital mobility.

Chapter 5 extends the Bond and Chen model by introducing a government budget constraint (*GBC*) on the host country's government. This chapter examines the effects of financing internal enforcement of illegal immigration by the host country's government on the welfare of the host country, the foreign country and the world, both in the absence and in the presence of international capital mobility.

Part II is composed of two chapters, in which we reintroduce the Bond and Chen model of illegal migrant workers using a Cobb-Douglas production function. In Chapter 6, the Bond and Chen model is modified to examine whether there is an optimal enforcement level of employer sanctions from the viewpoint of the host country's income in the presence (or absence) of international capital mobility. We assume here that the domestic firm can discern between legal domestic workers and illegal foreign workers. In Chapter 7, we extend the model of Chapter 6 by incorporating a government budget constraint on the host country (*GBC*), which model is essentially similar to that of Chapter 5. This chapter examines the effects on the welfare of the host country of the financing of internal enforcement of illegal immigration by the host country's government, both in the absence and in the presence of international capital mobility. We search for an optimal level of interior inspection in terms of the host country's welfare.

In Part III, we develop a standard (two-country, one good, two-factor) model of legal immigration, rather than illegal immigration as considered in Parts I and II. Chapter 8 examines the welfare effects of a profit-sharing plan by the host country's government, using a model in which there is unemployment in both the host (capital abundant) country and the foreign (labor abundant) country. We assume that the level of immigration to the host country is set under the Harris and Todaro (1970) hypothesis. We consider whether a profit-sharing scheme is justified from the viewpoint of global welfare.

Chapter 9 introduces a model like that of Chapter 8, in which legal immigrants form their own labor union in the host country. Chapter 9 analyzes the welfare effects of the profit-sharing policy, and also examines whether the policy is *a Pareto-improving policy* in terms of global income.

Chapter 10 examines the effects of introducing a profit-sharing scheme in the urban sectors of a less developed country (LDC). We use a generalized Harris and Todaro (1970) model in which the LDC has a dual economy, with urban-specific unemployment. We assume that the wage of urban labor is determined by a single labor union. We then introduce a profit-sharing scheme in the urban sector. We analyze whether or not profit-sharing can remedy the large-scale urban unemployment problems of LDCs and improve LDC welfare.

Appendix 1

Table 1.2 A summary of available estimates of the probability of undocumented alien apprehension along the Mexico-US border

Source	Estimate	Comments
More speculative		
Informal survey of Border Patrol agents (Borjas, Freeman & Lang 1991)	0.2	No time period or place referent given
Border Patrol (Fogel 1982)	0.16	No time period or place referent given
Chief Border Patrol agent in San Diego (Borjas, Freeman & Lang 1991)	0.5	No time period or place referent given
Based on numerous assumptions (Papademetriou, Lowell & Clark, 1991)	0.25–0.75	Probabilities are assumed to rise with successive attempts to cross the border on the same trip; based on cumulative migrant trips prior to 1982
Border Patrol agents (Fogel 1982; Dillin 1986; FAIR 1989; Borjas, Freeman & Lang 1991)	0.25–0.33	Reflects the INS aphorism that for every undocumented immigrant apprehended, 'two or three get away'; no time period given
More analytical		
Garcia y Griego & Giner de los Rios (1985)	0.5	Authors claim this estimate is an upper limit; based on data for 1984
Small nonrandom sample of Mexican male illegal immigrants in San Diego (Borjas, Freeman & Lang 1991)	0.4	Probability is lower for immigrants on a second or higher-order US trip than for immigrants in the US for the first time; based on cumulative migration experiences prior to summer 1986

Colegio de la Frontera Norte (Crane et al. 1990)	0.4	Upper bound on the probability of capture; based on a survey by COLEF conducted in 1988-89 (?)
Unpublished tabulations, Westat survey (Papademetriou, Lowell & Clark 1991)	0.25	The 1989 Westat survey was based on cumulative migrant trips prior to 1982
Westat survey final report (US INS 1992)	0.28	Represents an upper limit; based on cumulative migrant trips prior to 1982
CENIET and INS date (Garcia y Griego 1979)	0.18-0.29	Upper end of range represents probability of apprehension; lower end the probability of expulsion. Period studied, 1972-76
INS fingerprint experiment (California Department of Justice 1989)	0.25	Estimate biased down because of poor quality of fingerprint data; estimate based on migrants apprehended in June-August 1989
Border Patrol annual data on apprehensions (Crane et al. 1990)	0.3	Based on annual time series, 1970-1988, which exhibits little variation
CENIET data (Kossoudji 1992)	0.33	Median value; includes apprehension either at the border or in the US interior. Based on male migrant trips between January 1974 and January 1979
Mexican community studies (Donato, Durand & Massey 1992)	0.32	Sample mean based on 1,273 border crossings by migrants interviewed in 1987-90 about their cumulative US migration histories

(Source: Espenshade and Acevedo (1995))

Appendix 2

Table 1.3   Summary of studies that assess the impact of undocumented immigration on US labor markets

Source	Data	Approach	Control for skill level	Control for endogeneity[a]	Control for capital	Results
Empirically based studies (data on immigrants)						
Smith and Newman 1977	1970 US census	Regression analysis	Yes	No	No	Wages of low-skilled Mexican-Americans are more seriously affected than those of high-skilled workers as a result of Mexican-American concentration in labor markets.
DeFreitas and Marshall 1984	1970-78 Current Population Surveys	Regression analysis	Yes	No	No	Immigrants dampen the wages of low-skilled native workers in the manufacturing sector once immigrant concentration reaches 20 percent.
Simon and Moore 1984	Unemployment data (UI), Current Population Surveys, INS Annual Report	Regression analysis	No	No	No	No observed increase in unemployment due to total legal immigration in the United States.
Muller and Espenshade 1985	1970 and 1980 US census	Regression analysis	No	No	No	Mexican immigrants increase black family income and decrease black unemployment.
McCarthy and Valdez 1986	1970 and 1980 US census	Examination of earnings growth	No	No	No	Latino wage growth was less than the national average in areas with large Mexican immigrant population.
Stewart and Hyclack 1986	1970 1/100 public use sample, US census	Regression analysis	Yes	Yes	No	Immigrants from Mexico have no effect on the wages of central-city black males, while Cuban and West Indian migrants have complementary effects and all other immigrants have negative effects on black male wages.
Empirically based studies (date on undocumenteds)						
North and Houstoun 1976	Survey of apprehended undocumented	Inference based on characteristics and "authors' experience in the study of alien workers"	No	No	No	Undocumented workers displace low-skilled legal resident workers, depress educational and skill levels of the labor force, and create a new class of disadvantages workers based on national origin and immigration status.

Study	Data	Method				Findings
Van Arsdol et al. 1979	Nonapprehended undocumenteds in Los-Angeles	Comparisons of income with Hispanic workers	No	No	No	Undocumented males were not competitors with Hispanic population in Los Angeles. Female undocumenteds were crowded in same low-skill jobs as Hispanic females.
Model-based studies (data on immigrants)						
Grossman 1982	1970 US census	Translog production function	No	No	Yes	Total foreign-born persons:[b] second-generation wages -.2% third-generation wages -.3%
Borjas 1984	1970 1/100 public use sample and 1980 1/20 public use microdata sample-A (PUMS-A), US census	Generalized Leontief production function	Yes	Yes	Yes	Total immigrant males (1980)[b]: young white male earnings -1.2% old white male earnings +0.6% young black male earnings +2.7% old black male earnings +1.5% native females -1.5%
Borjas 1986b	1970 1/100 public use sample and 1980 1/20 PUMS-A, US census	Generalized Leontief production function	Yes	Yes	Yes	Total immigrant males have almost no effect on white males and are slightly complementary to black males.[b]
King et al. 1986	1970 public use sample, US census	Regression equation based on human capital and Leontief production function	Yes	No	No	Foreign-born Hispanic have little effect on the earnings of natives.
Borjas 1987	1980 1/20 PUMS-A, US census	Generalized Leontief production function	Yes	Yes	Yes	Total Hispanic immigrants:[b] white native wage 0% black native wage +1% Hispanic native wage +.2%
Model-based studies (data on undocumenteds)						
Bean et al. 1988	1980 US census	Generalized Leontief production function	Yes	Yes	No	Undocumented Mexican males:[b] Mexican-origin native US males 0% black males -.1% white males +.1% total females +.5%

[a] Endogeneity controls account for the fact that the labor supply may be endogenous rather than exogenous.
[b] Results expressed as the effect of a 10 percent increase in the number of immigrants.
(Source: Bean, Tells and Lowell (1987))

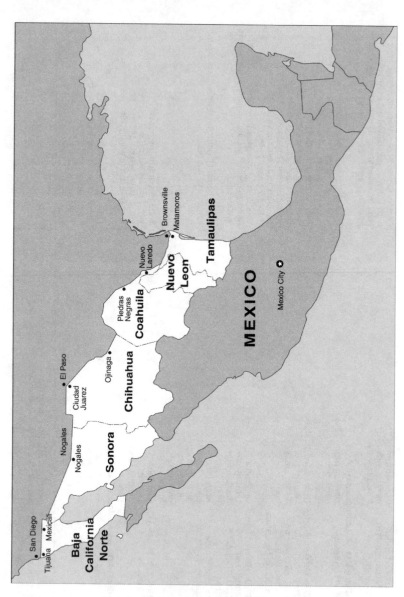

Map 1.1 Mexico's northern states
(Source: MapArt, Cartesia Software, NJ)

Map 1.2   European countries
(Source: The University of Texas at Austin, TX)

Notes

1   On 1st May, 2004, the following ten countries, Cyprus, Czech Republic, Estonia, Hungary, Latvia, Lithuania, Malta, Poland, Slovakia and Slovenia joined the EU. EU is now composed of 25 European countries: already joined 15 countries; Germany, France, Italy, Belgium, Holland, Luxembourg, United Kingdom, Denmark, Ireland, Greece, Spain, Portugal, Austria, Sweden , Finland and the 10 countries mentioned above. A total population in EU is about 4.5 hundred million. The 15 countries that have previously gained membership in the EU can regulate migration from eight of the newly entrant countries, except Cyprus and Malta. The total amount of gross domestic product (GDP) in the enlarged EU countries is approximately 9.731 trillion euro in 2003. The EU GDP ranks with US GDP which is 9.713 trillion euro in 2003. Furthermore, Bulgaria, Romania and Turkey are also seeking admission to the EU.

2   With the opening of trade, Mexican apparel producers are shifting from production for the domestic market to product assembly for US firms. This implies that NAFTA will not only shift apparel assembly jobs from the US to Mexico, but will also lead to substantial relocation of production within Mexico (Hanson (1996b)).

3   The paragraph was quoted from Salgado (1998).

4   Warren and Passel (1987) suggested that the population of undocumented Mexican aliens in the US in 1980 was in the one to two million range, and the total number of deportable aliens from all countries was in the range of two to four million.

5   Bratsberg (1995) estimated the response of immigration from Mexico to the US to increases in Mexico's GNP. He reported that a 10 (or 22) percent growth in Mexico's GNP would reduce legal immigration by 6.30 (or 12.7) percent, and illegal immigration by 8.30 (or 16.7) percent, or 10.30 (or 20.4) percent if special agriculture workers (SAW) are included. According to those estimates, he concluded that the NAFTA could have an effect on curbing both legal and illegal immigration flows to the US by spurring GNP growth in Mexico (cf. Acevedo and Espenshade (1992), Yoshida (1999), Hanson and Spilimbergo (1999)). Harper (1995) reported an estimate by the US Department of Commerce. He indicated that 16 months after the implementation of NAFTA, about 130,000 additional jobs were created within the US labor market as a result of increased exports from the US to Mexico, while job displacements caused by inflows of low-wage Mexican workers had been minimal. Also, Hanson (1996a) suggested that as labor-intensive assembly operations continued to relocate from the US to Mexico in order to employ cheaper Mexican labor, complementary manufacturing activities would continue to move from the US interior to US border cities, since trade barriers between the US and Mexico are much reduced by NAFTA. This implies that NAFTA, by further lowering trade barriers, will contribute to the expansion of US border cities, leading to increased manufacturing employment in these cities. Goto (1998) described that increases in imports of labor-intensive goods from less developed countries (LDCs) to Japan could substitute for foreign labor imports when higher tariffs and non-tariff barriers against labor-intensive goods imported from LDCs are reduced. He put this in another way as follows: trade liberalization by Japan could cause increases in income and employment in labor-exporting Asian countries.

6 We refer to Borjas (1990).

7 See Woodrow (1992).

8 See Briggs (1975), Fogel (1977), Contini (1982), Passel (1986), Weiss (1987), Contini (1989), Yanaihara and Yamagata (1992), the Ministry of Welfare (1993), Bangfu (1994), Palmer (1995) etc., on the specific situations facing illegal immigrants. Briggs (1975) outlined US immigration policies and showed the impact of illegal immigration. Fogel (1977) presented some of the problems faced by the US immigration authorities in controlling the entry of illegal aliens. We know from Contini (1982), Weiss (1987) and Contini (1989) that the majority of enterprises hiring undocumented, non-union workers in Western European countries are factories doing subcontract work, which supply half-finished goods or raw materials to holding companies. Passel (1986) explained the social, economic, and demographic characteristics of illegal immigrants in the US, most of whom are from Mexico. Yanaihara and Yamagata (1992) illustrated the role of Asian countries' economies and migration flows from developing Asian countries to developed nations. The Ministry of Welfare (1993) explained the recent massive migration to developed countries. Bangfu (1994) showed the relationships between would-be immigrants and brokers, called "snake-heads", who help immigrants safely enter their destination countries. Palmer (1995) described immigration from the English-speaking Caribbean to the US, and described the characteristics of immigrants settling in the US. He also concluded that 'only accelerated growth that reduces the disparity in living standards between the Caribbean and the United States can stem the flow of immigrants'.

9 Note in Table 1.1 that numbers are indicated in thousands; parts might not add to totals because of rounding.

10 This paragraph is deeply indebted to 2002 yearbook of immigration statistics published by US Department of Homeland Security for empirical data on apprehensions of unauthorized migrants.

11 Grazia (1982) elucidated the features and economic effects of clandestine employment in European countries.

12 Winegarden and Khor (1991), using an empirical model, showed that illegal immigration has not necessarily caused increases in unemployment among the youth and minority workers in the host country, although a small amount of job displacement is demonstrated (cf. Mühleisen and Zimmermann (1994), Dorantes and Huang (1997)).

13 Del Boca and Forte (1982) illustrated the employment conditions of unofficial workers in the Italian underground economy.

14 In the US, immigrants who have legally migrated to the country pay income taxes while illegal immigrants do not. However, both types of immigrants draw the same benefits, e.g., social or welfare services and the use of public facilities such as public schools and universities, hospitals and so on. This raises the question of why both should receive the same benefits when these benefits are largely financed by legal immigrants (including naturalized immigrants) and native-born workers. However, under current law, e.g., California's Proposition 187, undocumented immigrants are already barred from receiving most public benefits (see Munoz and Gottfried (1995), Robert (1996)). Schuck (1995) explained the details of California's Proposition 187, legislated in 1994, which is a melange of different schemes that restrict the

inflow of undocumented workers to California. It has caused about 1.4 million workers resident in the US to return to their mother countries.

15 Borjas (1996) explained that much of the wage gap between Mexican immigrants and US native-born workers could be attributed to the very low educational attainment of the Mexican immigrant population. Friedberg (2000) claimed that immigrants to Israel earn roughly one-quarter less than natives who have equivalent skill levels, and that education received abroad is more highly valued for migrants from Europe and the Western Hemisphere than for migrants from Asia and Africa. Clandestine workers do not necessarily receive lower wages than other workers. Davila, Bohara and Saenz (1993) found that, regardless of English proficiency, Mexican Americans speaking English with an accent in the US are likely to earn lower wages than their non-accented peers. They suggested that this could occur because employers perceive that accented (non-accented) Mexican Americans could be illegal (legal) workers (cf. Phillips and Massey (1999)).

16 In this section, we refer to the works of Hanami and Kuwahara (1993), Djajic (1997), Hanami (1997).

17 See http://www.takatalaw.com/us/iract96.html, prepared by the law office of Timothy D. Takata, for a summary of the major provisions of the 1996 immigration law.

18 We have referred to "EUROPA – Gateway to the European Union" at the web site of EU (http://europa.eu.int/index_en.htm).

19 We have cited those articles from the web site, EUROPA – Justice and Home Affairs – Freedom Security and Justice – Illegal immigration European Commission (http://europa.eu.int/comm/justice_home/fsj/immigration/illegal/fsj_immigration_illegal_en.htm).

20 Chiswick (1986b) showed that 'the gains in income to skilled workers and capital from the migration of low-skilled workers are likely to exceed the losses to native low-skilled workers. This means that as a result of low-skilled illegal immigration, the income of the native US population is increased!'.

21 Ethier (1986b) also analyzed the effects of restrictive immigration policies on the host country; Ethier (1986a) explored the impact of the policies more formally than Ethier (1986b).

22 IRCA-1986 enforces fines on employers who knowingly hire unofficial workers. These civil fines range from $250 to $2,000 for each illegal alien in the case of a first offense, and to criminal penalties of up to 6 months in prison for a 'pattern and practice' of hiring illegal workers (c.f. White, Bean and Espenshade (1990)).

23 Gill and Long (1989) analyzed the source of wage differentials between legal and illegal Hispanic workers in the Los Angeles garment industry – one of several industries that are familiar sources of employment for undocumented workers in Southern California. They concluded that such wage differentials are also caused by the coercive element of wage agreements between employers and undocumented workers. This implies that employers may discount productivity-based wage offers to illegal aliens, who may accept lower wage offers rather than risk possible apprehension while engaging in an extended job search (c.f. Donato and Massey (1993), p.539) because of their fear of possible exposure and deportation by the INS. Also, Chiswick (1978) reported that ten to fifteen years after immigration to the US, the earnings of

immigrants overtook those of native-born workers.

24 In the period following the 1986 IRCA implementation, most Mexican migrants gained employment in the US by using bogus documents – typically counterfeit "green cards" or *micas* (permanent legal immigrant credentials) and counterfeit US Social Security cards. Migrants can easily purchase such false documents both in their communities of origin in Mexico and in the US-Mexican border cities at an average cost of US$50. Most, however, obtain them at little or no cost through their social networks (especially relatives and friends in the US) (Cornelius (1989)). Therefore, we conclude from such findings that it is very difficult for employers in the US to discern whether an alien is a legal or illegal migrant.

25 See Appendix 1: 'Table 1.2 A summary of available estimates of the probability of undocumented alien apprehension along the Mexico-US border' in Espenshade and Acevedo (1995).

26 We know from White, Bean and Espenshade (1990) and Donato and Massey (1993) that: The INS reported a 42 percent decrease in the number of apprehensions of undocumented aliens by the US Border Patrol between 1986-1988. However, it is known that IRCA has had little impact on illegal immigration to the US and that apprehension statistics are down because many US Border Patrol agents have been reallocated to other assignments, including hunting for drug smugglers. It is also believed that the number of potential illegal aliens has fallen because migrants who previously went back and forth across the US-Mexico border illegally now do so legally, as a result of the SAWs legalization program and as a result of amnesty. These programs, which removed more than two million Mexicans from the stream of undocumented migrants regularly crossing the border, are components of IRCA.

According to Palmer (1995), we find that:

In the past, the 1917 Immigration Act provided for temporary work visas. Under this Act, the Florida sugar industry began importing workers from the West Indies in 1943 to replace southern blacks who had moved north to work in war-related industries. The Second World War also brought temporary workers from Mexico to meet wartime labor shortages in the southwestern US agricultural industry when the US government initiated the "bracero program" as the result of a 1942 agreement between Mexico and the US. In the post-war period, both the Mexican bracero program and the West Indies temporary worker program were authorized under section H-2 of the 1952 Immigration and Nationality Act. The bracero program was by far the larger of the two. The program came under attack from organized labor and was terminated by President Lyndon Johnson in December 1964. From 1942 to 1964 nearly 5 million temporary labor contracts were issued to Mexican citizens and apprehensions of Mexican workers working without documents numbered over 5 million. During the recession following the Korean War in 1954, the INS launched a deportation campaign, Operation Wetback, which arrested over one million illegal Mexican workers. Yet Mexican migration resumed during the late 1950s, when over four hundred thousand Mexican workers entered the US through the bracero program each year (cf. Alston and Ferrie (1993), Mills and Rockoff (1993), Hondagneu-Sotelo (1994)).

27   Espenshade and Acevedo (1995) reported that the more human and capital resources utilized by the INS to put US immigration policy into force, the higher the probability of apprehension for would-be illegal migrants.

28   The first half of the section is to some extent indebted to pp.662-664 in Wong (1995).

29   There are a lot of empirical studies on illegal immigration: Martin and Sehgal (1980), Robinson (1980), Wachter (1980), Beranek (1982), Corwin (1983), Sain, Martin and Paris (1983), Grossman (1984), Pearce and Gunther (1985), Torok and Huffman (1986), Chiswick (1986a and 1988b), Portes (1987), Bean, Tells and Lowell (1987), Bean, Lowell and Taylor (1988), Moehring (1988), Hill and Pearce (1990), Donato and Massey (1993), Cobb-Clark, Shiells and Lowell (1995) and so on. Most analyses focus mainly on the impact of illegal immigration and/or its restriction on the wages of low-skilled workers in the host country. Bean, Tells and Lowell (1987) summarized various empirical studies on the impact of illegal immigration on the US labor market (see Appendix 2). Also, Greenwood and McDowell (1986), Chiswick (1992) and Borjas (1994) attempted to examine the effect of *immigration* on wages and the employment of native unskilled workers.

30   Gerking and Mutti (1980), using cost-benefit analysis, examined the effects of illegal immigration on the income and employment of native low-skilled labor.

31   Yoshida (2000a) studied the effects of a profit-sharing policy on a less developed country's (LDC's) economy using a model similar to that of Gonzalez (1994).

32   In this paper, it appears that all immigration is assumed to be legal.

33   The major objective of IRCA was to reduce illegal immigration. Immigration authorities tried to achieve this goal using two strategies. The first strategy was the legalization of undocumented immigrants already settled in the US. This was done both through a regular legislation program and a legalization program for special agricultural workers called SAWs through the SAW program. The SAW program offered legal status to illegal aliens able to claim at least 90 days of employment as farm-workers in the US in the 12-month period ending May 1, 1986. The second strategy was the reduction of possible immigrants to the US through the imposition of penalties on employers who hired illegal workers (see Cornelius (1989), Bean, Edmonston and Passel (1990), White, Bean and Espenshade (1990)). About 1.3 million aliens applied as SAWs through IRCA during the apprehension period from June 1, 1987 to November 30, 1988. Of the applicants 82 percent were male and about 82 percent were Mexican. (US INS (1991) and Woodrow (1992)).

Part I
The Welfare Effects of Illegal Immigration

Part I
The Welfare Effects of Illegal Immigration

Part I

The Welfare Effects of
Illegal Immigration

2
The Global Welfare Effects of Illegal Immigration in the Absence of Capital Mobility*

The purpose of this chapter is to complement an earlier paper by Bond and Chen (1987). Our model consists of a two-country world in which the host country introduces an internal enforcement policy to catch illegal immigrants working in domestic firms. We examine the effects of this policy on the welfare of the host country, the foreign country and the world when capital is internationally immobile. Our main result is that the internal enforcement policy reduces the foreign country's welfare and global welfare and, under certain conditions, increases the host country's welfare.

2.1 Introduction

Ethier (1986a), Bond and Chen (1987) and Brecher and Choudhri (1987) developed models of illegal immigration. The Ethier model broke new ground by analyzing the effects of border enforcement and internal enforcement in a one-country model using a crime-theoretic analysis (Becker (1968)). In his model, Ethier examined how a small country could use domestic border control and internal enforcement policies to achieve domestic policy objectives regarding illegal immigration and income distribution.

Bond and Chen (1987) extended the Ethier model by constructing a two-country model. In their paper, they analyzed the effect of enforcement policies on the host-country's welfare. As we will see below, they showed that the host country's welfare may or may not be improved by the introduction of enforcement policies. Still in the case where the host country's welfare is improved, the welfare of the foreign (labor-exporting) country decreases to a greater extent. Thus, we can state that the global welfare effect of an imposition of an enforcement policy is unfavorable.

In the next section we briefly summarize the analysis of Bond and Chen (1987), and present our results using their model. Section 2.3 offers some concluding remarks.

2.2 The basic model and main results

First, we develop a simple two-country model of illegal immigration, following Bond and Chen (1987). Firms in both countries produce a single output, assumed to be the numeraire, using a constant returns to scale technology. Technologies may differ between countries. Output in both countries is produced using labor and capital inputs. The production functions of domestic and foreign firms are $F(L,K)$ and $F^*(L^*,K^*)$, respectively. We assume that labor is scarce in the host country relative to the foreign country, so that the domestic wage rate, w, exceeds the foreign wage rate, w^*, in the absence of factor mobility.

Furthermore, we assume the existence of legal barriers to factor mobility. Foreign workers are assumed to be indifferent between working in their native country and working illegally in the host country, provided they are given the same (expected) wage. In this chapter, we consider the implications when the domestic government determines the level of enforcement against domestic firms that employ illegal immigrant workers. These firms will be subject to penalties if they are caught employing illegal immigrants.

2.2.1 Factor market equilibrium

Following Bond and Chen (1987), we develop the standard (two-country, one-good, two-factor) model, in which foreign workers illegally migrate to the host country and in which capital is internationally immobile. In autarky, the host country is relatively capital abundant as compared to the foreign country. Both countries produce the same good using capital and labor and a constant returns to scale technology. Technologies differ between the two countries.

The domestic firm is risk neutral, and is indifferent between legal workers and illegal workers. The cost of employing an illegal immigrant consists of the worker's wage and the expected value of a fine if the firm is caught employing him. Namely, in equilibrium the following equation is obtained:

$$w = w^* + p(E)z , \qquad (2.1)$$

where $p(E)$ is the probability of detection, with $p(0) = 0$, $p \leq 1$, $p' > 0$

and $p'' < 0$; z is the fine which firms pay for each illegal worker caught by the government enforcement policy; and E is the level of enforcement. The notation p' denotes the first partial derivation, and p'' does the second partial derivation of the function $p(E)$.

The production function of the domestic firm can be rewritten as $F(L, K) = Kf(\lambda)$, where $\lambda = L/K$ and $f' > 0$, $f'' < 0$. Hence, the first order conditions for a firm's cost-minimization problem[1] given capital rental rates, r, and wage rates, w, are

$$f'(\lambda) = w \tag{2.2a}$$

and

$$f(\lambda) - \lambda w = r. \tag{2.2b}$$

From (2.2a) it is obvious that

$$\lambda = \lambda(w), \qquad d\lambda/dw = 1/f'' < 0. \tag{2.3}$$

By totally differentiating (2.1) and (2.2b), the effects of enforcement on w, r and w^* are given by

$$dr/dE = -\lambda dw/dE, \tag{2.4}$$

$$= -\lambda(dw^*/dE + p'z), \tag{2.5}$$

where it is assumed that λ has been chosen optimally. The effect of enforcement, E, on r is opposite in sign to its effect on w.

In the foreign country, firms minimize their total costs given their wage rate, w^*, and capital rental rate, r^*, with respect to labor and capital. Hence, we obtain equations similar to (2.3), (2.4) and (2.5):

$$\lambda^* = \lambda^*(w^*), \qquad d\lambda^*/dw^* = 1/f^{*''} < 0, \tag{2.6}$$

$$dw^* = -dr^*/\lambda^*. \tag{2.7}$$

From (2.4), (2.5) and (2.7), the relationship between the effects of enforcement, E, on w^* and r^* are derived as follows:

$$dr^*/dE = -\lambda^* dw^*/dE. \tag{2.8}$$

From (2.8), it is clear that the effect of enforcement on r^* is opposite in sign to its effect on w^*, as was the case in the host country.

Let us examine the equilibrium condition in factor markets. This condition for the domestic market is

$$\overline{K}(1-a)\lambda(w^* + p(E)z) = \overline{L}, \tag{2.9}$$

where $\overline{K}$ and $\overline{L}$ are the initial endowments of the host country, I is the number of illegal immigrants, and a, which is defined as $I/(\overline{L} + I)$, is the proportion of illegal immigrants in the host country's labor force.

In the foreign market equilibrium, the following equation holds:

$$\lambda^*(w^*)\overline{K}^* + a\lambda(w^* + p(E)z)\overline{K} = \overline{L}^*, \tag{2.10}$$

where $\overline{L}^*$ and $\overline{K}^*$ are the capital and labor endowments, respectively, of the foreign country.

From the total differentiation of (2.9) and (2.10), we know the effects of an increase in the enforcement level, E, on w^* and a to be:

$$dw^*/dE = -\overline{K}\lambda\overline{K}\lambda' p' z/\Delta < 0, \tag{2.11a}$$

$$da/dE = (1-a)\overline{K}\,\overline{K}^*\lambda'\lambda^{*'} p' z/\Delta < 0, \tag{2.11b}$$

where $\Delta = \overline{K}\lambda[\overline{K}\lambda' + \overline{K}^*\lambda^{*'}] < 0$. Therefore, from (2.11b) and the definition of a, the effect of the enforcement policy on illegal immigration, I, is

$$dI/dE = [\overline{K}\lambda/(1-a)]da/dE,$$

$$= \overline{K}^2\lambda\overline{K}^*\lambda'\lambda^{*'} p' z/\Delta < 0. \tag{2.12}$$

Next from (2.4), (2.5) and (2.11a),

$$dw/dE = dw^*/dE + p'z = \overline{K}^*\lambda^{*'}\overline{K}\lambda p' z/\Delta > 0. \tag{2.13}$$

The effects of E on r and r^* are obtained from (2.4), (2.8), (2.11a) and (2.13):

$$dr/dE = -\lambda\overline{K}^*\lambda^{*'}\overline{K}\lambda p' z/\Delta < 0, \tag{2.14}$$

and

$$dr^*/dE = \lambda^*\overline{K}\lambda\overline{K}\lambda' p' z/\Delta > 0. \tag{2.15}$$

With these comparative static results, Bond and Chen found that the enforcement policy will impose adverse (favorable) effects on domestic capital (labor) and foreign labor (capital). Higher E leads to lower I, higher w, lower w^*, lower r and higher r^*.

2.2.2 Welfare effects

In general, as pointed out by Bond and Chen, the welfare effect on the host country of an increase in the level of enforcement is ambiguous. Even when the enforcement level is initially zero, somewhat stringent conditions are necessary for the host country to improve its welfare as a result of the introduction of an enforcement policy. Bond and Chen have related these conditions to the magnitude of the marginal costs of enforcement, and to the magnitude of changes in foreign wages due to enforcement.

We briefly summarize the effect of internal enforcement on the host country's welfare, which is given by national income levels. The welfare of the host country is defined as

$$Y = w\overline{L} + r\overline{K} + (z - v)p(E)I - E .$$

Here, v denotes the fixed (per unit) cost associated with returning illegal immigrants to their native country and the cost of collecting fines from firms caught hiring illegal immigrants. E is the host country's cost of catching illegal immigrants.

The effect of internal enforcement on the host country's income is derived from differentiating Y with respect to E and making use of (2.4):

$$dY / dE = -Idw^* / dE + (z - v)p(E)dI / dE - (vp'I + 1).$$

If we evaluate the effect at the zero-enforcement level, $E = 0$, it is

$$dY / dE|_{E=0} = -Idw^* / dE - (vp'I + 1) .$$

On the right hand side of the equation above, we find that the sign of the first term is positive (from (2.11a)) and the sign on the second term is negative. Consequently, the welfare effect of the enforcement policy is ambiguous. However, the welfare effect is positive if the following condition is satisfied:

$$-Idw^* / dE > (vp'I + 1) . \tag{2C.1}$$

Condition (2C.1) implies that internal enforcement by the host country's government makes the host country better off, provided that the effect of enforcement on the foreign wage outweighs the marginal cost of enforcement.

Proposition 2.1 [Bond and Chen (1987)]

Internal enforcement by the host country's government will improve the host country's welfare if condition (2C.1) is satisfied.

When we turn to the welfare effects of enforcement on the foreign (labor-exporting) country and the two countries combined, we obtain unambiguous results. First, we consider the welfare of the labor-exporting country in terms of its national income. It is expressed as

$$Y^* = w^*(\overline{L}^* - I) + r^*\overline{K}^* + w^*I . \tag{2.16}$$

Y^* is composed of factor expenditures, $w^*(\overline{L}^* - I) + r^*\overline{K}^*$, and immigrant labor earnings, w^*I.

To examine the effect of enforcement on Y^*, the foreign country's welfare, we differentiate (2.16) with respect to E:

$$dY^* / dE = [\lambda^*\overline{K}^*dw^* / dE + \overline{K}^*dr^* / dE]$$

$$+[w^*\overline{K}^*\lambda^{*\prime}dw^*/dE+w^*dI/dE]$$

$$+Idw^*/dE. \tag{2.17}$$

The respective sums of terms within the first and second pairs of brackets in the right-hand side of (2.17) are both zero (from (2.8), (2.11a) and (2.12)), so that (2.17) can be rewritten as:

$$dY^*/dE=Idw^*/dE=-\overline{IK}\lambda\overline{K}\lambda'\,p'z/\Delta<0. \tag{2.18}$$

Y^* falls when the level of enforcement increases.

Proposition 2.2 [Yoshida (1993)]

The welfare of the labor-exporting country will decline when the enforcement policy is introduced in the host (labor-importing) country.

Next consider global welfare $(Y+Y^*)$, given by

$$Y+Y^*=[w\overline{L}+r\overline{K}+(z-v)p(E)I-E]$$

$$+[w^*(\overline{L}^*-I)+r^*\overline{K}^*+w^*I]. \tag{2.19}$$

Differentiating (2.19) with respect to E yields:

$$d(Y+Y^*)/dE=[(\overline{L}+I)dw/dE+\overline{K}dr/dE]$$

$$-Idw^*/dE+Idw^*/dE$$

$$+(z-v)pdI/dE-(vp'I+1). \tag{2.20}$$

Evaluating (2.20) at $E=0$, given that the sum within bracket in the right-hand side of (2.20) is zero (see (2.4)) gives:

$$d(Y+Y^*)/dE|_{E=0}=-(vp'I+1)<0. \tag{2.21}$$

Thus, we obtain the next proposition.

Proposition 2.3 [Yoshida (1993)]

Global income (welfare) will fall when the host country's government intro-duces an enforcement policy.

Thus, we have shown that the enforcement policy is undesirable in terms of global welfare when capital is immobile.

2.3 Concluding remarks

In this chapter we examined the global welfare effect of a domestic enforcement policy by the host (labor-importing) country. While the host country's welfare may or may not be improved by the introduction of an enforcement policy, we can unambiguously state that both the foreign country and the world are worse off following the introduction of the policy.

Bond and Chen (1987) have already noticed that the optimal level of enforcement is zero, unless the magnitude of the effects of enforcement on foreign wages is sufficiently large and the marginal cost of enforcement is sufficiently low. It should be emphasized that our results give further insights into the desirability of zero enforcement.

Mathematical appendix

We will show the cost minimization and profit maximization problems for a domestic firm. In addition, we introduce and verify the different theorems and lemmas normally associated with these problems.

Let us consider cost-minimization, in which a competitive domestic firm chooses L and K so as to maximize profit:

$$\text{Maximize:}\quad -(wL + rK)$$

$$\text{subject to:}\quad y \le Kf(\lambda),\quad L \ge 0 \text{ and } K \ge 0,$$

where y is the target level of output, and w, r and $y(>0)$ are taken as given. The *Lagrange* function, Φ, is

$$\Phi(L, K, \alpha; w, r, y) \equiv -(wL + rK) + \alpha[Kf(\lambda) - y], \tag{2A.1}$$

where $\alpha(\ge 0)$ is the *Lagrange* multiplier. Then, the Kuhn-Tucker conditions for this problem can be written as

$$\Phi_L \le 0, \qquad \Phi_L \cdot L = 0, \qquad L \ge 0, \tag{2A.2a}$$

$$\Phi_K \le 0, \qquad \Phi_K \cdot K = 0, \qquad K \ge 0, \tag{2A.2b}$$

$$\Phi_\alpha \ge 0, \qquad \Phi_\alpha \cdot \alpha = 0, \qquad \alpha \ge 0, \tag{2A.2c}$$

where subscripts indicate partial derivatives, e.g., $\Phi_L \equiv \partial\Phi / \partial L$.
The constraint set of this problem can be written as $S \equiv \{(L, K) : L \ge 0 \text{ and } K \ge 0, Kf(\lambda) \ge y\}$. We assume that $L \ge 0$ and $K \ge 0$ such that $Kf(\lambda) > y$, which is called Slater's condition.

If we assume that there are interior solutions, $\hat{L} > 0$, $\hat{K} > 0$ and $\hat{\alpha} > 0$, (2A.2a) through (2A.2c) are reduced to the following conditions:

$$w = \alpha f'(\lambda),\quad r = \alpha(f(\lambda) - \lambda f'(\lambda))\quad \text{and}\quad Kf(\lambda) = y, \tag{2A.2)'}$$

which determines the following demand conditions,

$$\hat{L} = L(w, r, y),\quad \hat{K} = K(w, r, y)\quad \text{and}\quad \hat{\alpha} = \alpha(w, r, y).$$

Let the maximum value function, $-C(w, r, y)$, and the function $\psi(w, r, y)$ be defined as

$$-C(w, r, y) \equiv -\{wL(w, r, y) + rK(w, r, y)\}, \tag{2A.3}$$

$$\psi(w, r, y) \equiv -\{wL(w, r, y) + rK(w, r, y)\}$$
$$+ \alpha(w, r, y)\{Kf(\lambda) - y\}. \tag{2A.4}$$

We call $C(w, r, y)$ the minimum cost function.

We can find the following relations using the Envelope Theorem,

$$-C_y(w, r, y) = \psi_y(w, r, y) = \Phi_y(w, r, y). \tag{2A.5}$$

Proof (recall that the production function, f, is homogeneous of degree one and that λ is the labor-capital ratio, L/K):

$$\psi_y = -(wL_y + rK_y) + \alpha[K_y f(\lambda) + \{Kf'(L_y K - K_y L)\}/K^2 - 1],$$

$$= -(wL_y + rK_y) + \alpha[fK_y + f'(L_y - K_y \lambda) - 1],$$

$$= -L_y(w - \alpha f') - K_y\{r + \alpha(\lambda f' - f)\} - \alpha,$$

$$= -\alpha, \text{ [since } w = \alpha f' \text{ and } r = \alpha(f - \lambda f') \text{ from (2A.2)'].}$$

$$= \Phi_y.$$

$$-C_y = -(wL_y + rK_y),$$

$$= -\alpha,$$

$$= \Phi_y.$$

We derive the following equation from (2A.2)',

$$K(w,r,y)f(L(w,r,y)/K(w,r,y)) - y = 0.$$

Differentiation of the above equation with respect to y gives

$$K_y f + Kf'((L_y K - K_y L)/K^2) - 1 = 0,$$

$$L_y f' + K_y(f - \lambda f') = 1,$$

$$wL_y + rK_y = \alpha. \qquad\qquad \text{[from (2A.2)']}$$

Hence, we know that $-C_y = -\alpha$. $\qquad\qquad\qquad\qquad\qquad \square$

By using the envelope theorem, the *Lagrange* multiplier, $\alpha(w,r,y)$, is equal to the marginal cost of output, C_y. Also, it can be seen from the equations that

$$C_w = L(w,r,y) \text{ and } C_r = K(w,r,y). \qquad\qquad (2A.6)$$

Those results are known as Shephard's Lemma (or the Shephard-McKenzie Lemma).

If we assume that $C(w,r,y)$ is twice continuously differentiable, then Young's theorem yields $C_{wr} = C_{rw}$, $C_{wy} = C_{yw}$, and $C_{ry} = C_{yr}$. In conjunction with Shephard's Lemma, we then obtain the following:

$$L_r = K_w, \quad L_y = \alpha_w, \text{ and } K_y = \alpha_r. \qquad\qquad (2A.7)$$

(2A.7) is known as Samuelson's reciprocity relation. Let us consider the following matrix S:

$$\begin{bmatrix} C_{ww} & C_{wr} \\ C_{rw} & C_{rr} \end{bmatrix}. \qquad\qquad (2A.8)$$

This matrix is called the substitution matrix; it is symmetric and defined as $S(w,r)$. The factor demands, $L(w,r,y)$ and $K(w,r,y)$, are homogeneous of degree zero in factor prices, w and r, since the following equation does not change, even if both the denominator and the numerator on the right and left hand sides are multiplied by any non-zero factor:

$$\frac{w}{r} = \frac{f'(\lambda)}{f(\lambda) - \lambda f'(\lambda)}.$$

Hence, by Euler's theorem,

$$L_w w + L_r r = 0,$$

$$K_w w + K_r r = 0.$$

In other words, $S(w,r) \cdot (w,r)' = 0$, where (w,r) is the factor price vector.

$C(w,r,y)$ is homogeneous of degree one in factor prices, since $C(w,r,y) \equiv wL(w,r,y) + rK(w,r,y)$, and the factor demands, $L(w,r,y)$ and $K(w,r,y)$, are homogenous of degree zero in the factor prices, w and r.

We define $l \equiv (L(w,r,y), K(w,r,y))$. This can be rewritten as $l \equiv l(h,y)$ where $h \equiv (w,r)$. Hence, $C(h,y) \equiv hl(h,y)$. Let $l^0 \equiv l(h^0, y)$, $l^* \equiv l(h^*, y)$ and $l^\theta \equiv l(h^\theta, y)$, where $h^\theta \equiv \theta h^0 + (1-\theta)h^*$, $0 \le \theta \le 1$. Then, $h^0 l^0 \le h^0 l^\theta$ and $h^* l^* \le h^* l^\theta$ by cost minimization, where $F(l^0) \ge y$, $F(l^*) \ge y$ and $F(l^\theta) \ge y$ by the definitions of l^0, l^* and l^θ.[2] Hence,

$$\theta h^0 l^0 + (1-\theta)h^* l^* \le \theta h^0 l^\theta + (1-\theta)h^* l^\theta = h^\theta l^\theta.$$

In other words, $\theta C(h^0, y) + (1-\theta)C(h^*, y) \le C(h^\theta, y)$, $0 \le \theta \le 1$, which ensures that $C(h,y)$ is concave with respect to h. Therefore, the Hessian of C in h is negative semidefinite. This implies that S is negative semidefinite (see (2A.8)). Namely, we have $qS(w,r)q \le 0$ for all $q \ne 0$. Since S is negative semidefinite, we know that $C_{ww} < 0$ and $C_{rr} < 0$.

Moreover, we can show that

$$C/y = \partial C / \partial y (= \alpha), \qquad \partial \alpha(w,r,y)/\partial y = 0. \tag{2A.9}$$

(2A.9) is known as the Shephard-Samuelson Theorem. The first condition of (2A.9) means that the average cost is equal to the marginal cost. We have

$$C = hl = wL + rK = \alpha[f'(\lambda)L + \{f(\lambda) - \lambda f'(\lambda)\}K]$$

$$= \alpha K f(\lambda) = \alpha y,$$

where $w = \alpha f'(\lambda)$, $r = \alpha(f(\lambda) - \lambda f'(\lambda))$ and $y = Kf(\lambda)$ from (2A.2)'.

Let us consider the profit maximization problem. The domestic firm chooses output, y, so as to

Maximize: $py - C(w,r,y)$,

where $C(w,r,y) \equiv wL(w,r,y) + rK(w,r,y)$. The solution of the problem is $p = C_y$, which implies that price equals marginal cost.

We assumed in the present chapter that output is treated as the numeraire. The price of output is one, and hence marginal cost (= the *Lagrange* multiplier α), C_y equals 1.

(2A.2)' is rewritten as

$$w = f'(\lambda), \tag{2A.2a}''$$

$$r = f(\lambda) - \lambda f'(\lambda), \tag{2A.2b}''$$

$$Kf(\lambda) - y = 0. \tag{2A.2c}''$$

(2A.2a)'' and (2A.2b)'' show that the wage rate of domestic labor equals the marginal product of labor, and the rental price of domestic capital equals the marginal product of capital.

We can generally consider the profit maximization problem, which is regarded as the problem of choosing inputs, L and K, and an output, y, as

Maximize: $py - (wL + rK)$

subject to: $Kf(\lambda) \geq y$, $L \geq 0$, $K \geq 0$ and $y \geq 0$,

where p, w and r are given.

The associated *Lagrange* function is:

$$\Phi(y,L,K,\gamma;p,w,r) \equiv py - (wL + rK) + \gamma\{Kf(\lambda) - y\}. \tag{2A.10}$$

The Kuhn-Tucker conditions for the problem are

$$\Phi_y \leq 0, \qquad \Phi_y \cdot y = 0, \qquad y \geq 0 \tag{2A.11a}$$

$$\Phi_L \leq 0, \qquad \Phi_L \cdot L = 0, \qquad L \geq 0 \tag{2A.11b}$$

$$\Phi_K \leq 0, \qquad \Phi_K \cdot K = 0, \qquad K \geq 0 \tag{2A.11c}$$

$$\Phi_\gamma \leq 0, \qquad \Phi_\gamma \cdot \gamma = 0, \qquad \gamma \geq 0 \tag{2A.11d}$$

When we assume that an interior solution exists, $\hat{y}, \hat{L}, \hat{K}$ and $\hat{\gamma}$, the equations are rewritten as follows:

$$p - \gamma = 0, \tag{2A.12a}$$

$$w = \gamma f'(\lambda), \tag{2A.12b}$$

$$r = \gamma\{f(\lambda) - \lambda f'(\lambda)\}, \tag{2A.12c}$$

$$Kf(\lambda) - y = 0. \tag{2A.12d}$$

Considering (2A.12a) through (2A.12d), we define the solution of the problem as

$$L \equiv L(p,w,r), \quad K \equiv K(p,w,r),$$
$$y \equiv y(p,w,r) \quad \text{and} \quad \gamma \equiv \gamma(p,w,r). \tag{2A.13}$$

Hence, the maximum profit function is defined as

$$\pi(p,w,r) \equiv py(p,w,r) - \{wL(p,w,r)$$
$$+rK(p,w,r)\}. \tag{2A.14}$$

We can obtain the following equations by using the Envelope Theorem:

$$\pi_p = y, \quad \pi_w = -L \quad \text{and} \quad \pi_r = -K. \tag{2A.15}$$

(2A.15) is known as Hotelling's Lemma.

If we assume that $\pi(p,w,r)$ is twice continuously differentiable, then the Hessian matrix is symmetric.[3] The following equations are derived from this:

$$L_r = K_w, \quad L_p = -y_w \quad \text{and} \quad K_p = -y_r. \tag{2A.16}$$

(2A.16) is known as Hotelling's symmetry relation.

Notes

* The chapter was first published in the Indian Economic Review 28, 111-115, 1993.
1 See mathematical appendix.
2 Recall that the production function of the domestic firm is transformed:
$$F(L,K) = KF(L/K,1) = Kf(\lambda).$$
3 Hessian matrix is:

$$\begin{bmatrix} \pi_{pp} & \pi_{pw} & \pi_{pr} \\ \pi_{wp} & \pi_{ww} & \pi_{wr} \\ \pi_{rp} & \pi_{rw} & \pi_{rr} \end{bmatrix},$$

from which we can find that it is symmetric.

3
The Global Welfare Effects of Illegal Immigration in the Presence of Capital Mobility*

Using the Bond and Chen (1987) model of illegal immigration, we re-examine the effects of internal enforcement by the host country's government on the welfare of the host (labor-importing) country, the foreign (labor-exporting) country and the world, when capital is internationally mobile between countries. Our main result is that the internal enforcement policy increases the foreign country's welfare and global welfare and, under certain conditions, increases the host country's welfare. Therefore, we conclude that enforcement is a *Pareto-improving policy* potentially.

3.1 Introduction

Chapter 2 used the Bond and Chen (1987) model to analyze the effects of introducing internal enforcement on the host country's welfare, on the foreign country's welfare and on global welfare (the combined welfare of the host country and the foreign country). Chapter 2 showed that the introduction of enforcement by the host country's government reduces the welfare of the foreign country and reduces global welfare when there is no international capital mobility.

However, Chapter 2 did not examine the welfare effects of internal enforcement *in the presence of international capital mobility between countries*. Using the Bond and Chen (1987) model, we examine the effects of enforcement on the welfare of the host country and the foreign country and on the combined (global) welfare of the two countries when capital is internationally mobile between the two countries.

In the presence of capital mobility, we show that enforcement improves the welfare of the host country under some circumstances, improves the welfare of the foreign country, and hence, improves the two countries' combined (global) welfare. This result is opposite to that of Chapter 2, in which enforcement reduces global welfare in the absence of international capital mobility. We conclude that internal enforcement by the host country's government is *a Pareto-improving policy* when international capital mobility exists.

In the next section, we summarize the comparative static analysis of Bond and Chen (1987) and present our results. Section 3.3 offers some concluding remarks.

3.2 The basic model and main results

Following Bond and Chen (1987), we introduce a standard (two-country, one-good, two-factor) model of illegal immigration, in which capital is assumed internationally mobile. Firms in both the host (domestic) country and the foreign country produce a single output, assumed to be the numeraire, using a constant returns to scale technology. Technologies are assumed to be the same in both countries. Output in both countries is produced using labor and capital inputs. The production functions of domestic and foreign firms are, respectively, denoted by $F(L,K)$ and $F^*(L^*,K^*)$, where L, K, L^* and K^* are domestic labor, domestic capital, foreign labor and foreign capital, respectively. We assume that labor is scarcer in the host country than in the foreign country, so that in the absence of factor mobility the host's wage rate, w, exceeds the foreign wage rate, w^*.[1,2]

Furthermore, we assume that there are legal barriers to factor mobility. Foreign workers are assumed to be indifferent between working in their native country and working illegally in the host country, when they face the same expected wages in both countries. The host country's government determines the enforcement level against domestic firms that employ illegal foreign workers. A firm must pay a penalty to the host government if it is caught employing an illegal foreign worker. The host country's government also levies a tax on the export of host country (domestic) capital.

3.2.1 Factor market equilibrium

Following Bond and Chen (1987), we develop the standard (two-country, one-good, two-factor) model of illegal immigration in which foreign labor illegally migrates to the host country and capital is internationally mobile. Technologies are the *same* between the two countries. In autarky, the host country is labor-scarce relative to the foreign country (i.e., the foreign country is capital-scarce relative to the host country). Each country produces a single good using labor and capital, and a constant returns to scale technology.

Domestic firms are indifferent between employing domestic labor and employing illegal foreign labor.[3] The cost of employing illegal workers is composed of these workers' wages and the expected value of the fine if caught employing illegal workers. Hence, in equilibrium[4] we have:

$$w = w^* + p(E)z , \qquad (3.1)$$

where $p(E)$ is the probability of detection, with $p(0) = 0$, $p \leq 1$, $p' > 0$ and $p'' < 0$, z is the fine which a domestic firm pays for each illegal worker caught by the host country's government during enforcement, and E is the level of enforcement. We exclude the possibility of $E = 0$ (see footnote 6 for explanation).

The production function for the domestic firm is expressed as $F(L, K) = Kf(\lambda)$, where $\lambda = L/K$ and $f' > 0, f'' < 0$. Thus, the first-order conditions for cost-minimization for domestic firms facing given wage rates, w, and given capital rental rates, r, are:

$$f'(\lambda) = w, \qquad (3.2a)$$

$$f(\lambda) - \lambda w = r . \qquad (3.2b)$$

From (3.2a) it is clear that

$$\lambda = \lambda(w), \quad \lambda' = 1/f'' < 0 . \qquad (3.3)$$

The total differentiation of (3.1) and (3.2b) yields the effects of enforcement, E, on w, r and w^*:

$$dr = -\lambda dw , \qquad (3.4)$$

$$= -\lambda(dw + p' z dE) , \qquad (3.5)$$

where λ is assumed to be chosen optimally.

In the foreign country, foreign firms minimize total costs given foreign wages and rental rates, w^* and r^*, with respect to labor and capital. Hence, we obtain equations similar to (3.3), (3.4) and (3.5):

$$\lambda^* = \lambda^*(w^*), \quad \lambda^{*\prime} = 1/f^{*\prime\prime} < 0 , \qquad (3.6)$$

$$dw^* = -dr^* / \lambda^* . \qquad (3.7)$$

If there were no barriers to capital mobility, then domestic capital would migrate to the foreign country until returns to capital were equalized; $r = r^*$. Under the assumption that both countries utilized the same production technology, this would cause the domestic and foreign wages to equalize in our model; $w = w^*$. Hence, there would be no illegal immigration. However, if the host country taxes capital exports, illegal immigration will exist. We assume the host country's government levies a tax on domestic capital located in the foreign country, K_F, so that the net return to domestic capital in the foreign country is $r^*(1-t)$, where t is the tax rate, and t is in $(0, 1)$. Thus, in equilibrium, there are both legal capital flows and illegal labor flows. Domestic capital migrates to the foreign country until the rental rate of domestic capital located in the host country equals the after-tax returns of domestic capital, K_F, located in the foreign country:[5]

$$r = r^*(1-t). \tag{3.8}$$

Let us examine the equilibrium conditions in factor markets.[6] This condition for the host (domestic) market is

$$(\overline{K} - K_F)(1-a)\lambda(w^* + p(E)z) = \overline{L}, \tag{3.9}$$

where $\overline{K}$ and $\overline{L}$ are the host country's initial capital and labor endowments, respectively, and a is defined as $I/(\overline{L}+I)$, where I is the level of illegal immigration. In the foreign market equilibrium we have

$$(\overline{K}^* + K_F)\lambda^*(w^*) + (\overline{K} - K_F)a\lambda(w^* + p(E)z) = \overline{L}^*, \tag{3.10}$$

where $\overline{L}^*$ and $\overline{K}^*$ are the foreign country's initial labor and capital endowments, respectively. The three equations, (3.8), (3.9) and (3.10), simultaneously determine w^*, a and K_F.

By totally differentiating (3.8) and making use of (3.5) and (3.7), we obtain the following equation:

$$[\lambda^*{}'(w^*)(1-t) - \lambda(w^* + p(E)z)]dw^* = r^*d(1-t) + \lambda p' z dE. \tag{3.11}$$

From (3.11), we see that an increase in the tax rate on exported domestic capital reduces the wages of foreign workers, provided $(\lambda^*(1-t) - \lambda) > 0$. Following Bond and Chen (1987), we assume that the sign of $(\lambda^*(1-t) - \lambda)$ is positive (see Jones (1971) and Neary (1978)).[7]

Total differentiation of (3.8), (3.9) and (3.10) yields the following three-equation system, after eliminating dw using (3.1):

$$\begin{bmatrix} \lambda^*(1-t) - \lambda & 0 & 0 \\ (\overline{K} - K_F)(1-a)\lambda' & -(\overline{K} - K_F)\lambda & -(1-a)\lambda \\ (\overline{K}^* + K_F)\lambda^{*'} + a\lambda'(\overline{K} - K_F) & (\overline{K} - K_F)\lambda & \lambda^* - a\lambda \end{bmatrix} \begin{bmatrix} dw^* \\ da \\ dK_F \end{bmatrix}$$

$$= \begin{bmatrix} -r^*dt + \lambda p' z dE \\ -(\overline{K} - K_F)(1-a)\lambda' p' z dE \\ -(\overline{K} - K_F)a\lambda' p' z dE \end{bmatrix}. \tag{3.12}$$

The determinant of the system (3.12) is

$$\Delta = (\lambda^*(1-t) - \lambda)((K - K_F)(\lambda - \lambda^*)\lambda),$$

where the sign of Δ is negative because the sign of $(\lambda^*(1-t) - \lambda)$ is assumed to be positive.

From (3.12) we obtain the effects of E on w^*, a and K_F:

$$dw^* / dE = \lambda p' z / (\lambda^*(1-t) - \lambda) > 0, \tag{3.13a}$$

$$da / dE = p' z[-\lambda^{*2}(1-t)(1-a)(\overline{K} - K_F)\lambda'$$
$$- \lambda^2(1-a)(\overline{K} - K_F)\lambda^{*'}] / \Delta < 0, \tag{3.13b}[8]$$

$$dK_F / dE = p' z[\lambda\lambda^*(1-t)(\overline{K} - K_F)^2 \lambda'$$
$$+ (\overline{K} - K_F)(\overline{K}^* + K_F)\lambda^2\lambda^{*'}] / \Delta > 0, \tag{3.13c}$$

Next from (3.4), (3.5) and (3.13a), the effect of E on w is:

$$dw / dE = dw^* / dE + p' z$$
$$= \lambda^*(1-t)p' z / (\lambda^*(1-t) - \lambda) > 0. \tag{3.14}$$

And the effects of E on r and r^* are obtained from (3.4), (3.7), (3.13a) and (3.14):

$$dr / dE = -\lambda\lambda^*(1-t)p' z / (\lambda^*(1-t) - \lambda) < 0, \tag{3.15}$$

and

$$dr^* / dE = -\lambda^* \lambda p' z / (\lambda^*(1-t) - \lambda) < 0. \tag{3.16}$$

With these comparative static results, Bond and Chen (1987) stated that under capital mobility, the enforcement policy has adverse effects on the returns to domestic and foreign capital, whereas it has favorable effects on the returns to domestic and foreign labor.

We find from (3.13a) that internal inspection by the host country's government causes an increase in the foreign country's wages. This arises because internal enforcement causes home capital to shift from the home country to the foreign country. Capital immobility causes a match of illegal foreign country labor and home country capital in the home country. Capital mobility causes a match of (legal) foreign country labor and home country capital in the foreign country. Thus, capital mobility allows the elimination of production penalties that would be incurred under capital immobility.

An increase in distortion, i.e., internal enforcement, will bring about further separation from the equilibrium point where the factor prices are equal between countries; $w = w^*$ and $r = r^*$. Since the home country's output is produced by a capital-intensive technique in a value-sense as long as $\lambda^*(1-t)-\lambda>0$, the enforcement causes a decrease in the capital costs for both the home and the foreign country.

Although we have derived the effects on the six endogenous variables, the four factor prices, the number of illegal immigrants, and the level of capital exports, we have yet to derive the effects of internal enforcement on the welfare of each of the two countries and on global welfare. In subsection 3.2.2, we examine these effects.

3.2.2 Welfare effects

In this subsection, we examine the effects of internal enforcement by the host country's government on the welfare of the host country, the foreign country and the two countries combined.

Firstly, we consider the labor-importing country's income, which is used to measure its welfare:

$$Y = w\overline{L} + r\overline{K} + p(E)(z-v)I + (r^* - r)K_F - E, \tag{3.17}$$

where v denotes the costs associated with the return of illegal workers to their native country and the collection of fines from firms, and E is the cost incurred by the host country's government in catching illegal workers. Y is composed of factor expenditures, $(wL + rK)$, and the host government's surplus, $[p(E)(z-v)I + (r^* - r)K_F - E]$.

Differentiating (3.17) with respect to E yields:

$$dY / dE = \overline{L}dw / dE + \overline{K}dr / dE + p'(z-v)I + p(z-v)dI / dE$$
$$+ K_F(dr^* / dE - dr / dE) + (r^* - r)dK_F / dE - 1. \tag{3.18}$$

By making use of (3.1), (3.4), (3.5) and (3.7), and noting that $\lambda = (\overline{L}+I)/(\overline{K}-K_F)$, (3.18) is rewritten as:

$$dY / dE = (r^* - r)dK_F / dE - Idw^* / dE - \lambda^* K_F dw^* / dE$$
$$+ p(z-v)dI / dE - (vp'I + 1). \tag{3.19}$$

We assume that

$$z > v, \tag{3A}$$

which implies that the fine that the domestic firm pays for each illegal worker caught is larger than the combined cost associated with the return of each illegal worker to his native country and the collection of fines from the penalized firm.

We find that the sign of (3.19) is indeterminate. However, it is clear from (3.13a), (3.13b), (3.13c) and (3A) that the sign of (3.19) is positive if the condition

$$(r^* - r)dK_F / dE > p(z - v)dI / dE + Idw^* / dE$$
$$+ \lambda^* K_F dw^* / dE + (vp'I + 1). \qquad (3C.1)$$

is satisfied for any defined $E(> 0)$ and t.[9] This condition implies that the marginal tax on revenue of domestic capital outflows from the introduction of enforcement, $(r^* - r)dK_F / dE$ outweighs the change in revenue from penalties net of the real resource costs due to changes in the number of illegal immigration, $p(z - v)dI / dE$, the effect of enforcement on the foreign labor wage rate, $Idw^* / dE + \lambda^* K_F dw^* / dE$, and the marginal costs of the enforcement, $(vp'I + 1)$.

Proposition 3.1 [Yoshida (1996)]
The host country's income will increase under (3C.1) when the host country's government introduces internal enforcement.

Secondly, we consider the effect of internal enforcement on the foreign country's income. The foreign country's welfare, or income, is expressed as:

$$Y^* = w^* \lambda^* (w^*)(\overline{K}^* + K_F) + r^* \overline{K}^* + Iw^*. \qquad (3.20)$$

Y^* consists of factor expenditures, $[w^* \lambda^* (w^*)(\overline{K}^* + K_F) + r^* \overline{K}^*]$, and immigrant earnings, Iw^*. By differentiating (3.20) with respect to E and using (3.7), the following equation is obtained:

$$dY^* / dE = Idw^* / dE + \lambda^* K_F dw^* / dE > 0. \qquad (3.21)$$

The sign of (3.21) is unambiguously positive from (3.13a). Y^* will rise when the level of enforcement increases.

Proposition 3.2 [Yoshida (1996)]
The welfare of the labor-exporting country will rise when the host country introduces an internal enforcement policy.

This result is opposite to Proposition 2.2 in Chapter 2, that 'the welfare of the labor-exporting country will decline when the enforcement policy is introduced in the host (labor-importing) country'.

Thirdly, we consider the effect of enforcement on global welfare $(Y + Y^*)$, or income. Global income, $(Y + Y^*)$, is derived from (3.17) and (3.20):

$$(Y + Y^*) = [w\overline{L} + r\overline{K} + p(E)(z - v)I + (r^* - r)K_F - E]$$
$$+ [w^* \lambda^* (w^*)(\overline{K} + K_F) + r^* \overline{K} + Iw^*], \qquad (3.22)$$

where Y and Y^* are expressed by the sums within the first and second pairs of brackets in the right-hand side of (3.22), respectively. Using (3.19) and (3.21), the differentiation of (3.22) with respect to E yields:

$$d(Y + Y^*)/dE = (r^* - r)dK_F/dE + p(z - v)dI/dE - (vp'I + 1). \qquad (3.23)$$

It is clear that the sign of (3.23) is positive if condition (3C.1) is satisfied for any defined $E(>0)$ and t. In short, the effect of enforcement on $(Y + Y^*)$ is positive when the marginal tax-revenue on domestic capital outflows, $(r^* - r)dK_F/dE$ outweighs the marginal expected revenue of fines net of the resource costs, $p(z - v)dI/dE$ and the marginal costs of enforcement, $(vp'I + 1)$. This result is opposite to Proposition 2.3 in Chapter 2 that 'global income (welfare) will fall when the host country's government introduces an enforcement policy'.

Proposition 3.3 [Yoshida (1996)]
Global income (welfare) will rise when the host country's government intro-duces an enforcement policy under (3C.1).

It has been shown from our welfare analyses that internal enforcement by the host country's government improves the host country's welfare under (3C.1), improves the foreign country's welfare, and hence, im-proves global welfare. We can conclude, therefore, that under the stated circumstances, internal enforcement is *a potentially Pareto-improving pol-icy*.

3.3 Concluding remarks

In the present chapter, using the Bond and Chen model, we examined the effects of internal enforcement by the host country's government on the welfare of the host country, on the welfare of the foreign country, and on global welfare, when capital was internationally mobile between countries. We showed that the introduction of the enforcement policy improves the host country's welfare under some circumstances and improves the foreign country's welfare, thereby improving global wel-fare. Hence, enforcement by the host country's government may be *a potentially Pareto-improving policy*. This result is opposite to Proposition 2.3, which states that introduction of enforcement will reduce global welfare when capital is not internationally mobile.

We state some economic interpretations of our results by comparing them with those of Chapter 2. The comments following Proposition 3.2 can be elaborated upon to indicate why this proposition differs from proposition 2.2 of Chapter 2. In Chapter 2, capital is immobile between countries, so an increase in enforcement reduces the wage rate in the foreign country. With capital mobility, an increase in enforcement raises the wage rate in the labor-exporting country. Thus, the fact that the terms of trade move in opposite directions in the two cases generates this difference in results. When capital is immobile, enforcement introduces a distortion into a previously Pareto optimal world economy, thereby reducing global welfare. When there is capital mobility and there is a capital export tax, the initial world economy faces a distortion. The introduction of a second distortion, the enforcement policy, can raise global welfare for the standard second-best reasons.

Mathematical appendix

We show the stability conditions of the equilibrium in the production factor markets. Following Chang (1981), we postulate the following dynamic adjustment process:

$$\dot{w} = \beta_1\{(\overline{K} - K_F)(1-a)\lambda(w) - \overline{L}\},$$

$$\dot{w}^* = \beta_2\{(\overline{K}^* + K_F)\lambda^*(w^*) + (\overline{K} - K_F)a\lambda(w) - \overline{L}^*\}, \quad (3A.1)$$

$$\dot{K}_F = \beta_3\{(1-t)r^* - r\},$$

$$\dot{a} = \beta_4\{w - w^* - p(E)z\},$$

where a dot over variables is the time derivative and β_i's are the speeds of adjustment, which are assumed to be positive constants.

Linearization of the differential equations around the equilibrium values in (3A.1) gives

$$
\begin{bmatrix} \dot{w} \\ \dot{w}^* \\ \dot{K}_F \\ \dot{a} \end{bmatrix} =
\begin{bmatrix}
\beta_1(\overline{K}-K_F)(1-a)\lambda' & 0 & \beta_1(1-a)\lambda & -\beta_1(\overline{K}-K_F)\lambda \\
\beta_2(\overline{K}^*-K_F)a\lambda' & \beta_2(\overline{K}^*+K_F)\lambda^{*'} & \beta_2(\lambda^*-a\lambda) & \beta_2(\overline{K}-K_F)\lambda \\
\beta_3\lambda & -\beta_3(1-t)\lambda^* & 0 & 0 \\
\beta_4 & -\beta_4 & 0 & 0
\end{bmatrix}
$$
$$
\times \begin{bmatrix} dw \\ dw^* \\ dK_F \\ da \end{bmatrix}.
$$

Let the coefficient matrix denote J. If J is a totally stable matrix, then J is a *Hicksian* matrix. The matrix implies that (1) every principal minor of J of even order is positive, (2) every principal minor of J of odd order is negative (see Quirk and Saposnik (1968)). Let J_i denote the ith principal minor. Then, we have

$$J_1 = \beta_1(\overline{K}-K_F)(1-a)\lambda' < 0,$$

$$J_2 = \beta_1\beta_2(\overline{K}-K_F)(\overline{K}^*+K_F)(1-a)\lambda'\lambda^{*'} > 0,$$

$$J_3 = \beta_1\beta_2\beta_3(1-a)\{(\overline{K}-K_F)\lambda'(1-t)\lambda^*(\lambda^*-a\lambda) + \lambda^2\lambda^{*'}(\overline{K}^*+K_F) + \lambda\lambda^*(1-t)(\overline{K}-K_F)a\lambda'\} < 0,$$

and

$$J_4 = \beta_1\beta_2\beta_3\beta_4(\overline{K}-K_F)\lambda(\lambda^*-\lambda)\{\lambda^*(1-t)-\lambda\}.$$

We can easily show that the signs of J_1, J_2 and J_3 are, respectively, negative, positive and negative. The sign of J_4 is indeterminate. However, from the total stability condition, the sign of J_4 must be positive. Therefore, we find that the sign of $\{\lambda^*(1-t)-\lambda\}$ must be positive, considering the sign of J_4 when the totally stable condition is satisfied. This implies that the foreign country is labor-abundant relative to the home country.

Notes

* The chapter was first published in the Journal of Economic Integration 11, 554-565, 1996.

1 From the assumption of the same technology in both countries, we find that in the absence of international factor mobility the wage rate (rental price) in the capital-abundant host country is higher (lower) than in the labor-abundant foreign country.

2 In our model, host country workers do not have incentives to legally or illegally migrate to the foreign country because their wage rate, w, exceeds the foreign wage rate, w^*, in the absence of factor mobility. The foreign country's government does not need to introduce either the border enforcement or the internal enforcement policies. Therefore, the expenditure levels on these enforcement policies by the foreign country's government are zero.

3 If the host country's government introduces border enforcement, workers attempting to illegally migrate will incur the penalty, k, if caught at the border between the two countries. If we assume that the probability of detection at the border is expressed as $g(B)$, where B is the expenditure on border enforcement by the host country's government, $g(0)=0, g<1, g'>0$ and $g^*<0$ then risk neutral illegal migrants determine their migration decisions so as to equate the expected reward from migration to the local wage, w^*:

$$(w^* - k)g + w^I(1-g) = w^*, \qquad \text{(i)}$$

where w^I is the wage earned by foreign workers who succeed in illegally immigrating and working in host country firms. Equation (i) is rewritten as:

$$w^I = w^* + k[g(B)/(1-g(B))]. \qquad \text{(ii)}$$

Thus, when the host country's government carries out border enforcement, the foreign illegal migrants who are not caught at the border earn the wage, w^I, which exceeds the foreign country's wage, w^*.

We can ignore $k[g(B)/(1-g(B))]$ in the right-hand side of equation (ii) since we assume that the level of border enforcement is constant throughout the chapter. Therefore, there is no wage differential between illegal working in the host country and legal working in the foreign country; $w^I = w^*$ (see Bond and Chen (1987)).

4 The number of illegal immigrants, $I(>0)$, is determined so that (3.1) is satisfied. If $w > w^* + p(E)z$ for any $E>0$, the domestic (host country) firm is willing to hire foreign illegal workers rather than domestic workers, and hence (3.1) holds. On the other hand, if it is not the case, the domestic firm would like to employ relatively more domestic workers than foreign workers, so (3.1) is satisfied. Therefore, in equilibrium (3.1) holds and thus $I(>0)$ is determined from (3.1).

When the level of internal enforcement, E becomes sufficiently high, the level of illegal immigration, I, is lower. Hence, it is possible that for some sufficiently large E, the number of illegal immigrants becomes zero; i.e. there is a corner solution with regard to labor mobility. However, we only assume the existence of an interior solution on labor movement for all E.

5   If a tax on capital exports is sufficiently high, so that $r > r^*(1-t)$, then the levels of capital exports may be zero; $K_F = 0$. Therefore, there might be a corner solution for capital mobility. But in our model, we assume the existence of an interior solution on capital exports.

6   There is the possibility that $w = w^*$ from (3.1) when the level of internal enforcement is zero; $E = 0$ (and a tax, t (which is $(0,1)$) is imposed on the returns of host country capital located in the foreign country), and hence the rental price of host country capital, r, becomes equal to the rental price of foreign capital, r^*. This implies that it may be possible for factor price equalization to occur, and hence *the level of illegal immigration, I, is independent of the enforcement level, E*.

However, we assume that the level of internal enforcement, E is initially set at some minimum level, $E_{min}(> 0)$. In short, we do not consider that the expenditure level of enforcement is zero since we exclude the possibility of factor price equalization from our consideration. Thus, there are two-way factor movements in equilibrium for any defined $E(> 0)$ and t.

7   See mathematical appendix on the condition.

8   From the definition of a and (3.13b), the effect of enforcement on the level of illegal immigration, I, is negative:

$$dI/dE = [(\overline{L} + I)/(1-a)] \cdot [da/dE] < 0.$$

9   Notice that (3C.1) is the necessary condition for the optimal enforcement policy to be positive where the objective function of the host country's government is the income of the host country.

4
The Welfare Effects of
Border Patrol on
Illegal Immigration*

This chapter extends Ethier's (1986a) one small-country model of illegal immigration by constructing a standard two-country, one-good, two-factor model. The host country introduces a border enforcement policy to catch illegal would-be migrants from the foreign country at the border between two countries. We examine the effects of this policy on the welfare of the host country, the foreign country, and the two countries combined (i.e. global welfare), both in the presence and in the absence of capital mobility. Our main result under capital immobility is that border enforcement reduces host country welfare, foreign country welfare and global welfare. Under capital mobility, we find that border enforcement increases foreign country welfare and global welfare and, under certain conditions, increases host country welfare.

4.1 Introduction

Ethier (1986a) pioneered a one-*small*-country model that focused on some issues of illegal immigration using a crime-theoretic analysis (Becker (1968)). Ethier examined the effects of a *border* enforcement policy by the host country's government on the host country's welfare in the one-small-country model. He concluded that border enforcement necessarily leads to a decrease in the host country's welfare, generating *a welfare cost* to the host country.

In this chapter, we extend the Ethier model of illegal immigration by constructing a standard two-country, one-good, two-factor model and explore some issues not considered by Ethier. We analyze the effects of an imposition of border enforcement on the welfare of the host country, the foreign country, and the two countries combined (i.e. global welfare) both in the presence and in the absence of capital mobility.

We obtain the following results: (4.a) When capital is not mobile between two countries, border enforcement causes a decrease in the welfare of both the host country and the foreign country, thereby causing a decrease in global welfare. (4.b) When capital is mobile between two countries, enforcement causes an increase in the welfare of the host country, under some circumstances, an increase in the foreign country's welfare, and hence, an increase in global welfare. Thus, we conclude that border enforcement may be a potentially *Pareto-inferior (improving) policy* in the absence (presence) of capital mobility.

In the next section, we examine the welfare effects of border enforcement in the absence of capital mobility. Section 4.3 examines the welfare effects of border enforcement in the presence of capital mobility. Section 4.4 offers some concluding remarks.

4.2 The basic model and main results

We introduce a standard two-country, one-good, two-factor model of illegal immigration, in which capital is assumed to be internationally immobile. Firms in both the home country and the foreign country produce a single output, using a constant returns to scale technology. Technologies are assumed to differ between the two countries. Output is produced using labor and capital inputs. The production functions of home and foreign firms are, respectively, denoted by $F(L,K)$ and $F^*(L^*,K^*)$ where L, K, L^* and K^* are the employment of home labor, home capital, foreign labor and foreign capital, respectively. The labeling of the two countries is chosen so that the home wage rate, w_B, exceeds the foreign wage rate, w_B^*, in the absence of factor mobility. The output is assumed to be the numeraire in our model.

Moreover, we assume that there are legal barriers to factor movements that prevent labor and capital from flowing freely between the two countries. Foreign labor may migrate illegally to the host country and work illegally in the domestic (host country) firm. Under border enforcement, the host country's government arrests any would-be illegal immigrants attempting to cross the border into the host country. The government then levies penalties against the arrested migrants. The illegal migrants who succeed in immigrating to the host country and finding employment may yet be caught due to an internal enforcement policy. Under internal enforcement, the host country's government fines any domestic firms caught employing illegal immigrant workers.[1] It determines the level of internal enforcement and the level of fines levied against such firms.

We abstract from the penalties suffered by the home firms when they are found hiring illegal foreign workers, since we assume that the level of internal enforcement is constant throughout the model. The policy tool of the host country's government is the level of border enforcement implemented to catch illegal foreign migrants who attempt to immigrate to the home country. The model excludes the possibility of legal immigration.

4.2.1 Factor market equilibrium

The home country's government puts border enforcement into effect at the frontier between the two countries. The foreign worker attempting to migrate illegally to the host country incurs a penalty, k, if caught at the border. We assume that the probability of detection at the border is expressed as $g(B)$, $g(0) = 0$, $g' > 0$, $g'' < 0$ and $g < 1$, where B is the expenditure on border enforcement by the host country's government. Foreign workers, who are assumed to be risk neutral, determine their migration decisions so as to equate the expected reward from migration to the local wage, w_B^*:

$$(w_B^* - k)g + w_B(1 - g) = w_B^*,$$

where w_B is the wage earned in the domestic firm by foreign workers who succeed in immigrating illegally to the host country. Note that they receive the same wage as the domestic workers' wage.

The above equation is rewritten as:

$$w_B = w_B^* + k[g(B)/(1 - g(B))]. \tag{4.1}$$

Thus, when the host country's government carries out border enforcement, foreign illegal immigrants who are not caught by border enforcement earn the higher wage, w_B, than the foreign country's wage, w_B^*.[2]

The production function for the home firm is expressed as $F(L, K) = Kf(\lambda)$, where $\lambda = L/K$ and $f' > 0$, $f'' < 0$. The first-order conditions for cost-minimization for domestic firms facing given wage rates, w_B, and capital rental rates, r, are:

$$f'(\lambda) = w_B, \tag{4.2a}$$

$$f(\lambda) - \lambda w_B = r. \tag{4.2b}$$

From (4.2a) it is clear that

$$\lambda = \lambda(w_B), \qquad \lambda' = 1/f'' < 0. \tag{4.3}$$

The total differentiation of (4.1) and (4.2b) gives the effects of enforcement, B, on w_B, r and w_B^*:

$$dr = -\lambda dw_B, \tag{4.4}$$

$$= -\lambda[dw_B^* + \{kg'/(1-g)^2\}dB], \tag{4.5}$$

where $\lambda > 0$ is assumed to be chosen optimally.

In the foreign country, foreign firms minimize total costs, given foreign wage and rental rates w_B^* and r^*, respectively. Hence, we obtain equations similar to (4.3), (4.4) and (4.5):

$$\lambda^* = \lambda^*(w_B^*), \qquad \lambda^{*\prime} = 1/f^{*\prime\prime} < 0, \tag{4.6}$$

$$dw_B^* = -dr^*/\lambda^*. \tag{4.7}$$

From (4.4), (4.5) and (4.7), we can derive the relationship between the effects of border enforcement B on w_B^* and r^*:

$$dr^*/dB = -\lambda^* dw_B^*/dB. \tag{4.8}$$

We find from (4.8) that the effect of enforcement, B, on r^* is opposite to the effect of B on w_B^*. Similarly, the effect of B on domestic rental rates is opposite to the effect of B on domestic wage rates.

Let us examine the equilibrium condition in factor markets. This condition for the home market is

$$\overline{K}(1-a)\lambda(w_B^* + kg/(1-g)) = \overline{L}, \tag{4.9}$$

where $\overline{K}$ and $\overline{L}$ are the initial capital and labor endowments, respectively, of the host country; $a = I/(\overline{L}+I)$ is the fraction of the host country's labor force that is comprised of illegal immigrant workers; and I is the number of illegal migrant-workers present in the host country. Note that $\lambda = (\overline{L}+I)/\overline{K}$. In the foreign market equilibrium, the following equation holds:

$$\lambda^*(w_B^*)\overline{K}^* + a\lambda(w_B^* + kg/(1-g))\overline{K} = \overline{L}^*, \tag{4.10}$$

where $\overline{L}^*$ and $\overline{K}^*$ are the capital and labor endowments of the foreign country, respectively. We know that $\lambda^* = (\overline{L}^* - I)/\overline{K}^*$ from (4.9) and (4.10).

Total differentiation of (4.9) and (4.10) yields the effects of an increase in the enforcement level, B, on w_B^* and a as follows:

$$dw_B^*/dB = \overline{K}\lambda\overline{K}\lambda' kg'/\Delta_1(1-g)^2 < 0, \tag{4.11a}$$

$$da/dB = -\overline{K}\overline{K}^*(1-a)\lambda'\lambda^{*\prime}kg'/\Delta_1(1-g)^2 < 0, \tag{4.11b}$$

where $\Delta_1 = -\overline{K}\lambda(\lambda^{*\prime}\overline{K}^* + \lambda'\overline{K}) > 0$. Therefore, from (4.11b) and the definition of a, the effect of border enforcement on the level of illegal immigration, I is

$$dI/dB = [(\overline{L}+I)/(1-a)][da/dB] < 0. \tag{4.12}$$

Next, from (4.4), (4.5) and (4.11a), the effect of an increase in enforcement, B, on w_B is:

$$dw_B / dB = dw_B^* / dB + kg' / (1-g)^2,$$

$$= -\overline{KK}^* \lambda \lambda^{*'} kg' / \Delta_1 (1-g)^2 > 0. \tag{4.13}$$

We find from (4.13) that the effect of B on w_B is positive. The effects of B on r and r^* are obtained from (4.4), (4.8), (4.11a) and (4.13):

$$dr / dB = \overline{KK}^* \lambda^2 \lambda^{*'} kg' / \Delta_1 (1-g)^2 < 0, \tag{4.14}$$

and

$$dr^* / dB = -\lambda^* \overline{K} \lambda \overline{K} \lambda' kg' / \Delta_1 (1-g)^2 > 0. \tag{4.15}$$

With these comparative static results, we can know that the border enforcement policy will have adverse (favorable) effects on domestic capital (labor) and foreign labor (capital).

4.2.2 Welfare effects

In this subsection, we examine the effects of border enforcement on the welfare of the host country, the foreign country and the world. Firstly, we consider the effect of the enforcement on the host country's welfare. Its welfare is expressed as follows:

$$Y_B = w_B \overline{L} + r\overline{K} - B. \tag{4.16}$$

The home country's welfare is composed of factor payments, $w_B \overline{L} + r\overline{K}$, minus the cost, B, of catching foreign illegal migrants at the frontier between the host country and the foreign country.[3]

By differentiating (4.16) with respect to B and making use of (4.4), we obtain the welfare effect of enforcement:

$$dY_B / dB = -Idw_B / dB - 1 < 0. \tag{4.17}$$

We find from (4.13) that the sign of (4.17) is negative. This implies that border enforcement by the host country's government causes the host country's welfare, as measured by its income, to decrease.

Proposition 4.1 [Ethier (1986a)]
In the absence of capital mobility, border enforcement by the host country's government will cause the host country's income to decrease.

Secondly, we examine the effect of border enforcement on the foreign country's welfare. Its welfare is defined as:

$$Y_B^* = \{w_B^*(\overline{L}^* - I) + r^* \overline{K}^*\} + w_B I - \{Ig / (1-g)\}k, \tag{4.18}$$

where the first term, $\{w_B^*(\overline{L}^* - I) + r^* \overline{K}^*\}$, on the right-hand side represents factor payments; the second term, $w_B I$, is illegal immigrant earnings, and the third term, $\{Ig /(1-g)\}k$, is the amount in penalties paid to the host country's government by would-be foreign migrants caught at the border.[4]

Now we examine the effect of an imposition of border enforcement, B, on Y_B^*. Differentiating (4.18) with respect to B and making use of (4.4), (4.5) and (4.8), its effect is derived as follows:

$$dY_B^* / dB = Idw_B^* / dB < 0. \tag{4.19}$$

We find from (4.11a) that the sign of (4.19) is negative.

Proposition 4.2 [Yoshida (1998)]
In the absence of international capital mobility, the labor-exporting country's welfare will decrease when the enforcement policy is introduced in the labor importing (host) country.

The effect of enforcement on global welfare, $(Y_B + Y_B^*)$ is obtained from (4.17) and (4.19):

$$d(Y_B + Y_B^*) / dB = -\{kg'I /(1-g)^2\} - 1 < 0. \tag{4.20}$$

It is clear that the sign of (4.20) is negative. Hence, we obtain the next proposition:

Proposition 4.3 [Yoshida (1998)]
In the absence of international capital mobility, global welfare will decrease when the host country's government introduces a border enforcement policy.

We have shown that border enforcement is undesirable in terms of global welfare and hence, it is *a Pareto-inferior policy*. For example, the Japanese Government's present border enforcement on possible immigrants would make the world economy worse off if capital were internationally immobile.

4.3 Capital mobility

In this section, we analyze the effects of border enforcement by the host country's government on the host country's welfare, the foreign country's welfare and global welfare, when capital is completely mobile between the host country and the foreign country. We first examine the comparative static effects of border enforcement. Then in subsection 4.3.2 we derive the welfare effects of an increase in the border enforcement level using the comparative static results derived in subsection 4.3.1.

4.3.1 Factor market equilibrium

We assume that the host country's government levies a tax on domestic capital located in the foreign country, K_F, so that the net return to domestic capital in the foreign country is $r^*(1-t)$, where t is the tax rate and t lies in the interval $(0,1)$. Firms in both countries are assumed to utilize the same production technology. Note that in equilibrium there are both capital flows and illegal labor flows between the two countries. Domestic capital flows to the foreign country, until the rental rates of domestic capital located in the host country equal after-tax returns of domestic capital, K_F, located in the foreign country:

$$r = r^*(1-t). \tag{4.21}$$

Let us examine the equilibrium conditions in factor markets. This condition for the home market is

$$(\overline{K} - K_F)(1-a)\lambda(w_B^* + kg/(1-g)) = \overline{L}. \tag{4.22}$$

In the foreign market equilibrium we have

$$(\overline{K}^* + K_F)\lambda^*(w_B^*) + (\overline{K} - K_F)a\lambda(w_B^* + kg/(1-g)) = \overline{L}^*. \tag{4.23}$$

The three equations (4.21), (4.22) and (4.23) simultaneously determine the equilibrium levels of w_B^*, a and K_F.

We examine the effects of border enforcement on w_B^*, a and K_F. By totally differentiating (4.21) and making use of (4.5) and (4.7), we obtain the following equation:

$$dw_B^*/dB = \lambda kg'/\{\lambda^*(1-t) - \lambda\}(1-g)^2. \tag{4.24}$$

We assume that the sign of $\{\lambda^*(1-t) - \lambda\}$ is positive (see Jones (1971) and Neary (1978)).[5] We find from (4.24) that the effect of enforcement on the foreign wage rate is positive.

Total differentiation of (4.21), (4.22) and (4.23) yield the following three-equation system, eliminating dw_B using (4.1):

$$\begin{bmatrix} \lambda^*(1-t) - \lambda & 0 & 0 \\ (\overline{K} - K_F)(1-a)\lambda' & -(\overline{K} - K_F)\lambda & -(1-a)\lambda \\ (\overline{K}^* + K_F)\lambda^{*'} + a\lambda'(\overline{K} - K_F) & (\overline{K} - K_F)\lambda & \lambda^* - a\lambda \end{bmatrix} \begin{bmatrix} dw_B^* \\ da \\ dK_F \end{bmatrix}$$

$$= \begin{bmatrix} \{\lambda kg'/(1-g)^2\}dB \\ -\{(\overline{K} - K_F)(1-a)\lambda' kg'/(1-g)^2\}dB \\ -\{(\overline{K} - K_F)a\lambda' kg'/(1-g)^2\}dB \end{bmatrix}. \tag{4.25}$$

The determinant of the system (4.25) is

$$\Delta_2 = \{\lambda^*(1-t) - \lambda\}(\overline{K} - K_F)(\lambda - \lambda^*)\lambda,$$

where the sign of Δ_2 is negative because the sign of $\{\lambda^*(1-t) - \lambda\}$ is assumed to be positive.

From (4.25) we can obtain the effects of B on a and K_F:

$$da/dB = -kg'(1-a)[(1-t)(\overline{K} - K_F)\lambda'\lambda^{*2}$$
$$+ (\overline{K}^* + K_F)\lambda^2\lambda^{*'}]/\Delta_2(1-g)^2 < 0, \qquad (4.26a)^6$$

$$dK_F/dB = kg'\lambda(\overline{K} - K_F)[(1-t)\lambda^*\lambda'(\overline{K} - K_F)$$
$$+ \lambda\lambda^{*'}(\overline{K}^* + K_F)]/\Delta_2(1-g)^2 > 0. \qquad (4.26b)$$

From (4.4), (4.5) and (4.24), the effect of B on w_B is:

$$dw_B/dE = dw_B^*/dE + kg'/(1-g)^2$$
$$= \lambda^*(1-t)kg'/\{\lambda^*(1-t) - \lambda\}(1-g)^2 > 0. \qquad (4.27)$$

The effects of B on r and r^* are obtained from (4.4), (4.8), (4.24) and (4.27):

$$dr/dB = -\lambda\lambda^*(1-t)kg'/\{\lambda^*(1-t) - \lambda\}(1-g)^2 < 0, \qquad (4.28)$$

and

$$dr^*/dB = -\lambda^*\lambda kg'/\{\lambda^*(1-t) - \lambda\}(1-g)^2 < 0. \qquad (4.29)$$

It can be seen from these comparative static results that under international capital mobility, border enforcement has adverse (favorable) effects on domestic and foreign capital (domestic and foreign labor).

4.3.2 Welfare effects

In this section, we examine the effects of border enforcement by the host country's government on the welfare of the host country, the foreign country and the world.

Firstly, we consider the (host) labor-importing country's welfare. This is defined as follows:

$$Y_B = w_B\overline{L} + r\overline{K} + (r^* - r)K_F - B. \qquad (4.30)$$

The host country's income, which measures its welfare, consists of (4.16) plus the tax earnings obtained from domestic capital located in the foreign country.

We examine the effect of enforcement on the host country's welfare. Differentiating (4.30) with respect to B and manipulating the resulting equation making use of (4.1), (4.4), (4.5), (4.8) and $\lambda = (\overline{L} + I)/(\overline{K} - K_F)$, we derive the effect of enforcement on Y_B:

$$dY_B / dB = (r^* - r)dK_F / dB - Idw_B / dB - \lambda^* K_F dw_B^* / dB - 1. \qquad (4.31)$$

We find from (4.24), (4.26b) and (4.27) that the sign of (4.31) is indeterminate. However, it is clear that the sign of (4.31) is positive if the following condition holds:

$$(r^* - r)dK_F / dB > Idw_B / dB + \lambda^* K_F dw_B^* / dB + 1. \qquad (4C.1)$$

This condition, (4C.1), is the necessary condition for the optimal enforcement level to be positive. It implies that the marginal tax-revenue of domestic capital outflows from enforcement, $(r^* - r)dK_F / dB$, surpasses the combined effects of enforcement on the wages of domestic and foreign workers, $Idw_B / dB + \lambda^* K_F dw_B^* / dB$, and the marginal costs of enforcement, 1.

Proposition 4.4 [Yoshida (1998)]
In the presence of capital mobility, border enforcement by the host country will increase the host country's welfare provided condition (4C.1) holds.

Next, we consider the effect of border enforcement on the foreign country's welfare, as measured by its income. The foreign country's welfare is expressed as:

$$Y_B^* = [w_B^*(\overline{L}^* - I) + r^* \overline{K}^*] + w_B I - \{Ig / (1 - g)\}k. \qquad (4.32)$$

Y_B^* consists of factor expenditures, $[w_B^*(\overline{L}^* - I) + r^* \overline{K}^*]$, and immigrant earnings, $w_B I$, less the sum of penalties that arrested would-be foreign-migrants pay to the host country's government, $\{Ig / (1 - g)\}k$.[7] By differentiating (4.32) with respect to B and using (4.4), (4.5) and (4.8), we obtain the foreign welfare effect of introducing enforcement:

$$dY_B^* / dB = Idw_B^* / dB + \lambda^* K_F dw_B^* / dB > 0. \qquad (4.33)$$

The sign of (4.33) is unambiguously positive from (4.24). Y_B^* will rise when enforcement is introduced.

Proposition 4.5 [Yoshida (1998)]
In the presence of international capital mobility, the welfare of a (foreign) labor-exporting country will rise when the (host) labor-importing country introduces border enforcement.

Finally, we consider the effect of border enforcement on global income $(Y_B + Y_B^*)$. From (4.31) and (4.33), and making use of (4.4) and (4.5), this effect is obtained:

$$d(Y_B + Y_B^*) / dB = (r^* - r)dK_F / dB - \{kg'I / (1 - g)^2\} - 1. \qquad (4.34)$$

It is clear that the sign of (4.34) is positive if condition (4C.1) is satisfied. In short, the effect of border enforcement on $(Y_B + Y_B^*)$ is positive when the marginal tax-revenue on home capital outflows, $(r^* - r)dK_F/dB$, outweighs the marginal opportunity costs (see footnote 4) of foreign would-be migrants being caught at the border, $kg'I/(1-g)^2$, plus the marginal costs of the enforcement, 1.

Proposition 4.6 [Yoshida (1998)]
In the presence of international capital mobility, global welfare will increase given condition (4C.1) when the host country's government introduces border enforcement.

Our welfare analysis shows that border enforcement by the host country's government increases the foreign country's welfare, and provided condition (4C.1) holds, it increases the host country's welfare and global welfare. We can conclude that in the presence of capital mobility, border enforcement is *a Pareto-superior policy* under some circumstances. That is, the present border enforcement by the Japanese Government on possible illegal immigrants may be desirable in terms of global welfare when capital is internationally mobile.

4.4 Concluding remarks

We have developed the standard model of illegal immigration. We examined the effects of border enforcement by the host country's government on the welfare of the host country, the welfare of the foreign country, and the combined welfare of both countries, both in the absence and the presence of international capital mobility. We obtained the following results. (4.a) When capital is not mobile between the two countries, an introduction of border enforcement reduces host country welfare and foreign country welfare and reduces global welfare. (4.b) When capital is mobile between two countries, enforcement increases foreign country welfare, and provided condition (4C.1) holds, enforcement increases host country welfare and global welfare.

We conclude from our results, (4.a) and (4.b), that border enforcement by the host country's government may be *a Pareto-inferior policy* in the absence of capital mobility, whereas it may be *a Pareto-improving policy* in the presence of capital mobility.

Notes

* The chapter was originally published by the Seoul Journal of Economics as an article in its Volume 11, No. 1 (1998) issue.

1 In our model, domestic workers do not have incentives to legally or illegally migrate to the foreign country because the domestic wage rate, w_B, exceeds the foreign wage rate, w_B^*, in the absence of factor mobility. The foreign country's government has no need to introduce either the border enforcement policy or the internal enforcement policy. Thus, the expenditure levels on those enforcement policies by the foreign government are zero.

2 We assume that foreign migrant workers, regardless of their success in illegally immigrating to the host country, incur a psychic cost, $\tilde{k}$, in attempting to emigrate. Moreover for each foreign would-be migrant, k is implicitly assumed to contain not only the penalty if caught at the border, but also this psychic cost. (4.1) can be rewritten as follows:

$$w_B = w_B^* + kg/(1-g) + \tilde{k} . \tag{4.1}'$$

Thus, the foreign illegal worker will receive a higher wage than the foreign country's wage, w_B^*, even if the level of border enforcement is zero; $B = 0$. Throughout the chapter, we ignore the psychic cost, $\tilde{k}$, since it is assumed to be constant.

3 From the assumption, (4.16) should include the amount of penalties levied on the foreign would-be migrants caught, $\{Ig/(1-g)\}k$. However, in fact the host country's government might not have been able to collect these penalties from the arrested foreign workers, because they might not have had the ability to pay the fine, given that they might not have worked. Hence, (4.16) excludes these penalties $\{Ig/(1-g)\}k$.

4 Although we assume k is zero (see footnote 3), foreign workers who were unsuccessful in their migration attempt could not have earned a wage during the time they spent on the failed immigration attempt. Hence, we can consider the penalty as the opportunity cost of being arrested.

5 By assuming the condition, stability of the equilibrium solutions, w_B^*, a and K_F is guaranteed. See also mathematical appendix in Chapter 3.

6 From the definition of a and (4.26a), the effect of border enforcement on the level of illegal immigration, I is negative:

$$dI/dB = [(\bar{L} + I)/(1-a)][da/dB] < 0.$$

7 See footnote 4.

5

The Welfare Effects of Financing the Internal Enforcement of Illegal Immigration

The present chapter re-examines the Bond and Chen (1987) model on illegal immigration, introducing a government budget constraint (*GBC*) on the host country's government. It examines the effects of financing internal enforcement of illegal immigration by the host-country's government on the welfare of the host (labor-importing) country, the foreign (labor-exporting) country and the world, both in the absence and in the presence of international capital mobility. The aim of this chapter is to determine whether internal enforcement may be *a Pareto-improving policy*.

5.1 Introduction

Ethier (1986a) introduced a one-country model of illegal immigration to examine the effects of border and internal enforcement policies using a crime-theoretic analysis (Becker (1968)). Using this model, Ethier analyzed how a small country could use these policies to achieve domestic policy objectives concerning the level of illegal immigration or concerning income distribution.

Any apparatus to finance an increase in the level of expenditure on internal enforcement, e.g., income taxation of domestic labor, may have direct effects on the disposable incomes of domestic and foreign workers, and on the rental prices of domestic and foreign capital. This device may have different influences on the host country's welfare and on income distribution.

We use an extended Bond and Chen model on illegal immigration, introducing financing constraints on regulatory policies. We assume the host country's government is restricted to financing regulatory policies under a balanced budget constraint. Internal enforcement may be financed by the host (domestic) government by imposing fines on firms caught employing illegal foreign workers or by levying income taxes on domestic workers or by a combination of these two financing measures. We examine the welfare effects of internal enforcement given these financing measures and the government budget constraint.

The following will be shown. (5.a) In the absence of capital mobility, enforcement does not always improve the host country's welfare and invariably harms the foreign country's welfare. Furthermore, (5.b) enforcement may become *a Pareto-improving (or inferior) policy* that improves (or worsens) global welfare, depending upon the signs and magnitudes of direct and indirect fiscal effects on the GBC of financing the regulatory policy. (5.c) In the presence of capital mobility, enforcement does not necessarily improve the host country's welfare, and inevitably improves the foreign country's welfare. Furthermore, (5.d) enforcement can become *a Pareto-improving policy* that under some circumstances improves global welfare.

In the next section, assuming capital is not internationally mobile, we analyze how the introduction of internal enforcement effects the financing tools used by the host country's government. In section 5.3 we present the welfare effects of financing enforcement. In section 5.4 we examine the welfare effects of enforcement, and show the behavior of the host country's government. Section 5.5 examines more welfare effects of financing enforcement. The final section offers some concluding remarks.

5.2 The basic model

We introduce a standard two-country, one-good, two-factor model of illegal immigration in which capital is assumed to be internationally immobile. Firms in both the host country and the foreign country produce the same output, which is assumed to be the numeraire. This single output is produced using labor and capital inputs and a constant returns to scale technology. Technologies are assumed to differ between the two countries. The production functions of domestic and foreign firms are denoted by $F(L,K)$ and $F^*(L^*,K^*)$ where L, K, L^* and K^* are domestic labor, domestic capital, foreign labor and foreign capital employment, respectively. The labeling of the two countries is chosen so that the domestic wage rate, w_b, exceeds the foreign wage rate, w_b^*, in the absence of factor mobility.

We assume that there are legal barriers to factor movements. Foreign workers are assumed to be indifferent between working in their native country and illegally working in the host country provided the wage rate is the same in both countries.[1] The host country's government determines the level of enforcement of domestic firms, and levies fines against those firms caught employing illegal foreign workers. We assume that the host country's government operates a balanced budget, so that the cost of enforcement is financed by income taxes extracted from domestic workers and by fines collected from domestic firms caught employing foreign workers.

5.2.1 Factor market equilibrium

We develop the standard (two-country, one-good, two-factor) model of illegal immigration, in which foreign labor illegally migrates to the host country and capital is internationally immobile. Technologies are assumed to differ between the two countries. In autarky, the host country is labor scarce relative to the foreign country (i.e., the foreign country is capital scarce relative to the host country). Firms in both countries produce the same output good using labor and capital inputs and a constant returns to scale technology.

Domestic firms are risk neutral, and are indifferent between employing domestic workers and illegal foreign workers.[2] The cost of employing an illegal worker is composed of the worker's wage and the expected fine. Hence, in equilibrium[3] we have:

$$w_b = w_b^* + p(E)z(E), \tag{5.1}$$

where E is the level of enforcement; $p(E)$ is the probability of detection, with $p(0) = 0$, $p \leq 1$, $p' > 0$ and $p'' < 0$; and $z(E)$ is the fine that domestic firms pay for each illegal worker caught by the host country's government, with $z'(E) \geq 0$. We assume that the host country's government introduces immigration reform and enacts employer sanctions similar to those in IRCA. It is generally accepted that employer sanctions increase both the costs of internal enforcement and increase the penalties levied on domestic firms found hiring illegal workers. Since the costs of enforcement and the level of penalties are simultaneously increased, $z'(E) \geq 0$.

The production function for the domestic firm is expressed as $F(L, K) = Kf(\lambda)$, where $\lambda = L/K$ and $f' > 0$, $f'' < 0$. Thus, the first-order conditions for cost-minimization by domestic firms facing given wage rates, w_b, and capital rental rates, r, are:

$$f'(\lambda) = w, \tag{5.2a}$$

$$f(\lambda) - \lambda w_b = r. \tag{5.2b}$$

From (5.2a) it is clear that

$$\lambda = \lambda(w_b), \quad \lambda' = 1/f'' < 0. \tag{5.3}$$

The total differentiation of (5.1) and (5.2b) gives the effects of enforcement, E, on w_b and w_b^*:

$$dr = -\lambda dw_b, \tag{5.4}$$

$$= -\lambda(dw_b^* + (p'z + pz')dE), \tag{5.5}$$

where $\lambda > 0$ is assumed to be chosen optimally.

In the foreign country, foreign firms minimize total costs with respect to labor and capital, given foreign wage and rental rates, w_b^* and r^*. Hence, we obtain equations similar to (5.3), (5.4) and (5.5):

$$\lambda^* = \lambda^*(w_b^*), \quad \lambda^{*\prime} = 1/f^{*\prime\prime} < 0, \tag{5.6}$$

$$dw_b^* = -dr^* / \lambda^*. \tag{5.7}$$

Let us examine the equilibrium condition in factor markets.[4] The condition for the domestic market is

$$\overline{K}(1-a)\lambda(w_b^* + p(E)z(E)) = \overline{L}, \tag{5.8}$$

where $\overline{K}$ and $\overline{L}$ are the initial capital and labor endowments, respectively, of the host country, $a = I/(L+I)$, and I is the level of illegal immigration. In the foreign market equilibrium we have

$$\overline{K}^* \lambda^*(w_b^*) + \overline{K}a\lambda(w_b^* + p(E)z(E)) = \overline{L}^*, \tag{5.9}$$

where $\overline{L}^*$ and $\overline{K}^*$ are the initial labor and capital endowments, respectively, of the foreign country. Equations (5.8) and (5.9) determine w_b^* and a.

By totally differentiating (5.8) and (5.9) we obtain the effects of E on w_b^* and a:

$$dw_b^* / dE = -\overline{K}^2 \lambda\lambda'(p'z + pz')/\Delta_1 < 0, \tag{5.10a}$$

$$da / dE = \overline{K}\overline{K}^* \lambda' \lambda^{*\prime}(1-a)(p'z + pz')/\Delta_1 < 0, \tag{5.10b}[5]$$

where $\Delta_1 \equiv \overline{K}\lambda[\overline{K}\lambda' + \overline{K}^* \lambda^{*\prime}] < 0$.

Next from (5.4), (5.5) and (5.10a) the effect of E on w_b is:

$$dw_b / dE = dw_b^* / dE + p'z + pz'$$

$$= \overline{K}\overline{K}^* \lambda\lambda^{*\prime}(p'z + pz')/\Delta_1 > 0. \tag{5.11}$$

The effects of E on r and r^* are obtained from (5.4), (5.7), (5.10a) and (5.11):

$$dr / dE = -\overline{K}\overline{K}^* \lambda^2 \lambda^{*\prime}(p'z + pz')/\Delta_1 < 0, \tag{5.12}$$

and

$$dr^* / dE = \overline{K}^2 \lambda \lambda^* \lambda'(p'z + pz') / \Delta_1 > 0. \tag{5.13}$$

We find from these comparative static results that under no capital mobility, the internal enforcement policy brings about adverse effects on domestic capital and foreign labor, whereas it brings about favorable effects on domestic labor and foreign capital.

5.2.2 Government budget constraint

In this subsection, following Bucci and Tenorio (1996), we explain the budget activity of the host country's government. The host government's surplus, GS is:

$$GS \equiv (w_b - w_b^* - vp(E))I - E + T(E)w_b\overline{L}$$
$$= (z(E) - v)p(E)I - E + T(E)w_b\overline{L}, \tag{5.14}$$

where v denotes the costs associated with the return of illegal workers to their native country and the collection of fines from firms; E is the cost of arresting illegal workers incurred by the host country's government; and $T(E)$ is the income tax imposed on domestic labor, where $T(E)$ is in the open interval $(0, 1)$.

We assume the host country's government maintains a balanced budget. The government budget constraint (GBC) is:

$$T(E)w_b\overline{L} + z(E)p(E)I = vp(E)I + E. \tag{5.15}$$

The left-hand side of (5.15) consists of income taxes from domestic workers, $T(E)w_b\overline{L}$, and expected fines from domestic firms, $z(E)p(E)I$. The right-hand side of (5.15) consists of the costs incurred returning apprehended illegal workers to the foreign country, $vp(E)I$, and the costs of internal enforcement, E.

An increase in the level of enforcement may alter the GBC, (5.15). Once a new level of enforcement is chosen, the host-country's government will need to finance this change in policy using the following tools: z, or z and T. The total differentiation of (5.15) with respect to E is:

$$T(E)\overline{L}dw_b / dE + (z - v)(p'I + pdI / dE) + z'pI - 1$$
$$= -T'(E)w_b\overline{L}. \tag{5.16}$$

The left-hand side of (5.16) expresses the effect on the GBC of increased enforcement and fines. The impact is the direct fiscal effect (DFE) of the policy. When the host country's government sets (E, z) so that enforcement is fully financed by penalties on domestic firms, $DFE = 0$, then no additional financing tool will be required. However, if $DFE \neq 0$, then an imposition of income taxes will be required to balance the budget. This adjustment in T, the right-hand side of (5.16), is called the indirect fiscal effect (IFE) of enforcement. In short, (5.16) implies that some financing tool, z, or both z and T, will be required to rebalance the government's budget, (5.16).

By carefully considering (5.16), we can classify direct and indirect fiscal effects, (5.A), into the following three cases:

$$\text{(i)} \quad \text{If } DFE = 0, \ T'(E) = 0,$$

$$\text{(ii)} \quad \text{If } DFE > 0, \ T'(E) < 0, \tag{5.A}$$

$$\text{(iii)} \quad \text{If } DFE < 0, \ T'(E) > 0,$$

where $T'(E) = 0, T'(E) < 0$ and $T'(E) > 0$ imply $IFE = 0, IFE < 0$ and $IFE > 0$, respectively.

5.3 Welfare effects

In this section, we examine the welfare effects of financing the host country's internal enforcement policy. In particular, we look at the effects on the host (labor-importing) country's welfare, the foreign (labor-exporting) country's welfare, and global welfare (the combined welfare of the two countries.)

Firstly, we consider the labor-importing country's welfare, as measured by its income:

$$Y_b = (1 - T(E))w_b\overline{L} + r\overline{K} + (z(E) - v)p(E)I$$
$$- E + T(E)w_b\overline{L}. \tag{5.17}$$

where Y_b is composed of factor incomes, $[(1 - T(E))w_b\overline{L} + r\overline{K}]$, and the host country's government surplus, $[(z(E) - v)p(E)I - E + T(E)w_b\overline{L}]$. By manipulating the GBC, the following equation is derived:

$$(z(E) - v)p(E)I - E = -T(E)w\overline{L}. \tag{5.18}$$

Substituting (5.18) into (5.17) yields:

$$Y_b = (1 - T(E))w_b\overline{L} + r\overline{K}. \tag{5.19}$$

The host country's income consists of the incomes of domestic workers net of income tax, $(1 - T(E))w_b\overline{L}$, and payments to domestic capital, $r\overline{K}$.

We examine the effect of enforcement on the host country's welfare, as measured by its income. This impact is obtained by differentiating (5.19) with respect to E and using (5.4) and (5.5):

$$dY_b / dE = -(T(E)\overline{L} + I)dw_b / dE - T'w_b\overline{L}. \tag{5.20}$$

It is clear from (5.A) that the sign of the *IFE*, $T'(E)$ is determined by the sign of *DFE* that has three patterns.

The first is when the case of (i) holds from (5.A), $T'(E) = 0$. Hence, the sign of (5.20) is negative from (5.11). The second is when the case of (ii) holds, $T'(E) < 0$. The sign of (5.20) is indeterminate since the first term in the right-hand side of (5.20) is negative from (5.11) and the second term is positive. However, the sign of (5.20) is positive if condition (5C.1):

$$\left| -T'w_b\overline{L} \right| > \left| -(T(E)\overline{L} + I)dw_b/dE \right| \tag{5C.1}$$

is satisfied. The condition sufficient for the optimal enforcement level of the host country to be positive implies that the marginal income tax revenue, $-T'w_b\overline{L}$ is larger than the effect on the domestic country's wage, $(T(E)\overline{L} + I)dw_b/dE$. The third is when the case of (iii) holds, $T'(E) > 0$. We find from (5.11) that the sign of (5.20) is negative.

Proposition 5.1
Internal enforcement will cause the host country's welfare to decrease under (a) DFE ≤ 0 and IFE ≥ 0, and will cause the host country's welfare to increase under (b) DFE > 0 and IFE < 0 if condition (5C.1) is satisfied.

Bond and Chen (1987) maintained that in order for penalties to improve the host country's welfare, the host country must be large enough to have an effect on the foreign wage, and the marginal costs of enforcement must be sufficiently low (see proposition 2.1 in Chapter 2).[6] However, by introducing the budget constraint of the host country's government into the model of Chapter 2, we can explicitly determine the impacts of financing enforcement on the host country's welfare, e.g., the welfare effect under case (a) in proposition 5.1, that enforcement will make the host country's welfare worse off. The effects on the host-country's income under case (a) are *contrary to* those in proposition 2.1. Also, it is possible for the host country's government program to improve the host country's welfare under some circumstances, that is, the case (b) in the proposition that is *different from* those by proposition 2.1.

Secondly, we consider the effect of internal enforcement on the foreign country's welfare, as measured by its income. The foreign country's welfare is expressed as:

$$Y_b^* = w_b^*(\overline{L}^* - I) + r^*\overline{K}^* + Iw_b^*. \tag{5.21}$$

Y_b^* consists of factor expenditures, $[w_b^*(\overline{L}^* - I) + r^*\overline{K}^*]$, and immigrant earnings, Iw_b^*. By differentiating (5.21) with respect to E and using (5.7), we obtain the following equation:

$$dY_b^* / dE = I dw_b^* / dE < 0. \tag{5.22}$$

The sign of (5.22) is unambiguously negative from (5.10a). We find that Y_b^* will decrease when the level of enforcement increases.

Proposition 5.2
The welfare of a labor-exporting country will decrease when the host country introduces internal enforcement.

Thirdly, we consider the effect of internal enforcement on global welfare, $(Y_b + Y_b^*)$, as measured by global income. Global income, $(Y_b + Y_b^*)$, is derived from (5.19) and (5.21):

$$(Y_b + Y_b^*) = [(1 - T(E))w_b\overline{L} + r\overline{K}]$$
$$+ [w_b^*(\overline{L}^* - I) + r^*\overline{K}^* + Iw_b^*], \tag{5.23}$$

where Y_b and Y_b^* are expressed in the first and second brackets on the right-hand side of (5.23), respectively. The differentiation of (5.23) with respect to E is derived from (5.20) and (5.22):

$$d(Y_b + Y_b^*) / dE = -T(E)\overline{L}dw_b / dE$$
$$- I(p'z + pz') - T'w_b\overline{L}. \tag{5.24}$$

The first and second terms on the right-hand side of (5.24) are both negative given (5.10a) and other assumptions, and the third term is indefinite. We find that the sign of (5.24) is negative if cases (i) and (iii) in (5.A) hold (i.e., if $DFE \leq 0$, $T'(E) \geq 0$), while it is indeterminate when case (ii) holds (i.e., if $DFE > 0$, $T'(E) < 0$). The sign of (5.24) is positive if condition (5C.2):

$$\left| T'w_b\overline{L} \right| > \left| T(E)\overline{L}dw_b / dE + I(p'z + pz') \right|$$

is satisfied where case (ii) holds. In other words, enforcement by the host country's government causes global welfare to increase only if the marginal wage tax revenue, $-T'w_b\overline{L}$, surpasses the combined increase in domestic wages, $T\overline{L}dw_b / dE$, and the marginal revenue of penalties, $I(p'z + pz')$.

Summarizing the above results, we obtain the following proposition:

Proposition 5.3
Internal enforcement by the host country's government will decrease global welfare when (a) DFE ≤ 0 and IFE ≥ 0, and will increase global welfare when

(b) DFE > 0 and IFE < 0 if condition (5C.2) is satisfied.

We can conclude that enforcement is *a Pareto-inferior policy* that causes global welfare to fall when case (a) in Proposition 5.3 holds, whereas when case (b) holds it is *a Pareto-improving policy* that improves global welfare, under some circumstances.

5.4 Capital mobility

We analyze the effects of an internal enforcement policy by the host country's government on the welfare of the host country, the foreign country and the world when capital is internationally mobile. Firms in both countries are assumed to use the same production technology. In the next subsection, we examine the comparative static effects of internal enforcement. In subsection 5.4.2 we consider the financing tools used by the host country's government. Finally, in section 5.5, we analyze the welfare effects of internal enforcement using the comparative static effects derived in subsection 5.4.1.

5.4.1 Factor market equilibrium

We assume that the host country's government levies a tax on domestic capital located in the foreign country, K_F, so that the net return on domestic capital in the foreign country is $r^*(1-t)$, where t is in $(0,1)$. Note that in equilibrium there are both capital movements and illegal labor flows. Domestic capital moves to the foreign country until the rental rates for domestic capital located in the host (domestic) country equal the after-tax returns on domestic capital located in the foreign country:

$$r = r^*(1-t). \tag{5.25}$$

Let us examine the equilibrium conditions in the factor markets of the two countries. The condition for the host country's factor market is

$$(\overline{K} - K_F)(1-a)\lambda(w_b^* + p(E)z(E)) = \overline{L}. \tag{5.26}$$

The left-hand side of (5.26) is labor demand in the host country's labor market, while the right-hand side is labor supply.

In the foreign country's market equilibrium we have

$$(\overline{K}^* + K_F)\lambda^*(w_b^*) + (\overline{K} - K_F)a\lambda(w_b^* + p(E)z(E)) = \overline{L}^*, \tag{5.27}$$

The left-hand side of (5.27) is labor demand in the foreign country's labor market, while the right-hand side is labor supply. The three equations (5.25), (5.26) and (5.27) determine w_b^*, a and K_F.

We examine the effects of enforcement on w_b^*, a and K_F by totally differentiating (5.25) through (5.27). By differentiating (5.25) and making use of (5.5) and (5.7), we can obtain the following equation:

$$dw_b^* / dE = (p'z + pz')\lambda / \{\lambda^*(1-t) - \lambda\}, \tag{5.28}$$

where the tax rate of capital, t, is assumed to be given. We assume that the sign of $\{\lambda^*(1-t) - \lambda\}$ is positive (see Jones (1971) and Neary (1978)).[7] Thus, we find from (5.28) that the effect of enforcement on foreign wages is positive.

By totally differentiating (5.25), (5.26) and (5.27) and eliminating dw_b using (5.1), we obtain the following three-equation system:

$$\begin{bmatrix} \lambda^*(1-t) - \lambda & 0 & 0 \\ (\overline{K} - K_F)(1-a)\lambda' & -(\overline{K} - K_F)\lambda & -(1-a)\lambda \\ (\overline{K}^* + K_F)\lambda^{*'} + a\lambda'(\overline{K} - K_F) & (\overline{K} - K_F)\lambda & \lambda^* - a\lambda \end{bmatrix} \begin{bmatrix} dw_b^* \\ da \\ dK_F \end{bmatrix}$$

$$= \begin{bmatrix} (p'z + pz')\lambda dE \\ -(\overline{K} - K_F)(1-a)\lambda'(p'z + pz')dE \\ -(\overline{K} - K_F)a\lambda'(p'z + pz')dE \end{bmatrix}. \tag{5.29}$$

The determinant of system (5.29) is

$$\Delta_2 = \{\lambda^*(1-t) - \lambda\}(\overline{K} - K_F)(\lambda - \lambda^*)\lambda,$$

where the sign of Δ_2 is negative, because the sign of $\{\lambda^*(1-t) - \lambda\}$ is assumed to be positive.

From (5.29) we can obtain the effects of E on a and K_F:

$$da/dE = -(1-a)(p'z + pz')[\lambda^{*2}\lambda'(1-t)(\overline{K} - K_F)$$
$$+ \lambda^2\lambda^{*'}(\overline{K}^* + K_F)]/\Delta_2 < 0, \tag{5.30a}[8]$$

$$dK_F/dE = (p'z + pz')(\overline{K} - K_F)\lambda[\lambda'\lambda^*(1-t)(\overline{K} - K_F)$$
$$+ \lambda\lambda^{*'}(\overline{K}^* + K_F)]/\Delta_2 < 0. \tag{5.30b}$$

From (5.4), (5.5) and (5.28), the effect of E on w_b is:

$$dw_b/dE = dw_b^*/dE + p'z + pz'$$
$$= \lambda^*(1-t)(p'z + pz')/\{\lambda^*(1-t) - \lambda\} > 0. \tag{5.31}$$

The effects of E on r and r^* are obtained from (5.4), (5.7), (5.28) and (5.31):

$$dr/dE = -\lambda\lambda^*(1-t)(p'z + pz')/\{\lambda^*(1-t) - \lambda\} < 0, \tag{5.32}$$

and

$$dr^* / dE = -\lambda\lambda^*(p'z + pz') / \{\lambda^*(1-t) - \lambda\} < 0. \tag{5.33}$$

These comparative static results demonstrate that in a world with international capital mobility, the introduction of an internal enforcement policy brings about adverse (favorable) effects on domestic and foreign capital (domestic and foreign labor).

5.4.2 Government budget constraint

In this subsection, by following the analysis of Bucci and Tenorio (1996) we explain the activity of the host country's government. The host government surplus, GS, is:

$$
\begin{aligned}
GS &\equiv (w_b - w_b^* - vp(E))I - E + T(E)w_b\overline{L} + tr^*K_F \\
&= (z(E) - v)p(E)I - E + T(E)w\overline{L} + tr^*K_F. \tag{5.34}
\end{aligned}
$$

Note that (5.34) is composed of (5.14) plus tax revenues from domestic capital exports, tr^*K_F.

We assume that the budget of the host country's government is balanced. The *GBC* is:

$$T(E)w_b\overline{L} + z(E)p(E)I + tr^*K_F = vp(E)I + E. \tag{5.35}$$

The left-hand side of (5.35) consists of income taxes collected from domestic workers, $T(E)w_b\overline{L}$, expected fines collected from domestic firms, $z(E)p(E)I$, and tax revenues from domestic capital outflows, tr^*K_F. The right-hand side of (5.35) consists of the cost of extraditing those illegal foreign workers apprehended, $vp(E)I$, and the cost of enforcement, E.

An increase in the level of enforcement will probably alter the *GBC*, (5.35). Once a new level of enforcement is chosen, the host-country's government will need to finance the cost of the policy by using the following tools, z, or z and T. Total differentiation of (5.35) with respect to E gives:

$$
\begin{aligned}
&T(E)\overline{L}dw_b / dE + (z - v)(p'I + pdI / dE) \\
&+ z'pI - 1 + tK_Fdr^* / dE + tr^*dK_F / dE \\
&= -T'(E)w_b\overline{L}. \tag{5.36}
\end{aligned}
$$

The left-hand side of (5.36) expresses the effect on the *GBC* of an increase in enforcement financed by an increase in fines. The impact is the *DFE* of the policy. When the host country's government sets (E,z) so that enforcement is fully financed by penalties on domestic firms, $DFE = 0$, no additional financing tool will be needed. However, if

$DFE \neq 0$, wage taxes will be required so as to balance the budget. This adjustment in T on the right-hand side of (5.36) is the *IFE*. By carefully considering (5.36), we can classify the difference between direct and indirect fiscal effects as indicated in (5.A).

5.5 Welfare effects

Using the comparative static results derived in subsection 5.4.1, we examine the welfare effects of internal enforcement by the host country's government when capital is assumed to be internationally mobile.

The labor-importing country's welfare is expressed as follows:

$$Y_b = (1 - T(E))w_b\overline{L} + r\overline{K} + (z(E) - v)p(E)I$$
$$- E + T(E)w_b\overline{L} + tr^*K_F . \qquad (5.37)$$

(5.37) consists of (5.17) and tax-revenue on capital exports tr^*K_F.

We can rewrite (5.37) by incorporating (5.35) into (5.37):

$$Y_b = (1 - T(E))w_b\overline{L} + r\overline{K} . \qquad (5.38)$$

The effect of enforcement on the host country's welfare is obtained by differentiating (5.38) with respect to E and using (5.4) and (5.5):

$$dY / dE = -(T(E)\overline{L} + I + \lambda K_F)dw_b / dE - T'w_b\overline{L} . \qquad (5.39)$$

Firstly, when case (i) in (5.A) holds, $T'(E) = 0$. Hence, the sign of (5.39) is negative from (5.31). Secondly, when case (ii) holds, $T'(E) < 0$. The sign of (5.20) is indeterminate, since the first term in the right-hand side of (5.39) is negative from (5.31) and the second term is positive. However, the sign of (5.20) is positive if condition (5C.3)

$$\left| T'w_b\overline{L} \right| > \left| (T(E)\overline{L} + I + \lambda K_F)dw_b / dE \right|$$

is satisfied. The condition sufficient for the optimal enforcement level by the host country to be positive implies that the marginal income tax revenue, $-T'w_b\overline{L}$, is larger than the effect on the domestic country's wage, $(T(E)\overline{L} + I + \lambda K_F)dw_b / dE$. Thirdly, when case (iii) holds, $T'(E) > 0$. We find from (5.31) that the sign of (5.39) is negative.

Proposition 5.4
When capital is internationally mobile, internal enforcement will cause the host country's welfare to decrease if (a) $DFE \leq 0$ and $IFE \geq 0$; and will cause the host country's welfare to increase under condition (5C.3), when (b) $DFE > 0$ and $IFE < 0$.

We now consider the effect of internal enforcement on the foreign country's welfare. The foreign country's welfare is expressed as:

$$Y_b^* = w_b^*(\overline{L}^* - I) + r^*\overline{K}^* + Iw_b^*. \tag{5.40}$$

Y_b^* consists of factor expenditures, $[w_b^*(\overline{L}^* - I) + r^*\overline{K}^*]$, and immigrant earnings, Iw_b^*. By differentiating (5.40) with respect to E and using (5.7), the following equation is obtained:

$$dY_b^* / dE = Idw_b^* / dE + \lambda^* K_F dw_b^* / dE > 0. \tag{5.41}$$

The sign of (5.41) is unambiguously positive from (5.28). We find that enforcement will improve the foreign country's welfare.

Proposition 5.5
In the presence of capital mobility, the welfare of the foreign (labor-exporting) country will increase when the host country introduces internal enforcement.

Finally, we consider the effect of enforcement on world welfare $(Y_b + Y_b^*)$, as measured by global income. Global income, $(Y_b + Y_b^*)$, is derived from (5.38) and (5.40):

$$(Y_b + Y_b^*) = [(1 - T(E))w_b\overline{L} + r\overline{K}] + [w_b^*(\overline{L}^* - I) + r^*\overline{K}^* + Iw_b^*]. \tag{5.42}$$

The differentiation of (5.42) with respect to E is derived from (5.39) and (5.41):

$$d(Y_b + Y_b^*)/dE = -(T(E)\overline{L} + I + \lambda K_F)dw_b/dE$$
$$+ (I + \lambda^* K_F)dw_b^*/dE - T'w_b\overline{L}. \tag{5.43}$$

The first term on the right-hand side of (5.43) is negative from (5.31), the second term is positive from (5.28), and the third term is indefinite.

When case (i) in (5.A) holds ($DFE = 0$ and $IFE = 0$), the sign of (5.43) is positive if the condition (5C.4):

$$\left|(I + \lambda^* K_F)dw_b^*/dE\right| > \left|-(T(E)\overline{L} + I + \lambda K_F)dw_b/dE\right|$$

is satisfied; that is, the effect on foreign wages, $(I + \lambda^* K_F)dw_b^*/dE$, outweighs the effect on domestic wages, $(T(E)\overline{L} + I + \lambda K_F)dw_b/dE$.

When case (ii) in (5.A) holds ($DFE > 0$ and $IFE < 0$), the sign of (5.43) is positive if condition (5C.5):

$$\left|(I + \lambda^* K_F)dw_b^*/dE - T'w_b\overline{L}\right| > \left|-(T(E)\overline{L} + I + \lambda K_F)dw_b/dE\right|$$

is satisfied; that is, the effect on foreign wages, $(I + \lambda^* K_F)dw_b^*/dE$ and the marginal revenue from income taxes, $-T'(E)w_b\overline{L}$, surpass the effect on home wages, $(T(E)\overline{L} + I + \lambda K_F)dw_b/dE$.

When case (iii) in (5.A) holds ($DFE < 0$ and $IFE > 0$), the sign of (5.43) is positive if condition (5C.6):

$$\left| (I + \lambda^* K_F) dw_b^* / dE \right| > \left| -(T(E)\overline{L} + I + \lambda K_F) dw_b / dE - T' w_b \overline{L} \right|$$

is satisfied; that is, the effect on the foreign country's wage, $(I + \lambda^* K_F)$ $\times dw_b^* / dE$, overweighs the effect on the host country's wage, $(T(E)\overline{L} + I + \lambda K_F) dw_b / dE$ and the marginal revenue of income tax, $T' w_b \overline{L}$.

We obtain the following proposition:

Proposition 5.6
In the presence of capital mobility, internal enforcement will improve global welfare, $Y_b + Y_b^*$, if (5C.4) is satisfied:

$$\left| (I + \lambda^* K_F) dw_b^* / dE \right| > \left| -(T(E)\overline{L} + I + \lambda K_F) dw_b / dE \right| ,$$

when case (i) in (5.A) holds (DFE = 0 and IFE = 0), or if (5C.5) is satisfied:

$$\left| (I + \lambda^* K_F) dw_b^* / dE - T' w_b \overline{L} \right| > \left| -(T(E)\overline{L} + I + \lambda K_F) dw_b / dE \right|,$$

when case (ii) in (5.A) (DFE > 0 and IFE < 0) holds, or if (5C.6) is satisfied:

$$\left| (I + \lambda^* K_F) dw_b^* / dE \right| > \left| -(T(E)\overline{L} + I + \lambda K_F) dw_b / dE - T' w_b \overline{L} \right|,$$

and when case (iii) in (5.A) (DFE < 0 and IFE > 0) holds.

We can conclude that when capital is internationally mobile, internal enforcement is *a Pareto-improving policy*, which improves global welfare under certain conditions. For example, the present US government policy on possible illegal immigrants will be desirable from the viewpoint of global welfare when capital is free to flow between countries.

5.6 Concluding remarks

We extended the Bond and Chen (1987) model on illegal immigration by introducing a government budget constraint (*GBC*) on the host country. We examined the effects of financing internal enforcement by the host country's government on the welfare of the host country, the welfare of the foreign country, and on global welfare. We performed this analysis both for when capital was assumed to be internationally mobile and for when capital was assumed to be immobile between the two countries.

We showed that in the absence of capital mobility, (5.a) enforcement does not always improve the host country's welfare, and invariably reduces the foreign country's welfare, and (5.b) enforcement may become *a Pareto-improving (or inferior) policy* that increases (or decreases) global welfare, depending upon the signs and magnitudes of the direct and indirect fiscal effects on the *GBC* of financing the enforcement. In the presence of capital mobility, (5.c) enforcement does not necessarily improve the host country's welfare and inevitably improves the foreign country's welfare, and (5.d) enforcement can become *a Pareto-improving policy* under some circumstances.

Notes

1   If we assume that the level of border enforcement is increased by the host country's government, we can suppose that there is a wage differential between illegal wages in the host country and legal wages in the foreign country. Since we allow the level of border enforcement to be fixed, we can ignore this wage differential in our model (see Bond and Chen (1987)).

2   If the host country's government introduces border enforcement, foreign would-be illegal immigrants incur the penalty, k, when they are caught at the border between the two countries. If we assume that the probability of detection at the border is expressed as $g(B)$ where B is the expenditure on border enforcement by the host country's government, $g(0) = 0$, $g' > 0$, $g'' < 0$ and $g < 1$, then risk-neutral illegal migrants alter their migration decisions so as to equate the expected reward from migration to the local wage, w_b^*:

$$(w_b^* - k)g + w^I(1 - g) = w_b^*, \tag{i}$$

where w^I is the wage that the illegal workers who succeed in moving into the host country earn by working illegally in the host country's firm. Equation (i) is rewritten as:

$$w^I = w_b^* + k[g(B)/(1 - g(B))]. \tag{ii}$$

Thus, when the host country's government carries out border enforcement, foreign illegal immigrants who escape detection at the border earn the wage, w^I, which is greater than the foreign country's wage, w_b^*.

We can ignore $k[g(B)/(1 - g(B))]$ on the right-hand side of equation (ii) since we assume that the level of border enforcement is constant throughout the model. Therefore, there is no wage differential between illegal working in the host country and legal working in the foreign country; $w^I = w_b^*$ (see Bond and Chen (1987)).

3   The number of illegal immigrants, $I(> 0)$, is determined so that (5.1) is satisfied. If $w_b > w_b^* + p(E)z(E)$ for any $E > 0$, the domestic firm is willing to hire foreign illegal workers rather than domestic workers. On the other hand, if $w_b < w_b^* + p(E)z(E)$, the domestic firm would like to employ relatively more domestic workers than foreign workers. Therefore, in equilibrium (5.1) holds and thus $I(> 0)$ is determined from (5.1).

When the level of internal enforcement, E becomes sufficiently high, the number of illegal immigrants, I is reduced. Hence, it is possible that for large E, the number of illegal immigrants becomes zero; there is a corner solution with regard to labor mobility. However, we only assume the existence of an interior solution on labor movement for all E.

4   There is a possibility that $w_b = w_b^*$ from (5.1) when the level of internal enforcement is zero; $E = 0$. This implies that *the number of illegal immigrants, I, is independent of the enforcement level, E*.

However, we assume that the level of internal enforcement, E, is initially set at some minimum level, $E_{min}(>0)$. In short, we do not consider that the expenditure level of enforcement is zero; $E = 0$ since we exclude the possibility of equality between domestic and foreign wages from consideration. Thus, there is an international labor movement in equilibrium for any defined $E(>0)$.

5   From the definition of a and (5.10b), the effect of enforcement on the level of illegal immigration, I is negative:

$$dI/dE = [(\overline{L} + I)/(1 - a)][da/dE] < 0.$$

6   Bond and Chen (1987) stated that 'a necessary condition for the optimal enforcement level to the positive is that $-I(dw^*/dE) - (vp'I + 1) > 0$'.

7   See also mathematical appendix in the Chapter 3.

8   From the definition of a and (5.30a), the effect of enforcement policy on the level of illegal immigration, I is negative:

$$dI/dE = [(\overline{L} + I)/(1 - a)][da/dE] < 0.$$

Part I: Final Conclusion

In the first part of this book, we have examined the welfare effects of internal enforcement and border enforcement on host country welfare, foreign country welfare and global welfare using the two-country (a host country and a foreign country) model of illegal immigration. We can categorize the global welfare effects under two scenarios.

Firstly, when there is no capital mobility, both internal enforcement and border enforcement introduce distortions into an initial Pareto Optimal world economy, and hence, make the world economy worse off. Secondly, when there is capital mobility as well as a tax on domestic capital located in the foreign country, a distortion exists in equilibrium prior to the introduction of any enforcement policy. The introduction of a second distortion, internal enforcement or border enforcement, could raise global welfare for the standard second-best reasons.

We conclude that in the presence (or absence) of capital mobility an internal enforcement policy or a border enforcement policy will be desirable (or undesirable) in terms of its impact on global welfare.

Part II

The Optimal Enforcement of Employer Sanctions

6
The Optimal Enforcement of Immigration Law*

Bond and Chen (1987) developed a two-country, one-good, two-factor model of illegal immigration. Bond and Chen concluded that in the absence of capital mobility between the two countries, employer sanctions against home firms knowingly employing illegal foreign workers by a host country's government might increase the host country's welfare given certain necessary conditions. We reintroduce the Bond and Chen model utilizing a Cobb-Douglas production function. We find an optimal level of the enforcement for the host country's welfare when capital is mobile between the countries. The purpose of this chapter is to complement the work of Bond and Chen. When there is capital mobility as well as a tax on home capital located in a foreign country, a distortion exists in equilibrium prior to the introduction of the enforcement. The introduction of the enforcement as a second distortion can increase the host country's income for some standard second-best reasons.

6.1 Introduction

The Ethier (1986a) model carved out new ground by analyzing the effects of border patrol and employer sanctions policies whose purposes are to reduce illegal immigration in a small one-country (host country) model using crime-theoretic analysis (Becker (1968)). In his model, Ethier examined how the host country could use home border control and internal enforcement policies to attain home policy objectives regarding the number of illegal immigration and income distribution.

Bond and Chen (1987) extended the Ethier model by constructing a two-country, one-good, two-factor model. In their paper they analyzed the effect of the employer sanctions that capture undocumented workers at home firms that knowingly hire the irregular workers by a home country's government on the home country's welfare. They showed that the imposition of this enforcement policy by the home government might improve their country's welfare if the country was large enough to affect the foreign wage and if marginal enforcement costs were sufficiently low when capital was immobile between the two countries. They also found an optimal enforcement level of the interior inspections that maximizes the host country's income in the absence of capital flows.

We reintroduce the Bond and Chen model using a Cobb-Douglas production function, and specifying a probability for illegal workers to be detected by a home immigration authority. We consider the case where capital is immobile between countries, as well as the case in which capital is allowed to be mobile between the two countries. The aims of this chapter are to discover an optimal level of the enforcement from the viewpoint of the home country's income especially in the presence of capital mobility, and to complement the work of Bond and Chen. When there is capital mobility as well as a tax on home capital located in the foreign country, a distortion exists in equilibrium prior to the introduction of the enforcement. The introduction of the enforcement as a second distortion can increase the host country's income for some standard second-best reasons.

In the next section, assuming capital is not internationally mobile, we analyze how internal enforcement effects the home country. In section 6.3, we present the welfare effects of the enforcement policy. In section 6.4 we examine the economic effects of enforcement in the presence of capital mobility. Section 6.5 examines additional welfare effects, and the final section offers some concluding remarks.

6.2 The basic model

We reintroduce a two-country, one good, two-factor model of illegal immigration using a Cobb-Douglas production function, following Bond and Chen (1987), in which foreign labor illegally migrates to the home country and capital is immobile between the two countries. The home country's economy produces a single good, F, produced using labor and capital inputs under a constant returns to scale technology. The production function is specified as a Cobb-Douglas production function:

$$F(L,K) = L^{\alpha}K^{1-\alpha}, \tag{6.1}$$

where L denotes employment of unskilled labor composed of home unskilled labor and foreign illegal labor, K represents the employment of native skilled workers and home real capital, and α is a parameter contained in $(0, 1)$.[1] Note that home unskilled workers and illegal foreign workers are perfect substitutes in production. Technologies are assumed to differ between the countries. The labeling of the countries is chosen so that in the presence of factor immobility, the home wage rate, w, exceeds the foreign wage rate, w^*. In autarky, the home country is labor scarce relative to the foreign country (i.e., the foreign country is capital scarce relative to the receiving country). We treat the home output as the numeraire.

Because of the existence of labor mobility restrictions determined by immigration laws (i.e., employer sanctions) implemented by the home immigration authority, there is a positive probability, p, that a foreign illegal worker will be detected and apprehended.[2] The probability increases with the effort that the authority devotes to internal inspection:

$$p = (E / R)^{1/\beta}, \quad p' > 0, \quad p'' < 0, \quad p(0) = 0, \quad p \leq 1, \qquad (6.2)$$

where $E(\geq 0)$ is the effort expended on internal enforcement, $R(> 0)$ is an initially given national budget of the host country, and is assumed that $E \leq R$, and the parameter β is larger than unity. Once a Congress in the home country ratifies a budget that the immigration department needs so as to catch unlawful foreign workers, the host country's government allocates the budget to the department. Suppose the authority behaves as a budget-maximizing bureau. E is equal to the budget distributed to the bureau. Note that if the tougher immigration policy against the foreign illegal workers is adopted, then the level of E is larger.

The policy that the home (labor-importing) country's government utilizes is part of their immigration law. Risk-neutral home firms are subject to penalties, z (whose level is constant), which they pay to the home government for each arrested illegal foreign worker found hired by the firm during inspection by the immigration authorities. We assume that home firms can completely distinguish between legal home workers and illegal foreign workers. Thus, the illegal workers must bear the burden of the fines. The wage paid to an illegal foreign worker will be equal to the wage of a legal home worker, w, minus the expected penalty $(E / R)^{1/\beta} \cdot z$. Home firms are indifferent between hiring legal home workers and illegal foreign workers. In equilibrium, the illegal aliens receive the same wage everywhere:

$$w - (E / R)^{1/\beta} \cdot z = w^*. \qquad (6.3)$$

The formula in (6.3) also implies that the expected cost of hiring a legal home worker, w, is the same as that of hiring an illegal foreign worker, $w^* + (E/R)^{1/\beta} \cdot z$.

Home competitive firms hire legal home labor, illegal foreign labor, and home capital in order to minimize the cost of producing a given level of output. The cost function, C, of a home firm is:

$$C \equiv wL + rK , \qquad (6.4)$$

where w and r are, respectively, home factor prices for labor and capital, which are assumed to be given. Solving the cost minimization problem for the firm, the following equilibrium conditions are obtained:

$$w = \alpha[(\overline{L}+I)/\overline{K}]^{\alpha-1} , \qquad (6.5a)$$

$$r = (1-\alpha)[(\overline{L}+I)/\overline{K}]^{\alpha} , \qquad (6.5b)$$

where $\overline{L}$ and $\overline{K}$ are the fixed initial endowments of labor and capital of the home country. Note that in the absence of capital mobility, $K = \overline{K}$, since we assume that home capital is fully employed in the home country. Furthermore, labor employment in the home country, L, is equal to $\overline{L}+I$, which is the fixed initial endowment of home labor plus the level of illegal foreign labor.

In the foreign country, the following equilibrium conditions, similar to that of the home country, are derived from solving the cost minimization problem for the foreign firm:

$$w^* = \alpha A[(\overline{L}^* - I)/\overline{K}^*]^{\alpha-1} , \qquad (6.6a)$$

$$r^* = (1-\alpha)A[(\overline{L}^* - I)/\overline{K}^*]^{\alpha} , \qquad (6.6b)$$

where w^* and r^* are the foreign wage rate and the foreign capital rental rate, $\overline{L}^*$ and $\overline{K}^*$ are the fixed initial endowments of labor and capital in the foreign (labor exporting) country, and A is level of technology in $(0, 1)$. Note that L^* and K^* are equal to $\overline{L}^* - I$ and $\overline{K}^*$, respectively.

Five endogenous variables, I, w, r, w^* and r^* are determined from (6.3), (6.5a), (6.5b), (6.6a) and (6.6b) given the level of internal enforcement, E. We solve for the effects of an increase in E, totally differentiating the five formulas:

$$dI/dE = (z/R\beta) \cdot (E/R)^{(1-\beta)/\beta} / \alpha(\alpha-1)\Delta_1 < 0 , \qquad (6.7)$$

$$dw/dE = (z/R\beta)(1/\overline{K})[(\overline{L}+I)/\overline{K}]^{\alpha-2} \cdot (E/R)^{(1-\beta)/\beta} / \Delta_1 > 0 , \qquad (6.8)$$

$$dr/dE = -(z/R\beta)(1/\overline{K})[(\overline{L}+I)/\overline{K}]^{\alpha-1} \cdot (E/R)^{(1-\beta)/\beta} / \Delta_1 < 0 , \qquad (6.9)$$

$$dw^*/dE = -A(z/R\beta)(1/\overline{K}^*)[(\overline{L}^* - I)/\overline{K}^*]^{\alpha-2} \cdot (E/R)^{(1-\beta)/\beta} / \Delta_1 < 0 , \quad (6.10)$$

$$dr^*/dE = A(z/R\beta)(1/\overline{K}^*)[(\overline{L}^* - I)/\overline{K}^*]^{\alpha-1} \cdot (E/R)^{(1-\beta)/\beta} / \Delta_1 > 0 , \qquad (6.11)$$

where $\Delta_1 \equiv [(\overline{L}+I)/\overline{K}]^{\alpha-2} \cdot (1/\overline{K}) + A[(\overline{L}^*-I)/\overline{K}^*]^{\alpha-2} \cdot (1/\overline{K}^*) > 0$. We notice from (6.8) and (6.9) that

$$dr/dE = -((\overline{L}+I)/\overline{K})dw/dE. \tag{6.12}$$

Tougher employer sanctions may increase the apprehended illegal aliens, and increase the numbers of irregular foreign workers deported back to the foreign country. A decrease in the home labor/capital ratio will arise, since home labor force involves illegal foreign workers. This causes a decline in the home rental rate of capital (see (6.9)). In the foreign country, foreign firms may employ the deported foreign workers, which increases the foreign labor/capital ratio. Thus, the increase in internal enforcement will cause foreign workers to be worse off and foreign capital to be better off as foreign wages fall and the foreign rental rate of capital rises (see (6.10) and (6.11)).

6.3 The welfare analysis of internal enforcement

Suppose that a policy maker in the home (labor receiving) country is concerned with the country's GNP (Gross National Product), composed of home factor expenditures and the surplus of the home country's government. This implies a social welfare function of the form:

$$Y(E) = [w\overline{L} + r\overline{K}] + [R + (z-v)p(E)I - E], \tag{6.13}$$

where the surplus consists of the initially endowed budget of the home government and expected penalties less the costs associated with both catching and deporting arrested illegal workers and collecting fines from home firms caught employing these illegal workers.

We analyze whether or not there is a level of enforcement, E, that maximizes home social welfare. Differentiation of (6.13) with respect to E, using (6.2), (6.7), (6.8), (6.9) and (6.12), yields:

$$dY/dE = -Idw^*/dE + (E/R)^{1/\beta} \cdot (z-v) \cdot dI/dE$$
$$- \{(v/R\beta) \cdot (E/R)^{(1-\beta)/\beta} \cdot I + 1\}. \tag{6.14}$$

The first term on the right-hand side of (6.14) is positive from (6.10), and the third term is negative. The sign of the second term is negative from (6.7), since $(E/R)^{1/\beta} \cdot (z-v)(>0)$ is the difference between the domestic and foreign wages, net of the resource costs regarding the relegation of arrested illegal aliens and the collections of fines (see Bond and Chen (pp. 320-321, 1987)).

If we evaluate (6.14) at the zero enforcement level, $E = 0$, then we can confirm that an introduction of the enforcement makes the host country's welfare better off, if the following condition (6C.1) is satisfied:

$$dY/dE|_{E=0} = -Idw^*/dE - \{(v/R\beta)\cdot(E/R)^{(1-\beta)/\beta}\cdot I + 1\} > 0, \quad (6.14.1)$$

if

$$-Idw^*/dE > \{(v/R\beta)\cdot(E/R)^{(1-\beta)/\beta}\cdot I + 1\}. \quad (6C.1)$$

As shown in (6.14.1) and (6C.1), Bond and Chen (1987) have explicitly described a necessary condition for the optimal enforcement level to be the positive. The condition is that 'the home country must be large enough to have an effect on the foreign wage, and the marginal costs of enforcement must be sufficiently low'. Moreover, they showed that the optimal level of enforcement would be set at the level where both marginal costs and marginal benefits of enforcement are equal, provided that the necessary condition is satisfied.

The optimal level of the interior enforcement such that $dY/dE = 0$ is maintained, is obtained by setting equation (6.14) equal to zero and solving the resuting equation for E, given the condition (6C.1):

$$\overline{E} = [(-I/\Delta_1)\{A((\overline{L}^* - I)/\overline{K}^*)^{\alpha-2}\cdot(z/R\beta)\cdot(1/\overline{K}^*)\cdot(E/R)^{(1-\beta)/\beta}\}$$
$$+(v/R\beta)(E/R)^{(1-\beta)/\beta}\cdot I + 1/(1/\alpha(\alpha-1)\Delta_1)\{(z/R\beta)(E/R)^{(1-\beta)/\beta}\}]^\beta$$
$$\times R > 0. \quad (6.14.2)$$

Bond and Chen (1987) have found where the optimal level of the enforcement in terms of the home country's income exists in the equation (12), p.320 of their paper. In (6.14.2), we have *implicitly* discovered the optimal enforcement level, $\overline{E}$ of the employer sanctions by using a Cobb-Douglas production function and specifying a probability of detection of undocumented aliens.

6.4 International capital mobility

We now relax the assumption of capital immobility between the two countries. Technologies are assumed to be the same between the two countries. We assume that the home country's government imposes a tax on returns to home capital located in the foreign country. Home capital migrates to the foreign country until the return, net of taxes, is equal to the return to home capital employed in the home country:

$$r = r^*(1-t), \quad (6.15)$$

where t is the tax rate, contained in $(0,1)$. We confirm that there are both capital movements and illegal immigration in equilibrium by considering (6.3) and (6.15). We define the level of home capital exports as K_F.

The firms in each country employ labor and capital located in their country. The equilibrium conditions facing factor markets in the home and foreign countries are determined in a manner similar to equation (6.5a), (6.5b), (6.6a) and (6.6b):

$$w = \alpha[(\overline{L} + I)/(\overline{K} - K_F)]^{\alpha - 1},\tag{6.16a}$$

$$r = (1 - \alpha)[(\overline{L} + I)/(\overline{K} - K_F)]^{\alpha},\tag{6.16b}$$

$$w^* = \alpha[(\overline{L}^* - I)/(\overline{K}^* + K_F)]^{\alpha - 1},\tag{6.17a}$$

$$r^* = (1 - \alpha)[(\overline{L}^* - I)/(\overline{K}^* + K_F)]^{\alpha}.\tag{6.17b}$$

Note that the technology level for the foreign production, A is unity from the assumption. The six unknown variables, w, r, w^*, r^*, I and K_F are endogenously determined from (6.3), (6.15), (6.16a), (6.16b), (6.17a) and (6.17b), given the level of expenditure on the enforcement policy.

Totally differentiating (6.16a) and (6.16b), we obtain the following formulas:

$$dw = \alpha(\alpha - 1)[(\overline{L} + I)/(\overline{K} - K_F)]^{\alpha - 2} \cdot \{1/(\overline{K} - K_F)^2\}\{(\overline{K} - K_F)dI$$
$$+ (\overline{L} + I)dK_F\},\tag{6.18a}$$

$$dr = \alpha(1 - \alpha)[(\overline{L} + I)/(\overline{K} - K_F)]^{\alpha - 1} \cdot \{1/(\overline{K} - K_F)^2\}\{(\overline{K} - K_F)dI$$
$$+ (\overline{L} + I)dK_F\}.\tag{6.18b}$$

Carefully considering (6.18a) and (6.18b), a relation between dw and dr is derived as follows:[3]

$$dr = -[(\overline{L} + I)/(\overline{K} - K_F)]dw.\tag{6.19}$$

The total differentiation of (6.17a) and (6.17b) is:

$$dw^* = \alpha(\alpha - 1)[(\overline{L}^* - I)/(\overline{K}^* + K_F)]^{\alpha - 2} \cdot \{1/(\overline{K}^* + K_F)^2\}$$
$$\times \{-(\overline{K}^* + K_F)dI - (\overline{L}^* - I)dK_F\},\tag{6.20a}$$

$$dr^* = \alpha(1 - \alpha)[(\overline{L}^* - I)/(\overline{K}^* + K_F)]^{\alpha - 1} \cdot \{1/(\overline{K}^* + K_F)^2\}$$
$$\times \{-(\overline{K}^* + K_F)dI - (\overline{L}^* - I)dK_F\}.\tag{6.20b}$$

We can also find a connection between dw^* and dr^* similar to (6.19) by looking at (6.20a) and (6.20b):

$$dr^* = -[(\overline{L}^* - I)/(\overline{K}^* + K_F)]dw^*.\tag{6.21}$$

Note that (6.21) is the cost-minimization condition (see footnote 3).

We can derive the effect of E on the foreign wage, totally differentiating (6.3) and (6.15) and making use of (6.19) and (6.21):

$$dw^* / dE = [(\overline{L} + I)/(\overline{K} - K_F)](z/R\beta)(E/R)^{(1-\beta)/\beta}$$

$$/[(1-t)((\overline{L}^* - I)/(\overline{K}^* + K_F)) - ((\overline{L} + I)/\overline{K} - K_F))] . \quad (6.22)$$

The denominator in the right-hand side of (6.22) is assumed to be positive, because we assume the stability of the equilibrium in the two-country model under two-way factor mobility (see Yoshida (p.45, 2000b)). We therefore know from (6.22) that stricter enforcement increases the wage of foreign workers. We also find the effect on the home wage, totally differentiating (6.3):

$$dw / dE = dw^* / dE + (z/R\beta)(E/R)^{(1-\beta)/\beta}$$

$$= (1-t)[(\overline{L}^* - I)/(\overline{K}^* + K_F)](z/R\beta)(E/R)^{(1-\beta)/\beta}$$

$$/[(1-t)((\overline{L}^* - I)/(\overline{K}^* + K_F)) - ((\overline{L} + I)/(\overline{K} - K_F))] > 0 . \quad (6.23)$$

By considering (6.18a), (6.20a) and (6.23), we can derive the effects of E on the number of illegal foreign workers, I, as well as on the amount of capital export, K_F:

$$\alpha(\alpha-1)\begin{bmatrix} \{(\overline{L}+I)/(\overline{K}-K_F)\}^{\alpha-2} \cdot \{1/(\overline{K}-K_F)\} & \{(\overline{L}+I)/(\overline{K}-K_F)\}^{\alpha-2} \cdot \{(\overline{L}+I)/(\overline{K}-K_F)^2\} \\ \{(\overline{L}^*-I)/(\overline{K}^*+K_F)\}^{\alpha-2} \cdot \{1/(\overline{K}^*+K_F)\} & \{(\overline{L}^*-I)/(\overline{K}^*+K_F)\}^{\alpha-2} \cdot \{(\overline{L}^*-I)/(\overline{K}^*+K_F)^2\} \end{bmatrix}$$

$$\times \begin{bmatrix} dI/dE \\ dK_F/dE \end{bmatrix} = \begin{bmatrix} dw^*/dE + (z/R\beta)(E/R)^{(1-\beta)/\beta} \\ dw^*/dE \end{bmatrix}, \quad (6.24)$$

where the determinant of the coefficient matrix on the left-hand side of (6.24), Δ_2, is

$$\Delta_2 \equiv -\alpha^2(\alpha-1)^2[(\overline{L}+I)/(\overline{K}-K_F)]^{\alpha-2} \cdot [(\overline{L}^*-I)/(\overline{K}^*+K_F)]^{\alpha-2}$$

$$\times \{1/(\overline{K}-K_F)\} \times \{1/(\overline{K}^*+K_F)\} \times [\{(\overline{L}^*-I)/(\overline{K}^*+K_F)\}$$

$$-\{(\overline{L}+I)/(\overline{K}-K_F)\}] < 0.$$

$$dI/dE = -[(dw^*/dE + (z/R\beta)(E/R)^{(1-\beta)/\beta})\alpha(\alpha-1)((\overline{L}^*-I)$$

$$/(\overline{K}^*+K_F))^{\alpha-2}((\overline{L}^*-I)/(\overline{K}^*+K_F)^2) + (dw^*/dE)\alpha(\alpha-1)((\overline{L}+I)$$

$$/(\overline{K}-K_F))^{\alpha-2}((\overline{L}+I)/(\overline{K}-K_F)^2)]/\Delta_2 < 0, \quad (6.25a)$$

$$dK_F/dE = \alpha(\alpha-1)[(dw^*/dE)((\overline{L}+I)/(\overline{K}-K_F))^{\alpha-2} \cdot (1/(\overline{K}-K_F))$$

$$+((dw^*/dE) + (z/R\beta)(E/R)^{(1-\beta)/\beta})((\overline{L}^*-I)/(\overline{K}^*+K_F))^{\alpha-2}$$

$$\times (1/(\overline{K}^*+K_F))]/\Delta_2 > 0 . \quad (6.25b)$$

It can be seen from these comparative static results, (6.22), (6.23), (6.25a) and (6.25b), that given international capital mobility, internal inspection brings about adverse (favorable) effects on home and foreign capital (home and foreign labor).

We find from (6.22) that the employer sanction by the home country's government causes an increase in the foreign country's wages. This arises because enforcement causes home capital to migrate from the home country to the foreign country. Capital immobility causes a match of irregular foreign country labor and home country capital in the home country. Capital mobility causes a match of (regular) foreign country labor and home country capital in the foreign country. Thus, capital mobility allows the elimination of production penalties that would be incurred under capital immobility.

An increase in the distortion, i.e., internal enforcement, will bring about further separation between the equilibrium points. Since the home country's output is produced by a capital-intensive technique in a value-sense as long as $((\overline{L}^* - I)/(\overline{K}^* + K_F))(1-t) - ((\overline{L} + I)/(\overline{K} - K_F)) > 0$, enforcement causes a decrease in the capital costs for both the home and the foreign country.

6.5 Optimal enforcement

We explore whether or not there is an optimal level of enforcement of immigration law. In the presence of capital mobility, we assume that the home (labor-receiving) country's government is concerned about their social welfare defined as:

$$Y(E) \equiv [w\overline{L} + r\overline{K}] + [R + p(E)(z - v)I - E + tr^* K_F]. \tag{6.26}$$

This social welfare contains factor payments, $[w\overline{L} + r\overline{K}]$, and the government's budget surplus, $[R + p(E)(z - v)I - E + tr^* K_F]$. Note that the form of (6.26) is equal to (6.13) plus tax revenues obtained from capital exports, $tr^* K_F$.

The host country's government, by maximizing $Y(E)$ with respect to E, chooses an optimal level of enforcement of the law. The first order condition for a maximum is obtained from (6.18a) through (6.21):

$$
\begin{aligned}
dY/dE = {}& tr^* dK_F/dE + p(z-v)dI/dE \\
& - \{I + ((\overline{L}^* - I)/(\overline{K}^* + K_F))K_F\}dw^*/dE - (vp'I + 1) \\
= {}& (dI/dE)[-\alpha(1-\alpha)((\overline{L}^* - I)/(\overline{K}^* + K_F))^\alpha \cdot \{K_F((\overline{L}^* - I) \\
& /(\overline{K}^* + K_F)^2) + I((\overline{K}^* + K_F)/(\overline{L}^* - I)^2)\}] + (dK_F/dE)(1 - \alpha) \\
& \times [((\overline{L}^* - I)/(\overline{K}^* + K_F))^\alpha (1/(\overline{L}^* - I)(\overline{K}^* + K_F)) \cdot \{((\overline{L}^* - I) - \alpha I) \\
& \times ((\overline{K}^* + K_F) - \alpha K_F) + \alpha^2 IK_F\} - ((\overline{L} + I)/(\overline{K} - K_F))^\alpha] - ((v/R\beta) \\
& \times (E/R)^{(1-\beta)/\beta} \cdot I + 1) + (dI/dE) \cdot (E/R)^{1/\beta} \cdot (z - v) = 0, \tag{6.27}
\end{aligned}
$$

where the possible fine-cost gap,

$$(E/R)^{1/\beta} \cdot (z - v) > 0,$$

and

$$((\overline{L}^* - I) - \alpha I)((\overline{K}^* + K_F) - \alpha K_F) > 0.$$

The first and second (positive) terms in (6.27) are the welfare gains in the home country for the marginal increase in enforcement level. The third (negative) term is the marginal cost of enforcement, and the fourth term is the decrease in the penalty revenues, net of the resource cost of the enforcement.

A necessary condition for a slight rise in the employer sanction to be welfare-improving for the home country is that $dY/dE > 0$ at the initial pre-enforcement level, i.e., at $E = 0$.

The formula in (6.27) leads to the necessary condition:

$$-(dI/dE)[\alpha(1 - \alpha)((\overline{L}^* - I)/(\overline{K}^* + K_F))^\alpha \cdot \{K_F((\overline{L}^* - I)/(\overline{K}^* + K_F)^2)$$
$$+ I((\overline{K}^* + K_F)/(\overline{L}^* - I)^2)\}] + (dK_F/dE)(1 - \alpha)[((\overline{L}^* - I)/(\overline{K}^* + K_F))^\alpha$$
$$\times (1/(\overline{L}^* - I)(\overline{K}^* + K_F)) \cdot \{((\overline{L}^* - I) - \alpha I)((\overline{K}^* + K_F) - \alpha K_F) + \alpha^2 I K_F\}$$
$$- ((\overline{L} + I)/(\overline{K} - K_F))^\alpha] > ((v/R\beta)(E/R)^{(1-\beta)/\beta} \cdot I + 1). \qquad (6C.2)$$

It turns out from (6C.2) that the effects of an increment in internal enforcement on illegal immigration and capital flow outweigh the marginal costs of enforcement.

We obtain the optimal enforcement level, $\overline{\overline{E}}$, from (6.27) given the necessary condition (6C.2):

$$\overline{\overline{E}} = [[\{\alpha(1 - \alpha)(dI/dE)((\overline{L}^* - I)/(\overline{K}^* + K_F))^\alpha \cdot \{(K_F(\overline{L}^* - I)/(\overline{K}^* + K_F)^2)$$
$$+ (I(\overline{K}^* + K_F)/(\overline{L}^* - I)^2)\} - (1 - \alpha)(dK_F/dE)\{((\overline{L}^* - I)/(\overline{K}^* + K_F))^\alpha$$
$$\times (1/(\overline{L}^* - I)(\overline{K}^* + K_F)) \cdot (((\overline{L}^* - I) - \alpha I)((\overline{K}^* + K_F) - \alpha K_F) + \alpha^2 I K_F)$$
$$- ((\overline{L} + I)/(\overline{K} - K_F))^\alpha\} + ((v/R\beta)(E/R)^{(1-\beta)/\beta} \cdot I + 1)]$$
$$/(z - v)dI/dE]^\beta \cdot R > 0, \qquad (6.28)$$

where $(1/R\beta)(E/R)^{(1-\beta)/\beta}$ is the marginal probability of detection, $p'(E)$, and the fine-cost gap, $(z - v)$ is assumed to be positive (see the comments below (6.14)).

Proposition 6.1 [Yoshida (1999)]

There is an optimal enforcement level of an immigration law against illegal aliens by the immigration authority of a home country if condition (6C.2) holds, when capital is internationally mobile.

The implication behind this proposition is that the US DHS can optimally carry out internal enforcement to improve US welfare when a slight increase in enforcement promotes deportation of illegal immigrants, given capital mobility and sufficiently low marginal costs of enforcement. The DHS must make an effort to curtail expenditures on the enforcement of employer sanctions, they should implement innovations in the techniques of detecting and arresting illegal foreign workers, and they should recover the cost of inspecting home firms knowingly hiring illegal aliens.

Bond and Chen (1987) have found how the host country's government can optimally enforce, when capital is immobile between the two countries. Considering the NAFTA between the US, Canada and Mexico came into effect in 1994, there are large scale capital exports from the US to Mexico, for example, *maquiladora* (cf. Arreola and Curtis (1993), Bratsberg (1995), Gianaris (1998), Gonzalez-Arechiga (1992), Greenwood, Hunt and Kohli (1997), Massey et. al. (1998) and OECD (1997)). The increments in the capital exports caused by stronger employer sanctions (see (6.25b)) might have enlarged employment opportunities for the labor-exporting country's workers. This should have forced undocumented immigration from Mexico to the US to decrease. We obtained the optimal level of the internal inspections from the viewpoint of the home country's welfare when there are capital flows between the countries. Therefore, we complemented the work of Bond and Chen.

6.6 Conclusion

We developed the two-country model of illegal aliens using a Cobb-Douglas production function, and particularly defining a probability of detection of an unlawful foreign worker. We considered whether or not there is an optimal level of internal enforcement from the point of view of the home country's welfare, both when capital is internationally mobile or when it is internationally immobile.

Bond and Chen (1987) showed an optimal enforcement level of internal inspections given the necessary condition for the enforcement level of internal inspections to be positive when there is no capital mobility. We rigorously searched for the optimal level of the employer sanctions in view of a host country's welfare using our model.

We also determined that in the presence of capital mobility, the immigration authority of the home country could optimally set the level of internal inspection when condition (6C.2) is satisfied. Condition (6C.2) requires that the US government should put the following policies into practice (see the comments below the proposition). First, the government must try to encourage US firms to shift capital to the source country of the illegal immigrant workers, e.g., Mexico. Second, the administration must attempt to reduce the costs of inspection of home firms intentionally employing illegal foreign workers.[4]

Notes

*   The chapter was first published in 'Business & Economics for the 21st Century - Volume III', ISBN #: 0-9659831-2-9, Library of Congress Catalog Card#: 99-097613, Worcester, MA, USA,1999.

1   We regard skilled workers as human capital.

2   In the US, DHS (formerly INS) enforces the internal enforcement policy against US firms that knowingly hire illegal aliens (Calavita (1998)).

3   Considering (6.5a) and (6.5b), we can rewrite (6.4) as follows:

$$\tilde{C}(w,r) \equiv wL(w,r) + rK(w,r).$$

We obtain (6.19) by making use of the cost-minimization condition:

$$d\tilde{C} \equiv \tilde{C}_w dw + \tilde{C}_r dr = Ldw + Kdr = (\overline{L}+I)dw + (\overline{K}-K_F)dr = 0.$$

4   Sanctions against employers are also introduced in European countries, e.g. Germany, France, Austria, Netherlands, Sweden, Norway, Italy, Hungary, etc (see Brochmann and Hammar (1999)). Therefore, it is possible to extrapolate the effects of enforcing the employer sanction examined in section 6.4 and 6.5 to the European countries.

7
The Optimal Enforcement of a Finance-Constrained Immigration Law*

We extend the Bucci and Tenorio (1996) model of illegal immigration by constructing a two-country, one-good, two-factor model, and analyze political issues not considered in their work. We consider the case where capital is immobile between the two countries, as well as the case in which capital is mobile between them. Our main result is that the host country's government can, under some circumstances, optimally enforce employer sanctions in order to maximize the host country's welfare under both capital mobility and immobility.

7.1 Introduction

Prosperous countries have recently tended to restrict an inflow of foreign migrants. This has caused illegal immigration from poorer, less developed countries to wealthier, developed countries. Illegal immigration is usually considered to be the problem of the labor-receiving or host country.

The governments of developed countries deal with the problem of illegal foreign workers mainly through the use of the following two immigration enforcement policies: border patrol and internal enforcement. Border patrol involves the prevention of attempted illegal migration at the border. Internal enforcement involves apprehending foreign workers who are working illegally in domestic firms.

An example of an internal enforcement policy is the Immigration Reform and Control Act passed by the US Congress in 1986 (IRCA–1986). The IRCA provisions provided three fundamental measures to reduce illegal immigration to the US: (1) employer sanctions for knowingly hiring undocumented aliens; (2) amnesty programs for long-term resident illegal immigrants; (3) increased resources for border patrols (Gimpel and Edwards Jr. (1999)).

Employer sanctions include civil fines and criminal penalties for employers who knowingly hire illegal immigrants. For a first offense, these fines range from $250 to $2,000 for each illegal immigrant worker. Criminal penalties include prison sentences of up to 6 months if an employer is convicted for a 'pattern and practice' of hiring illegal foreign workers (cf. White, Bean and Espenshade (1990), Woodrow (1992) and Calavita (1998)).

The work of Bucci and Tenorio (1996) initially perceived that immigration reforms such as the employer sanction provision of the US IRCA-1986 prescribed simultaneous increases in both the costs of enforcement and employer fines. Bucci and Tenorio then examined the effects of financing internal enforcement on the host country's welfare by using *a one-small-country model*. Therefore, we could assume that the host country's government would raise the employer penalties so as to satisfy the budget constraint in accordance with an increase in the enforcement level. Bucci and Tenorio, however, did not examine whether there was an optimum level of financed internal enforcement in terms of the host country's income.

We extend the Bucci and Tenorio model by constructing a two-country, one-good, two-factor model, and use a Cobb-Douglas production function and define a home immigration authority who enforces the interior inspections as a budget-maximizing bureau to analyze some political issues not considered in their work. We consider the case where capital is immobile between the two countries, as well as the case in which capital is mobile between them. If there is a level of finance-constrained interior enforcement that maximizes the host country's welfare, then we can derive the optimum level of enforcement from the model. We assume in our model that there is an income tax rate imposed on home legal workers. Therefore, a distortion exists in equilibrium prior to the introduction of any enforcement policy. The introduction of a second distortion, the internal enforcement, can *improve* the host country's welfare for some standard second-best reasons.

We briefly introduce the other interesting researches on illegal immigration. Ethier (1986a) pioneered the new model on illegal immigrants by analyzing the effects of border and internal enforcement schemes in a one-country model using crime-theoretic analysis (Becker (1968)). Bond and Chen (1987) extended the Ethier model by constructing a standard, two-country, one-good, two-factor model. They analyzed the effect of interior inspections by the host country's government on the host country's welfare when capital is immobile between the two countries. Bandyopadhyay and Bandyopadhyay (1998) have modeled the source country of illegal immigration and employer sanctions at length. In a recent paper, Gaytan-Fregoso and Lahiri (2000) have developed a new model in which the decision to migrate is made at families with *no risk* for illegal immigrants to be apprehended by border patrol or employer sanctions so as to explore the effect of foreign aid on undocumented immigration. Yoshida (2000b) used the Bond and Chen model to explore the effects of the internal enforcement on the host and foreign countries' incomes in the presence of capital mobility. The papers introduced above have used a generalized production function with a constant returns to scale technology and a generalized function of probability for the illegal labor to be arrested. However, unlike the above-mentioned paper, the present chapter considers a framework in which the production function is defined as the Cobb-Douglas, and the functions of the probability of detection of illegal aliens and the fine imposed on the home firm are specified by considering the home immigration department as the budget-maximizing government bureau. Moreover, none of the already presented papers has discovered the optimal level of the immigration restrictions in view of the home country's welfare.

In the next section, we analyze the effects of internal enforcement on the host country when capital is not internationally mobile. In section 7.3, we examine how enforcement affects the financing tools used by the host country's government. In section 7.4 we present the welfare effects of financing enforcement. In section 7.5 we consider the welfare effects of enforcement when there is capital mobility. Section 7.6 further examines the welfare effects of financing enforcement. The final section offers some concluding remarks.

7.2 The basic model

We introduce a two-country, one good, two-factor model of illegal immigration, using a Cobb-Douglas production function, in which foreign labor illegally migrates to the host country and capital is immobile between the two countries. The host country's economy produces a single good, F, produced using labor and capital inputs under a constant returns-to-scale technology. The production function specified is a Cobb-Douglas production function:

$$F(L,K) = L^{\alpha} K^{1-\alpha}, \qquad (7.1)$$

where L denotes employment of labor composed of domestic labor and illegal foreign labor, K represents the employment of domestic real capital, and α is a parameter contained in $(0, 1)$. Note that domestic workers and illegal foreign workers are perfect substitutes in production. Technologies are assumed to differ between the countries. The labeling of the countries is chosen so that in the presence of factor immobility, the domestic wage rate, w, exceeds the foreign wage rate, w^*. In autarky, the domestic or host country is labor scarce relative to the foreign country (i.e., the foreign country is capital scarce relative to the receiving country). We treat the domestic output as the numeraire.

Because of restrictions on labor mobility determined by immigration laws (i.e., employer sanctions) implemented by the domestic immigration authority, there is a positive probability, p, that an illegal foreign migrant worker will be detected and apprehended.[1] The probability increases with the effort that the authority devotes to internal inspection:

$$p = (E/R)^{1/\beta}, \quad p' > 0, \quad p'' < 0, \quad p(0) = 0, \quad p \le 1, \qquad (7.2a)$$

where $E(\ge 0)$ is the effort expended on internal enforcement by the immigration bureau, $R(> 0)$ is an initially endowed national budget of the host country, and the parameter β is larger than unity. We assume that the home country's government determines to allocate a part of the national budget, E, for the immigration department, and hence $E \le R$. The immigration authority behaves as a budget-maximizing government bureau. We assume that arrested illegal aliens are removed from the domestic labor force through deportation.

The policy that the host (labor-importing) country's government utilizes is part of their immigration law. We assume that the host country's government introduces immigration reform and enacts employer sanctions similar to those in IRCA. It is generally accepted that employer sanctions increase both the costs of internal enforcement and the penalties levied on domestic firms found hiring illegal workers. Since the costs of enforcement and the level of penalties are simultaneously increased, $z'(E) \ge 0$.

Therefore, risk-neutral domestic firms are subject to penalties,

$$z(E) \equiv (E/\bar{I})^\rho, \qquad (7.2b)$$

where $\rho(> 0)$ is a positive constant, and $\bar{I}$ is the initial given number of illegal foreign workers in the labor-importing country.[2] (7.2b) implies that the cost of inspecting the home firm is financed by a fine imposed on an illegal worker found and apprehended by the immigration authority. Domestic firms pay the domestic government for each illegal foreign worker that is caught and arrested during an inspection of the firm by the immigration authorities.

We assume that domestic firms can completely distinguish between legal domestic workers and illegal foreign workers. Thus, illegal workers must bear the burden of the firms' fines. The wage paid to an illegal foreign worker will be equal to the wage of a legal domestic worker, w, minus the expected penalty $(E/R)^{1/\beta} \cdot (E/\bar{I})^{\rho}$. Domestic firms are indifferent between hiring legal domestic workers and illegal foreign workers. In equilibrium, illegal aliens receive the same wage in both countries:

$$w - (E/R)^{1/\beta} \cdot (E/\bar{I})^{\rho} = w^*. \qquad (7.3)$$

The formula in (7.3) also implies that the expected cost of hiring a legal domestic worker, w, is the same as that of hiring an illegal foreign worker, $w^* + (E/R)^{1/\beta} \cdot (E/\bar{I})^{\rho}$.

Domestic competitive firms hire legal domestic labor, illegal foreign labor, and domestic capital in order to minimize the cost of producing a given level of output. The cost function, C, of a domestic firm is:

$$C \equiv wL + rK, \qquad (7.4)$$

where w and r are, respectively, factor prices for labor and capital, which are assumed to be given. Solving the cost minimization problem for the firm, the following equilibrium conditions are obtained:

$$w = \alpha[(\bar{L} + I)/\bar{K}]^{\alpha-1}, \qquad (7.5a)$$

$$r = (1-\alpha)[(\bar{L} + I)/\bar{K}]^{\alpha}, \qquad (7.5b)$$

where $\bar{L}$ and $\bar{K}$ are the fixed initial endowments of labor and capital of the host country. Note that in the absence of capital mobility, $K = \bar{K}$, since we assume that domestic capital is fully employed in the host country. Furthermore, labor utilization in the domestic country, L, is equal to $\bar{L} + I$, which is the fixed initial endowment of domestic labor plus the population of illegal foreign labor.

In the foreign country, competitive firms choose levels of labor and capital so that the costs of the firms are minimized, given the foreign wage rate and the foreign capital rental rate, w^* and r^*. The following equilibrium conditions, similar to those of the domestic country, are derived from solving the cost minimization problem for the firm:

$$w^* = \alpha A[(\bar{L}^* - I)/\bar{K}^*]^{\alpha-1}, \qquad (7.6a)$$

$$r^* = (1-\alpha)A[(\bar{L}^* - I)/\bar{K}^*]^{\alpha}, \qquad (7.6b)$$

where $\bar{L}^*$ and $\bar{K}^*$ are the fixed initial endowments of labor and capital in the foreign (labor exporting) country, and A is the level of technology in $(0, 1)$. Note that L^* and K^* are equal to $\bar{L}^* - I$ and $\bar{K}^*$, respectively.

The five equations, (7.3), (7.5a), (7.5b), (7.6a) and (7.6b), have five endogenous variables, I, w, r, w^* and r^*, which are determined from these equations given the level of internal enforcement, E. We examine the effects of increments in the level of effort, E, expended on internal enforcement. Totally differentiating the five equations with respect to E and solving gives us the effects on the five variables of changes in enforcement effort:

$$dI / dE = \psi / \alpha(\alpha - 1)\Delta_1 < 0, \tag{7.7}$$

$$dw / dE = ((\overline{L} + I) / \overline{K})^{\alpha - 2} \cdot (1 / \overline{K}) \cdot \psi / \Delta_1 > 0, \tag{7.8}$$

$$dr / dE = -((\overline{L} + I) / \overline{K})^{\alpha - 1} \cdot (1 / \overline{K}) \cdot \psi / \Delta_1 < 0, \tag{7.9}$$

$$dw^* / dE = -A((\overline{L}^* - I) / \overline{K}^*)^{\alpha - 2} \cdot (1 / \overline{K}^*) \cdot \psi / \Delta_1 < 0, \tag{7.10}$$

$$dr^* / dE = A((\overline{L}^* - I) / \overline{K}^*)^{\alpha - 1} \cdot (1 / \overline{K}^*) \cdot \psi / \Delta_1 > 0, \tag{7.11}$$

where

$$\Delta_1 \equiv [(\overline{L} + I) / \overline{K}]^{\alpha - 2}(1 / \overline{K}) + A[(\overline{L}^* - I) / \overline{K}^*]^{\alpha - 2}(1 / \overline{K}^*) > 0,$$

and

$$\psi \equiv (1 / R\beta)(E / R)^{(1 - \beta) / \beta} \cdot (E / \overline{I})^{\rho} + (\rho / \overline{I})(E / R)^{1 / \beta} \cdot (E / \overline{I})^{\rho - 1}.$$

We notice from (7.8) and (7.9) that

$$dr / dE = -((\overline{L} + I) / \overline{K})dw / dE. \tag{7.12}$$

Tougher employer sanctions may improve the identification of illegal aliens, and increase the number of illegal foreign workers deported back to their home country. This will bring about a decrease in the domestic labor/capital ratio, since illegal foreign workers are considered part of the employed domestic labor force. The result is a decline in the domestic rental rate of capital (see (7.9) and Razin and Sadka (1995), Chapter 16). In the foreign country, foreign firms may hire the deported foreign workers, which increases the foreign labor/capital ratio. Thus, the increase in internal inspection efforts will cause foreign workers to be worse off and foreign capital to be better off as foreign wages fall and the foreign rental rate of capital rises (see (7.10) and (7.11)) (see Razin and Sadka (1995), Chapter 16).

7.3 Government budget constraint

In this section, following Bucci and Tenorio (1996), we examine the budget activity of the host country's government. The host government's surplus,

GS, is:

$$GS \equiv R + (w - w^* - vp(E))I - E + T(E)w\overline{L}$$
$$= R + (z(E) - v)p(E)I - E + T(E)w\overline{L}, \qquad (7.13)$$

where v denotes the costs associated with the return of illegal workers to their native country and the collection of fines from firms; E is the cost of arresting illegal workers incurred by the host country's government; and $T(E)$ is the income tax levied on domestic labor, where $T(E)$ is in the open interval $(0, 1)$.

We assume the host country's government maintains a balanced budget. The government budget constraint (*GBC*) is:

$$R + T(E)w\overline{L} + z(E)p(E)I = vp(E)I + E. \qquad (7.14)$$

The left-hand side of (7.14) consists of the initially endowed national budget, R, income taxes from domestic workers, $T(E)w\overline{L}$, and expected fines from domestic firms, $z(E)p(E)I$. The right-hand side of (7.14) consists of the costs incurred deporting apprehended illegal workers back to the foreign country, $vp(E)I$, and the costs of internal enforcement, E.

An increase in the level of enforcement may alter the *GBC*, (7.14). Once a new level of enforcement is chosen, the host country's government will need to finance this change in policy using the following tools: z, or z and T. The total differentiation of (7.14) with respect to E is:

$$T(E)\overline{L}dw/dE + (z - v)(p'I + pdI/dE) + z'pI - 1 = -T'(E)w\overline{L} \qquad (7.15)$$

The left-hand side of (7.15) expresses the effect on the *GBC* of increased enforcement and fines. The impact is the direct fiscal effect (*DFE*) of the policy. When the host country's government sets (E, z) so that enforcement is fully financed by penalties on domestic firms, $DFE = 0$, then no additional financing tool will be required. However, if $DFE \neq 0$, then an imposition of income taxes will be required to balance the budget. This adjustment in T, the right-hand side of (7.15), is called the indirect fiscal effect (*IFE*) of enforcement. In short, (7.15) implies that some financing tool, z, or both z and T, will be required to rebalance the government's budget, (7.15).

By carefully considering (7.15), we can classify direct and indirect fiscal effects, (A), into the following three cases:

      (i)   If $DFE = 0$, $T'(E) = 0$,
      (ii) If $DFE > 0$, $T'(E) < 0$,   (7.A)
      (iii) If $DFE < 0$, $T'(E) > 0$,

where $T'(E) = 0$, $T'(E) < 0$ and $T'(E) > 0$ imply $IFE = 0$, $IFE < 0$ and $IFE > 0$, respectively.

7.4 A welfare analysis of interior inspections

Suppose that a social planner in the host (labor receiving) country is concerned with the country's GNP (Gross National Product), composed of domestic factor expenditures and the surplus of the host country's immigration authority. This implies a social welfare function of the form:

$$Y(E) = [(1 - T(E))w\overline{L} + r\overline{K}] + [R + (z - v)p(E)I - E + T(E)w\overline{L}], \quad (7.16)$$

where $Y(E)$ consists of domestic factor payments net of income tax, $(1 - T(E))w\overline{L} + r\overline{K}$, the budget surplus of the host country's government, $R + (z(E) - v)p(E)I - E + T(E)w\overline{L}$. Since we assume that the domestic national budget should be balanced (see (7.14)), (7.16) is changed as follows:

$$Y(E) = (1 - T(E))w\overline{L} + r\overline{K}. \quad (7.17)$$

We analyze whether or not there is a level of enforcement, E, that maximizes domestic social welfare. Differentiation of (7.17) with respect to E, using (7.8), (7.9) and (7.12), yields:

$$dY / dE = -(T(E) + I)dw / dE - T'w\overline{L}. \quad (7.18)$$

First, we consider the case (i) in (7.A), which means that $DFE = 0$ and $T'(E) = 0$. Hence, (7.18) is

$$dY / dE = -(T(E) + I)dw / dE < 0. \quad (7.19a)$$

We find from (7.8) that the sign of (7.19a) is negative. When revenues from penalties imposed on domestic firms directly finance the costs of employer sanctions, tougher internal enforcement makes the domestic country worse off. The higher wages received by domestic workers following stricter internal enforcement (see (7.8)) are more than offset by higher domestic income taxes.

Second is case (ii) in (7.A), which implies that $DFE > 0$ and $T'(E) < 0$. Let the income tax rate be denoted by $T(E) \equiv (E/R)^{\eta}$, where $\eta \gtreqless 0$ in accordance with each case in (7.A). This implies that the income tax rate must finance a portion of the budget distributed to the immigration department so as to maintain the balanced government budget, (7.14). The sign of (7.18) is unclear from (7.8) and $IFE < 0$. However, evaluating (7.18) at the zero enforcement level, $E = 0$, it is clear how enforcement affects the host country's well-being:

$$dY / dE\big|_{E=0} = -(\tilde{\eta} / R)(E / R)^{\tilde{\eta}-1} \cdot w\overline{L} > 0, \qquad (7.19b)$$

where the value of $\tilde{\eta}$ is negative, and $(\tilde{\eta} / R)(E / R)^{\tilde{\eta}-1}(< 0)$ is the gradient of $T(E)$ in a $T - E$ space. The sign of (7.19b) is positive. Here, we expect that there is an optimum level of domestic inspection in terms of the host country's income. (7.18) is re-written using (7.8) and the definition of the income tax rate:

$$dY / dE = [-\{(E / R)^{\eta} \cdot \overline{L} + I\}((\overline{L} + I) / \overline{K})^{\alpha-2} \cdot (1 / \overline{K})\{(1 / R\beta)(E / R)^{(1-\beta)/\beta}$$

$$\times (E / \overline{I})^{\rho} + (\rho / \overline{I})(E / R)^{1/\beta} \cdot (E / \overline{I})^{\rho-1}\} - (\tilde{\eta} / R)(E / R)^{\eta-1} \cdot w\overline{L}$$

$$\times \{((\overline{L} + I) / \overline{K})^{\alpha-2}(1 / \overline{K}) + A((\overline{L}^* - I) / \overline{K}^*)^{\alpha-2} \cdot (1 / \overline{K}^*)\} / \Delta_1$$

$$= 0. \qquad (7.19c)$$

We discover the optimum level of internal enforcement, $\overline{E}$ such that $dY / dE = 0$:

$$\overline{E} = [[\{(E / R)^{\eta} \cdot \overline{L} + I\}((\overline{L} + I) / \overline{K})^{\alpha-2} \cdot (1 / \overline{K})\{(1 / R\beta)(E / R)^{(1-\beta)/\beta} \cdot (E / \overline{I})^{\rho}\}$$

$$+ (\tilde{\eta} / R)(E / R)^{\eta-1} \cdot w\overline{L} \cdot \{((\overline{L} + I) / \overline{K})^{\alpha-2} \cdot (1 / \overline{K}) + A((\overline{L}^* - I) / \overline{K}^*)^{\alpha-2}$$

$$\times (1 / \overline{K}^*)\}]/[-\{(E / R)^{\eta} \cdot \overline{L} + I\}((\overline{L} + I) / \overline{K})^{\alpha-2}$$

$$\times (1 / \overline{K}) \cdot (\rho / \overline{I}) \cdot (E / \overline{I})^{\rho-1}]]^{\beta} \cdot R. \qquad (7.19d)$$

The implication behind (7.19d) is that the US DHS (formerly INS) can optimally enforce internal inspection to improve US welfare when case (ii) in (7.A) holds.

We should note that the necessary condition for the optimum $\overline{E}$ to be positive is that $DFE > 0$. This implies that the marginal income tax revenues, $T(E)\overline{L}dw / dE$, plus marginal expected penalties levied on discovered domestic firms, $(z'pI + zIp' + zpdI / dE)$ surpass marginal costs on enforcing employer sanctions, $(vp'I + vpdI / dE + 1)$. The US must therefore make as much effort as possible to accurately levy income taxes on domestic legal workers. The DHS should minimize expenditures on the enforcement of employer sanctions by implementing innovative techniques to detect and apprehend illegal foreign workers. Furthermore, they should recover the cost of inspecting domestic firms that knowingly hire illegal aliens, and they should minimize the costs of deporting illegal aliens back to their native country.

Third, case (iii) in (7.A) is considered. Case (iii) has $DFE < 0$ and $T'(E) > 0$. We can verify from (7.18) that once internal inspection is brought into effect, the host country's income will go down. The more stringent the internal inspection, the larger the tax burden on domestic labor.

Proposition 7.1 [Yoshida (2004)]

In the absence of capital mobility, (a) internal inspection of domestic firms by the immigration authority of the labor-importing (domestic) country is costly to the domestic country in terms of domestic social welfare, when we apply $DFE \leq 0$ and $IFE \geq 0$ to the model. Also, (b) there is an optimal level of enforcement in terms of domestic income, when $DFE > 0$ and $IFE < 0$.

We note from proposition 7.1 that outcome (a) is essentially identical with Bucci and Tenorio (1996); nevertheless, result (b) is a *new* one, not previously discovered.

Illegal workers are omitted from the definition of domestic welfare (see (7.17)). Illegal workers usually live in fear of exposure to the immigration authority. It has been shown that deportable aliens may receive social services, e.g., city water, transportation facilities, roads, hospitals, schools, etc, since they may possess counterfeit social security cards (cf. Yoshida (2000b)), which explains how illegal workers receive services without paying taxes in the host country. However, we can treat fines imposed on domestic firms as the equivalent of taxes on illegal aliens, because domestic employers initially set the wage of illegal labor at a lower level than that received by legal domestic labor (see (7.3)). Hence, it is desirable from the viewpoint of tax fairness for the labor importing country's government to implement internal enforcement.[3]

If stronger employer sanctions can be implemented without cost, as described above, then internal enforcement may be well-organized immigration law. Yet the probability of US enforcement agencies detecting illegal aliens is said to be approximately 2-3% (see Figure 1.1). It goes without saying that internal enforcement has little effect on the apprehension of illegal workers.

Although employer sanctions have little effect on the apprehension of illegal foreign workers, the US authorities can set an optimal level of interior inspection. However, they must raise the probability of catching illegal foreign workers, increase revenues from wage taxes on legal domestic labor, increase penalties on domestic firms found employing illegal workers, and reduce the costs of collecting income taxes and penalties.

7.5 International capital mobility

We now relax the assumption of capital immobility between the two countries. We assume that the host country's government imposes a tax on returns to domestic capital located in the foreign country. Domestic capital migrates to the foreign country until the return, net of taxes, is equal to the return to domestic capital employed in the domestic country:

$$r = r^*(1-t), \tag{7.20}$$

where t is the tax rate, contained in $(0, 1)$. We confirm that both capital movements and illegal immigration are in equilibrium, given (7.3) and (7.20). We define the level of domestic capital exports as K_F.

Firms in each country employ labor and capital located in their country. Technologies between the two countries are assumed to be same. The equilibrium conditions facing factor markets in the domestic and foreign countries are determined in a manner similar to equations (7.5a), (7.5b), (7.6a) and (7.6b):

$$w = \alpha[(\bar{L} + I)/(\bar{K} - K_F)]^{\alpha-1}, \tag{7.21a}$$

$$r = (1-\alpha)[(\bar{L} + I)/(\bar{K} - K_F)]^{\alpha}, \tag{7.21b}$$

$$w^* = \alpha[(\bar{L}^* - I)/(\bar{K}^* + K_F)]^{\alpha-1}, \tag{7.22a}$$

$$r^* = (1-\alpha)[(\bar{L}^* - I)/(\bar{K}^* + K_F)]^{\alpha}. \tag{7.22b}$$

The six unknown variables, w, r, w^*, r^*, I and K_F are endogenously determined from (7.3), (7.20), (7.21a), (7.21b), (7.22a) and (7.22b), given the level of expenditure on the enforcement policy.

Totally differentiating (7.21a) and (7.21b), we obtain the following formulae:

$$dw = \alpha(\alpha-1)[(\bar{L} + I)/(\bar{K} - K_F)]^{\alpha-2}$$
$$\times \{1/(\bar{K} - K_F)^2\}\{(\bar{K} - K_F)dI + (\bar{L} + I)dK_F\}, \tag{7.23a}$$

$$dr = \alpha(1-\alpha)[(\bar{L} + I)/(\bar{K} - K_F)]^{\alpha-1}$$
$$\times \{1/(\bar{K} - K_F)^2\}\{(\bar{K} - K_F)dI + (\bar{L} + I)dK_F\}. \tag{7.23b}$$

Carefully considering (7.23a) and (7.23b), a relation between dw and dr is derived as follows[4]:

$$dr = -[(\bar{L} + I)/(\bar{K} - K_F)]dw. \tag{7.24}$$

The total differentiation of (7.22a) and (7.22b) is:

$$dw^* = \alpha(\alpha-1)[(\bar{L}^* - I)/(\bar{K}^* + K_F)]^{\alpha-2}$$
$$\times \{1/(\bar{K}^* + K_F)^2\}\{-(\bar{K}^* + K_F)dI - (\bar{L}^* - I)dK_F\}, \tag{7.25}$$

$$dr^* = \alpha(1-\alpha)[(\bar{L}^* - I)/(\bar{K}^* + K_F)]^{\alpha-1}$$
$$\times \{1/(\bar{K}^* + K_F)^2\}\{-(\bar{K}^* + K_F)dI - (\bar{L}^* - I)dK_F\}. \tag{7.26}$$

We also find a relationship between dw^* and dr^* similar to (7.24) by looking at (7.25) and (7.26):

$$dr^* = -[(\overline{L}^* - I)/(\overline{K}^* + K_F)]dw^*. \tag{7.27}$$

Note that (7.27) is the cost-minimization condition (cf. footnote 4).

We derive the effect of E on the foreign wage, totally differentiating (7.3) and (7.20) and making use of (7.24) and (7.27):

$$dw^* / dE = [(\overline{L} + I)/(\overline{K} - K_F)] \cdot \{(1/R\beta)$$
$$\times (E/R)^{(1-\beta)/\beta} \cdot (E/\overline{I})^\rho + (\rho/\overline{I}) \cdot (E/R)^{1/\beta} \cdot (E/\overline{I})^{\rho-1}\}$$
$$/[(1-t)((\overline{L}^* - I)/(\overline{K}^* + K_F)) - ((\overline{L} + I)/(\overline{K} - K_F))] > 0. \tag{7.28}$$

The denominator in the right-hand side of (7.28) is assumed to be positive, because we assume stability of the equilibrium in the two-country model under two-way factor mobility (see Yoshida (2000b)). We therefore know from (7.28) that stricter enforcement increases the welfare of foreign workers (see Bond and Chen (1987)). We also find the effect on the domestic wage, totally differentiating (7.3):

$$dw / dE = dw^* / dE + \{(1/R\beta) \cdot (E/R)^{(1-\beta)/\beta} \cdot (E/\overline{I})^\rho$$
$$+ (\rho/\overline{I}) \cdot (E/R)^{1/\beta} \cdot (E/\overline{I})^{\rho-1}\}$$
$$= (1-t)[(\overline{L}^* - I)/(\overline{K}^* + K_F)] \cdot \{(1/R\beta) \cdot (E/R)^{(1-\beta)/\beta}$$
$$\times (E/\overline{I})^\rho + (\rho/\overline{I}) \cdot (E/R)^{1/\beta} \cdot (E/\overline{I})^{\rho-1}\}$$
$$/[(1-t)((\overline{L}^* - I)/(\overline{K}^* + K_F)) - ((\overline{L} + I)/(\overline{K} - K_F))] > 0. \tag{7.29}$$

By considering (7.23a), (7.25) and (7.29), we derive the effects of E on the number of illegal foreign workers, I, as well as on the amount of capital exports, K_F:

$$\alpha(\alpha - 1) \begin{bmatrix} a_{11} & a_{12} \\ a_{21} & a_{22} \end{bmatrix} \begin{bmatrix} dI/dE \\ dK_F/dE \end{bmatrix} = \begin{bmatrix} b_1 \\ b_2 \end{bmatrix}, \tag{7.30}$$

where

$$a_{11} = \{(\overline{L} + I)/(\overline{K} - K_F)\}^{\alpha-2} \cdot \{1/(\overline{K} - K_F)\},$$
$$a_{12} = \{(\overline{L} + I)/(\overline{K} - K_F)\}^{\alpha-2} \cdot \{(\overline{L} + I)/(\overline{K} - K_F)^2\},$$
$$a_{21} = -\{(\overline{L}^* - I)/(\overline{K}^* + K_F)\}^{\alpha-2} \cdot \{1/(\overline{K}^* + K_F)\},$$
$$a_{22} = -\{(\overline{L}^* - I)/(\overline{K}^* + K_F)\}^{\alpha-2} \cdot \{(\overline{L}^* - I)/(\overline{K}^* + K_F)^2\},$$
$$b_1 = dw^* / dE + (1/R\beta) \cdot (E/R)^{(1-\beta)/\beta} \cdot (E/\overline{I})^\rho + (\rho/\overline{I})$$
$$\times (E/R)^{1/\beta} \cdot (E/\overline{I})^{\rho-1},$$

$$b_2 = dw^* / dE \, ,$$

and the determinant of the coefficient matrix on the left-hand side of (7.30), Δ_2, is

$$\Delta_2 \equiv -\alpha^2 (\alpha - 1)^2 [(\overline{L} + I)/(\overline{K} - K_F)]^{\alpha - 2} \cdot [(\overline{L}^* - I)/(\overline{K}^* + K_F)]^{\alpha - 2}$$
$$\times \{1/(\overline{K} - K_F)\}\{1/(\overline{K}^* + K_F)\}[\{(\overline{L}^* - I)/(\overline{K}^* + K_F)\}$$
$$- \{(\overline{L} + I)/(\overline{K} - K_F)\}] < 0 \, .$$

$$dI/dE = -\alpha(\alpha - 1)[\{dw^*/dE + (1/R\beta) \cdot (E/R)^{(1-\beta)/\beta} \cdot (E/\overline{I})^{\rho}$$
$$+ (\rho/\overline{I}) \cdot (E/R)^{1/\beta} \cdot (E/\overline{I})^{\rho - 1}\}((\overline{L}^* - I)/(\overline{K}^* + K_F))^{\alpha - 2}$$
$$\times ((\overline{L}^* - I)/(\overline{K}^* + K_F)^2) + (dw^*/dE) \cdot ((\overline{L} + I)/(\overline{K} - K_F))^{\alpha - 2}$$
$$\times (\overline{L} + I)/(\overline{K} - K_F)^2]/\Delta_2 < 0 \, , \tag{7.31a}$$

$$dK_F/dE = \alpha(\alpha - 1)[(dw^*/dE)((\overline{L} + I)/(\overline{K} - K_F))^{\alpha - 2} \cdot (1/(\overline{K} - K_F))$$
$$+ \{(dw^*/dE) + (1/R\beta) \cdot (E/R)^{(1-\beta)/\beta} \cdot (E/\overline{I})^{\rho}$$
$$+ (\rho/\overline{I}) \cdot (E/R)^{1/\beta} \cdot (E/\overline{I})^{\rho - 1}\}$$
$$\times ((\overline{L}^* - I)/(\overline{K}^* + K_F))^{\alpha - 2} \cdot (1/(\overline{K}^* + K_F))]/\Delta_2 > 0 \, . \tag{7.31b}$$

It can be seen from these comparative static results, (7.24), (7.27), (7.28) and (7.29), that given international capital mobility, internal inspection brings about adverse (favorable) effects on domestic and foreign capital (domestic and foreign labor) (cf. Bond and Chen (1987)).

We find from (7.28) that employer sanctions by the domestic country's government cause an increase in the foreign country's wages. This arises because enforcement causes domestic capital to migrate from the domestic country to the foreign country. Capital immobility creates a match between (illegal) foreign workers and domestic capital in the domestic country. Capital mobility causes a match between (regular) foreign labor and domestic capital in the foreign country. Thus, capital mobility allows the elimination of the production penalties that would be incurred under capital immobility (see Bond and Chen (1987)).

7.6 Optimal enforcement

We explore whether there is an optimal level of enforcement of immigration law. If it exists, we also explore whether the optimal level can be determined.

In the presence of capital mobility, we assume that the domestic (labor-receiving) country's government is concerned about their social welfare, defined as:

$$Y(E) \equiv [(1 - T(E))w\overline{L} + r\overline{K}] + [R + p(E)(z - v)I$$
$$- E + T(E)w\overline{L} + tr^* K_F]. \tag{7.32}$$

Note that the form of (7.32) is equal to (7.16) plus tax revenues obtained from capital exports, $tr^* K_F$.

Suppose that the budget constraint of the labor receiving country's government is satisfied (cf. (7.14) in section 7.3). The income of the host country is:

$$Y(E) = (1 - T(E))w\overline{L} + r\overline{K}. \tag{7.33}$$

Note that (7.33) is the same as (7.17). It is easy to determine that more austere internal inspection causes the host country's income to fall, given conditions (a) and (c) in (A), $DFE \leq 0$ and $IFE \geq 0$ ($T'(E) \geq 0$) (cf. Bucci and Tenorio (1996)). In contrast, given the conditions in (b) $DFE > 0$ and $IFE < 0$, we find that there is an optimal level of internal enforcement, $\overline{\overline{E}}$ from the point of view of the domestic country's welfare. The level of $\overline{\overline{E}}$ is derived from the definition of $T(E)$ and (7.29):

$$\overline{\overline{E}} = [[\{((E/R)^{\eta} \cdot \overline{L} + I + ((\overline{L} + I)/(\overline{K} - K_F)) \cdot K_F\}(1-t)((\overline{L}^* - I)/(\overline{K}^* + K_F))$$
$$\times (1/R\beta)(E/R)^{(1-\beta)/\beta} \cdot (E/\overline{I})^{\rho} + \{(1-t)((\overline{L}^* - I)/(\overline{K}^* + K_F))$$
$$- ((\overline{L} + I)/(\overline{K} - K_F))\}(\widetilde{\eta}/R)(E/R)^{\eta-1} \cdot w\overline{L}]/[-\{((E/R)^{\eta} \cdot \overline{L} + I$$
$$+ ((\overline{L} + I)/(\overline{K} - K_F)) \cdot K_F\}(1-t)((\overline{L}^* - I)$$
$$/(\overline{K}^* + K_F))(\rho/\overline{I})(E/\overline{I})^{\rho-1}]]^{\beta} \cdot R, \tag{7.34}$$

where $\overline{\overline{E}}$ is the level of enforcement such that $dY/dE = 0$.[5]

Proposition 7.2 [Yoshida (2004)]

When there is capital mobility between a labor importing (host) country and a labor exporting country, the immigration department in the host country can optimally put employer sanctions into effect, in terms of the host country's welfare, only if $DFE > 0$ and $IFE < 0$.

The implication behind this proposition is that the US authorities can optimally carry out internal enforcement to improve US welfare. This requires that the costs of enforcement - levying fines on domestic firms and collecting income taxes on legal domestic workers - be fully financed by revenues from the penalties and from income taxes. Therefore, government authorities must make an effort to minimize expenditure on the enforcement of employer sanctions, implement innovative techniques to detect and apprehend illegal foreign workers, recover the cost of inspecting domestic firms, and minimize the cost of collecting income taxes from domestic workers.

We should also note that the 1994 NAFTA between US, Canada and Mexico regulated the removal of all tariff and non-tariff barriers between these countries. NAFTA was expected to accelerate capital exports from the US to Mexico, for example, *maquiladora*, and therefore expedite economic growth in Mexico (cf. Arreola and Curtis (1993), Bratsberg (1995), Gianaris (1998), Gonzalez-Arechiga (1992), Greenwood, Hunt and Kohli (1997), Massey et. al. (1998) and OECD (1997)). This should have reduced illegal immigration from Mexico to the US (see the comments below (7.31b)).

7.7 Conclusion

We developed a two-country model of illegal immigration, using a Cobb-Douglas production function, and specifically defined functions of probability of apprehension of illegal aliens and fines against the home firms who knowingly hire them. We considered whether there is an optimal level of internal enforcement from the point of view of the host or domestic country's income, both when capital is internationally mobile and when it is internationally immobile.

We found that in both the presence and absence of capital mobility, the labor receiving country can optimally implement internal enforcement when its government can directly finance expenditure on enforcement through receipts from the penalties and income taxes.

Considering the relationship between the US and Mexico, we present the following proposals. First, the US government must endeavor to encourage US firms to shift capital to the home country of the illegal immigrant workers, i.e., Mexico. Second, the administration must try to reduce the cost of inspection of domestic firms intentionally employing illegal foreign workers, and increase the probability of apprehending illegal aliens. Most of the illegal workers in the US are Mexicans, who are estimated to make up 54% of all illegal immigrants working in the US (cf. US INS (1997)). [6]

Notes

*   The chapter was first published in Open Economies Review 15, 57-62, 2004.
1   In the US, the DHS (formerly INS) enforces the internal enforcement policy against US firms that knowingly hire illegal aliens (Calavita (1998)).
2    $\bar{I}$ is the number of illegal immigration that the host country's government

can perceive, when the government determines to allocate a budget for the immigration division.

3 We do not explicitly incorporate a public good in this model. However, It is implicitly assumed that the home country is endowed with the public good that offers public services. Hence, We abstract a production structure of the public supply from the model.

4 Considering (7.21a) and (7.21b), we can rewrite (7.4) as

$$\tilde{C}(w,r) \equiv wL(w,r) + rK(w,r),$$

and obtain (7.24) by making use of the cost-minimization condition:

$$d\tilde{C} \equiv \tilde{C}_w dw + \tilde{C}_r dr = Ldw + Kdr = (\bar{L} + I)dw + (\bar{K} - K_F)dr = 0.$$

5 In a similar way to (7.19b), we can ensure that there is a positive enforcement level of the employer sanctions that maximizes the home country's welfare, since the effect of the enforcement on the home country's welfare evaluated at $E = 0$ is positive.

6 DHS has taken over all the functions of INS on 1 March, 2003.

Part II: Final Conclusion

In Chapter 6, we re-introduced the Bond and Chen (1987) model of illegal immigration making use of a Cobb-Douglas production function. Chapter 7 incorporated a budget constraint on the host country into the model of Chapter 6.

In Chapter 6, we obtained useful information on an optimal enforcement of the employer sanctions. When capital is immobile between a labor-importing and a labor-exporting country, there is not the optimal level of an employer sanctions from the viewpoint of the host country. The tougher interior inspections cause the income of home labor to increase, while they depress the rental price of home capital. A loss in the home capital may offset a gain in the home labor. Once the inspections are strengthened, the costs of it, e.g., enforcement and deportation costs, are enlarged. Therefore, the stricter enforcement may bring about negative effects on the home country's welfare.

When capital is mobile between countries, there is an optimal level of the interior enforcement under some circumstances. To put it concretely, the US DHS must satisfy some necessary conditions to optimally carry out the internal enforcement in view of US welfare. Those conditions are that (1) a slight increase in the enforcement promotes deportation of illegal immigrants; (2) an increment in it urges the home capital to shift to the labor-sending country; and (3) DHS endeavors to retrench the costs of the enforcement.

Chapter 7 provided some facts in optimally carrying out the finance-constrained interior inspections. If the costs of internal enforcement are assumed to be directly financed by the penalties levied on home firms caught employing illegal foreign workers, then this is called the direct fiscal effect (DFE). If the $DFE = 0$, no additional financing is needed. However, if the $DFE \neq 0$, other financing methods are required to ensure a balanced budget, such as income taxation of home workers.

In the presence of capital immobility, the enforcement will be optimally put into force in terms of the host country's welfare when $DEF > 0$ and $IFE < 0$. Otherwise, there is not an optimal enforcement when $DFE \leq 0$ and $IFE \geq 0$. Pre-enforcement equilibrium involves an income tax distortion (see equation (7.17)). The internal enforcement introduces a second distortion that may improve the labor-receiving country's income for standard second-best reasons. When the DFE is positive, it will

125

cause the *IFE* to decrease. In short, the *DFE* lessens the degree of the initial income tax distortion. A *DFE* > 0 implies that the migrant-receiving country benefits from the enforcement, since revenues from the enforcement penalties and income tax gains are larger than the costs of enforcement. Thus, under certain conditions, an immigration bureau of the host country can optimally enforce the internal inspections from the perspective of the host country's welfare.

In the presence of capital mobility, we get results essentially similar to those in the absence of capital mobility. Unless *DFE* > 0 and *IFE* < 0, the immigration authority cannot optimally enforce employer sanctions in view of the labor-importing country's welfare. In order to optimally put the interior investigations into operation to augment the donee country's welfare, the immigration department must make efforts to keep the following requirements. The requirements are that the immigration bureau should (1) inexpensively enforce employer sanctions, (2) improve abilities to find out and arrest irregular aliens, (3) retrieve the cost of investigating home firms and (4) economize on the cost of gathering income taxes from home workers.

The immigration authority does not control proceeds from employer sanctions (see Davila, Pagan and Grau (1999)). The authority usually maximizes the total number of apprehensions subject to a resource constraint. However, we examined whether or not there is an enforcement level of employer sanctions that maximizes the host country's welfare. As mentioned in Chapters 6 and 7, the intense enforcement forces the level of unlawful foreign workers to decrease. Especially in Chapter 7, we presented the immigration department of which a budget conduct is in a finance-constrained fashion. Hence, our model includes the behavior of the immigration bureau, which Davila et al. (1999) introduced.

We also assessed the internal enforcement from the viewpoint of the migrant-importing country's welfare. We found in Chapter 7 that it was desirable for the immigration authority to put the interior enforcement into effect irrespective of capital mobility, if the authority satisfies some necessary conditions to improve the host country's welfare. However, the immigration bureau must rather endeavor to keep some necessary conditions as stated above.

Part III
The Welfare Effects of a Profit-Sharing Policy

8
Unemployment, International Migration and Profit-Sharing

We develop the standard (two-country, one-good, two-factor) model of international immigration, in which we have unemployment in the host (capital abundant) country and in the foreign (labor abundant) country. Our main result is that the introduction of a profit-sharing plan by the host country causes: (1) Employment of domestic labor increases, (2) immigration decreases, (3) the domestic (foreign) country's welfare rises (falls), and, under certain circumstances, (4) global welfare rises in the presence of international capital immobility.

8.1 Introduction

In recent years, the *re-structuring* performed by many industries in the US has increased the profits and decreased the level of employment in many US firms. In addition, large migration flows from low-wage countries, such as Mexico and other Latin-American countries, to a high-wage country such as the US have caused severe competition between home and immigrant workers for domestic *unskilled* jobs in the US labor market (see Brecher and Choudhri (1987)). This has exacerbated the shortage of work faced by many US workers. As a consequence, it may be necessary for the US government to create employment opportunities for domestic labor. Extending this analogy, it may be necessary for any high-wage country facing large-scale immigration and domestic unemployment to create employment opportunities for domestic labor.

Weitzman (1983, 1985, 1987), Pohjola (1987), Jackman (1988), Fung (1989a, b) and others have claimed that a profit-sharing policy may be an effective tool to increase employment levels in such a country.[1] In this chapter, we extend their models by constructing a two-country model to examine the effects of a profit-sharing scheme implemented by the host country's government. In particular, we look at the welfare and labor market effects of such a scheme on the host country and on the foreign country.

We begin by introducing a standard (two-country, one-good, two-factor) general equilibrium model in which both the host country and the foreign country face unemployment, and foreign labor legally migrates to the host (capital-abundant) country.[2] We consider the effects on both countries of a profit-sharing scheme by the host country when capital is internationally immobile. We conclude that the host country's profit-sharing scheme has the following results. (8.1.a) Unemployment of domestic labor decreases; (8.1.b) immigration from the foreign country falls; (8.1.c) the domestic (foreign) country's welfare increases (decreases); and under some circumstances, (8.1.d) the welfare of the world (the two countries combined) increases.

Secondly, we consider the effects of such a profit-sharing scheme when capital is internationally mobile. The host country's profit-sharing scheme has the following results. (8.2.a) Employment of domestic labor increases; (8.2.b) immigration from the foreign country decreases; and (8.2.c) the outflow of domestic capital to the foreign country increases. In addition, (8.2.d) the host country's welfare increases; (8.2.e) the foreign country's welfare decreases; and (8.2.f) the global welfare effect, composed of the sum of the host country's welfare and the foreign country's welfare, is ambiguous.

Section 8.2 introduces a model of international factor movements. We examine the effects of the host country's profit-sharing scheme when capital is internationally immobile. In section 8.3 we examine the effects of the host country's profit-sharing scheme when capital is internationally mobile, and Section 8.4 offers some concluding remarks.

8.2 The basic model

We consider first a case in which there is no capital mobility between the two countries. Our model is explained as follows. The firms in the host and foreign countries are perfectly competitive. The domestic (foreign) firm produces a single good using domestic labor, migrant labor and domestic capital (foreign labor and capital) using a concave production function.[3,4] The domestic firm has a domestic-labor union that can extract economic rent and a part of the firm's profit (see Fung (1989a, b)), and it can monopolistically determine its members' wage. The foreign firm does not have a (foreign) labor union. Since both countries are assumed to adopt minimum wage legislation, employed domestic (foreign) labor receives any wage above a domestic minimum wage (a foreign minimum wage), and therefore both domestic and foreign workers face the possibility of unemployment in their native countries.

Following Brecher and Choudhri (1987), we assume that the host country uses lump-sum taxes to provide domestic labor with a package of unemployment insurance and welfare benefits, which have a real value of $\bar{w}$ per worker. Hence, domestic labor would not accept employment with a wage of less than $\bar{w}$. In equilibrium, foreign migrant workers in the host country receive the expected wage of their native country (see Harris and Todaro (1970)) and, hence, are fully employed (cf. Brecher and Choudhri (1987)). There is assumed to be full employment of capital in each country.

We introduce the two-country model of international factor movements in the next subsection, 8.2.1. In subsection 8.2.2 we examine the welfare effects of a profit-sharing scheme implemented by the host country's government in the two-country model introduced in subsection 8.2.1.

8.2.1 The domestic and foreign economies

In the domestic economy, the domestic firm produces a single good using domestic labor, L, foreign migrant labor, M, and domestic capital, K, with a strictly concave production function, $F(L,M,K)$, that has a decreasing returns to scale technology.[5] The domestic firm chooses L, M and K so as to maximize its profit, given factor prices for domestic labor, foreign migrant labor and domestic capital, w, v and r. The first-order conditions for the profit- maximization of the domestic firm are:

$$F_L(L,M,K) = w, \tag{8.1a}$$

$$F_M(L,M,K) = v, \tag{8.1b}$$

$$F_K(L,M,K) = r, \tag{8.1c}$$

where subscripts are partial derivatives, e.g., $F_L(L,M,K) \equiv \partial F(L,M,K) / \partial L$.

Let $\bar{K}$ be the initial endowment of domestic capital. Then, in the domestic capital market, $K = \bar{K}$. Substituting this equation into (8.1a), (8.1b) and (8.1c), the following equations are obtained:

$$F_L(L,M,\bar{K}) = w, \tag{8.2a}$$

$$F_M(L,M,\bar{K}) = v, \tag{8.2b}$$

$$F_K(L,M,\bar{K}) = r. \tag{8.2c}$$

In the foreign economy, the foreign firm produces a single good, using foreign labor L^* and foreign capital K^* under the production function,

$F^*(L^*,K^*)$.[6] The foreign firm chooses L^* and K^* so as to maximize its profit, given factor prices for foreign labor, $\overline{w}^*$, and foreign capital, r^*. The wage rate, $\overline{w}^*$, is assumed to be the regulated minimum wage in the foreign economy. The employed foreign worker earns the foreign minimum wage, which is above the market-clearing wage. Hence, we have some unemployment of foreign labor in the foreign economy. Similarly in the domestic economy, the initial endowment of foreign capital, $\overline{K}^*$, is assumed to be fully employed. Then, in the foreign capital market, $K^* = \overline{K}^*$.

The first-order conditions for profit-maximization of the foreign firm are:

$$F_L^*(L^*,\overline{K}^*) = \overline{w}^*, \tag{8.3a}$$

$$F_K^*(L^*,\overline{K}^*) = r^*. \tag{8.3b}$$

It is clear from (8.3a) that L^* is constant and r^* in (8.3b) is fixed.

The expected wage, w^{e^*} for the foreign worker in the foreign economy is:

$$w^{e^*} = \overline{w}^* L^* /(\overline{L}^* - M^*)$$
$$= e\overline{w}^*, \tag{8.4}$$

where $\overline{L}^*$ is the initial endowment of foreign labor in the foreign country and $e = L^* /(\overline{L}^* - M)$ which is the employment rate of foreign labor in the foreign country. Note that some foreign workers, M, emigrate from their native country to the host country. Migration will cease only when the following equilibrium condition is established (see Harris and Todaro (1970)):

$$v = \overline{w}^* L^* /(\overline{L}^* - M). \tag{8.4'}$$

(8.4)' implies that, in equilibrium, foreign migrant workers in the domestic economy earn a wage equal to that which they expected in their native economy. Incorporating (8.4)' into (8.2b), we obtain the following equation:

$$F_M(L,M,\overline{K}) = \overline{w}^* L^* /(\overline{L}^* - M). \tag{8.2b'}$$

We now know from the above arguments that the endogenous variables, L, M, r, L^* and r^*, are determined by the equilibrium equations, (8.2a), (8.2b)', (8.2c), (8.3a) and (8.3b). Specifically, two endogenous variables, L and M, are determined from (8.2a) and (8.2b)' where w, $\overline{w}$, $\overline{K}$ and $\overline{w}^*$ are exogenous variables and L^* is fixed from (8.3a). The wage of domestic labor, w, is assumed to be monopolistically determined by the domestic labor union.

Let us examine the effects of w on L and M as determined by the domestic labor union. These effects are obtained by differentiating (8.2a) and (8.2b)' with respect to w:

$$dL / dw = [F_{MM} - L^* \overline{w}^* / (\overline{L}^* - M)^2] / \Delta_1 < 0, \qquad (8.5)$$

$$dM / dw = -F_{ML} / \Delta_1 > 0, \qquad (8.6)$$

where $\Delta_1 \equiv (F_{LL} F_{MM} - F_{LM}^2) - F_{LL} L^* \overline{w}^* / (\overline{L}^* - M)^2 > 0$ and subscripts are partial derivatives, e.g., $F_{LL} \equiv \partial^2 F(L, M, \overline{K}) / \partial L^2$. Since the sign of $[F_{LL} F_{MM} - F_{LM}^2]$ is positive, and the sign of $[F_{LL}]$ is negative from the concavity of the production function (see footnote 4), the sign of Δ_1 is clearly positive. Hence, the sign of $[dL / dw]$ is unambiguously negative from (8.5) because $F_{MM} < 0$ by the concavity assumption. The sign of $[dM / dw]$ is positive from (8.6) because by assumption, $F_{ML} < 0$. Then, the effect of w on the employment rate of foreign labor in the foreign economy, e, is given by:

$$de / dw = [L^* / (\overline{L}^* - M)^2] dM / dw > 0. \qquad (8.7.1)$$

Since $L \equiv L(w)$ and $M \equiv M(w)$ from (8.5) and (8.6), $r \equiv r(w)$ in (8.2c). Hence, by differentiating (8.2c) with respect to w, the effect of w on r is obtained:

$$dr / dw = F_{KL} dL / dw + F_{KM} dM / dw > 0. \qquad (8.7.2)$$

Because $F_{KL} < 0$ and $F_{KM} > 0$, the sign of $[dr / dw]$ is positive from (8.5) and (8.6). Our technological assumptions, $F_{KL} < 0$ and $F_{KM} > 0$, imply that domestic capital and labor are substitutes, and domestic capital and foreign migrant labor are complements (see Takayama (1985)).

Having examined the effects of w on L, M, r, L^* and r^*, we now consider how w, the wage of domestic labor, is determined. In the domestic economy, we assume that a domestic labor union operates in the domestic firm. We assume this labor union can extract the economic rent, $w - \overline{w}$, and a part of the firm's profit, $\theta\pi$, as well as monopolistically determine the wages of its members at a level above the minimum wage, $\overline{w}$. θ is assumed to lie in the closed interval $[0, 1]$, and is exogenously determined by the host country's government.

The economic rent extracted by the domestic labor union is:

$$R = (w - \overline{w}) L(w) + \theta\pi(w), \qquad (8.8)$$

where $\pi(w)$ is $F(L(w), M(w), \overline{K}) - \{wL(w) + w^{e^*}(w)M(w) + r(w)\overline{K}\}$.[7] The domestic labor union chooses the wage rate, w, that maximizes its economic rent, R. The first-order condition for rent maximization by the domestic labor union is:

$$R_w = L + (w - \overline{w})dL/dw - \theta\pi_w,$$

$$= L + (w - \overline{w})dL/dw - \theta(L + Mde/dw + \overline{K}dr/dw) = 0, \tag{8.9}$$

where R_w is dR/dw. The domestic labor union determines the wage rate, w, so that (8.9) is satisfied.

Following Fung (1989a,b), we assume that the domestic government can operate a profit-share, θ, as its policy device. Now, let us examine the effects of θ on w by totally differentiating (8.9):

$$dw/d\theta = -R_{w\theta}/R_{ww} < 0, \tag{8.10}$$

where $R_{w\theta} = -(L + Mde/dw + \overline{K}dr/dw)$, the sign of which is negative from (8.7.1) and (8.7.2). Since the sign of R_{ww} is negative from the second-order condition of rent maximization, the sign of $dw/d\theta$ is negative. The profit-sharing scheme of the domestic government causes the wage rate of domestic labor, w, to fall. Since w is a function of θ from (8.10), by using the chain rule we can examine the effects of θ on L, M, r and w^{e^*} from (8.4), (8.5), (8.6), (8.7.1), (8.7.2) and (8.10):

$$dL/d\theta = (dL/dw)\cdot(dw/d\theta) > 0, \tag{8.11a}$$

$$dM/d\theta = (dM/dw)\cdot(dw/d\theta) < 0, \tag{8.11b}$$

$$de/d\theta = (de/dw)\cdot(dw/d\theta) < 0, \tag{8.11c}$$

$$dr/d\theta = F_{KL}dL/d\theta + F_{KM}dM/d\theta < 0, \tag{8.11d}$$

$$dw^{e^*}/d\theta = \overline{w}^*(de/dw)\cdot(dw/d\theta) < 0. \tag{8.11e}$$

From (8.10) through (8.11e), we can establish the following proposition:

Proposition 8.1 [Yoshida and Ohta (1994)]
The introduction of a profit-sharing scheme by the domestic government causes the following. Wages of domestic workers and foreign migrant workers fall; employment of domestic labor increases; the number of immigrants falls; the employment rate of foreign labor in the foreign country falls; and the rental rate of domestic capital falls.

8.2.2 Welfare effects

We examine the effects of a profit-sharing plan introduced by the domestic government on the welfare of the host country, the foreign country and the world. Firstly, we define the host country's welfare and consider how it would be affected by a profit-sharing scheme. The host country's welfare, Y, is:

$$Y \equiv F(L,M,\overline{K}) - w^{e^*}M, \tag{8.12}$$

where $F(L,M,\overline{K})$ is domestic output and $w^{e^*}M$ is the earnings of foreign migrant labor. Y equals domestic output minus the earnings of migrant labor. By differentiating (8.12) with respect to θ, the effect of θ on the host country's welfare, Y, is obtained:

$$dY/d\theta = wdL/d\theta - M\overline{w}^* de/d\theta > 0. \tag{8.13}$$

From (8.11a) and (8.11e), the sign of $dY/d\theta$ is positive. A profit-sharing scheme introduced by the domestic government increases the host country's welfare.

Secondly, we consider the foreign country's welfare. The foreign country's welfare, Y^* is defined as:

$$Y^* \equiv F^*(L^*,\overline{K}^*) + w^{e^*}M, \tag{8.14}$$

where $F^*(L^*,\overline{K}^*)$ is foreign output. The foreign country's welfare equals foreign output plus the earnings of foreign migrant labor. Let us examine the effect of θ on Y^*. By differentiating (8.14) with respect to θ, this effect is obtained:

$$dY^*/d\theta = w^{e^*}dM/d\theta + M\overline{w}^* de/d\theta < 0. \tag{8.15}$$

From (8.11b) and (8.11e), the sign of $dY^*/d\theta$ is negative. A profit-sharing scheme by the domestic government causes a fall in the foreign country's welfare.

Now, let us examine the effect of θ on global welfare, $Y + Y^*$. From (8.13) and (8.15), its effect is:

$$d(Y + Y^*)/d\theta = wdL/d\theta + w^{e^*}dM/d\theta. \tag{8.16}$$

By substituting (8.5), (8.6), (8.11a) and (8.11b) into (8.16), (8.16) is rewritten:

$$d(Y + Y^*)/d\theta = [\{wF_{MM} - w^{e^*}F_{ML} - wL^*\overline{w}^*/(\overline{L}^* - M)^2\}/\Delta_1]$$
$$\times[dw/d\theta]. \tag{8.16'}$$

The sign of the first bracket on the right-hand side of (8.16)' is indeterminate, because $F_{MM} < 0$ and $F_{ML} < 0$, by assumption. Hence, the effect of θ on the global income, $Y + Y^*$, is ambiguous. However, if $w \geq w^{e^*}$ and $|F_{MM}| \geq |F_{ML}|$, the sign of the first bracket on the right-hand side of (8.16)' is negative, hence (8.16)' is positive due to $\Delta_1 > 0$ and (8.10). The first necessary condition for the effect of θ on $(Y + Y^*)$ to be positive requires that the wage rate of domestic labor, w, be greater than the expected wage of foreign labor in the foreign country, w^{e^*}. It is natural that this condition $w \geq w^{e^*}$ holds, since the host country is assumed to be labor-scarce relative to the foreign country. The second necessary condition requires that the absolute value of the own effect, $|F_{MM}|$, is larger than the cross effect, $|F_{ML}|$.

By summarizing the above results, we obtain the following proposition:

Proposition 8.2 [Yoshida and Ohta (1994)]
In the presence of international capital immobility, a profit-sharing scheme introduced by the domestic government increases the host country's welfare, decreases the foreign country's welfare, and, under certain conditions, increases global welfare.

8.3 Capital mobility

We consider the case in which capital is internationally mobile, and examine the economic effects of a profit-sharing scheme introduced by the domestic government. In subsection 8.3.1, we examine the comparative static effects of a profit-sharing scheme. In subsection 8.3.2, we consider the effects of a profit-sharing scheme on the host country's welfare, the foreign country's welfare and on global welfare.

8.3.1 Effects of a profit-sharing scheme

First, we derive the equilibrium equation system using the same method as in section 8.2.1:

$$F_L(L, M, \overline{K} - K_F) = \overline{w}, \tag{8.17a}$$

$$F_M(L, M, \overline{K} - K_F) = \overline{w}^* L^* / (\overline{L}^* - M), \tag{8.17b}$$

$$F_K(L, M, \overline{K} - K_F) = r, \tag{8.17c}$$

$$F_L^*(L^*, \overline{K}^* + K_F) = \overline{w}^*, \tag{8.17d}$$

$$F_K^*(L^*, \overline{K}^* + K_F) = r^*, \tag{8.17e}$$

$$r = r^*, \tag{8.17f}$$

where K_F is the export of domestic capital from the domestic economy to the foreign economy. Domestic capital is exported to the foreign country until the rental rate of domestic capital, r, equals the rental rate of foreign capital, r^*. Hence, in equilibrium, (8.17f) is established. By incorporating (8.17f) into (8.17c), we obtain the following equation:

$$F_K(L, M, \overline{K} - K_F) = r^*. \tag{8.17c}'$$

The five endogenous variables, L, M, K_F, L^* and r^*, are determined from (8.17a) through (8.17e) with (8.17c) replaced by (8.17c)' where w, $\overline{K}$, $\overline{w}^*$, $\overline{L}^*$ and $\overline{K}^*$ are exogenously given. We denote these equations as equation system (8A).

Secondly, we examine the effects of w on L, M, K_F, L^* and r^*. By totally differentiating equation system (8A) with respect to w, its effects are (see Appendix for derivations):

$$dL / dw < 0, \quad dM / dw > 0, \quad dK_F / dw < 0, \quad dL^* / dw > 0$$

and

$$dr^* / dw > 0, \tag{8.18}$$

where $dr^* / dw = dr / dw > 0$ from (8.17f). By differentiating e with respect to w, the effect of w on the employment rate of foreign labor in the foreign country, e is:

$$de / dw = [(\overline{L}^* - M)dL^* / dw + L^* dM / dw]/(\overline{L}^* - M)^2 > 0, \tag{8.19}$$

where $e = L^* /(\overline{L}^* - M)$. From (8.18), we find that (8.19) is positive.

Thirdly, we examine how the wage rate of domestic labor, w is determined. The economic rent extracted by the domestic labor union is:

$$R \equiv (w - \overline{w})L(w) + \theta\pi(w), \tag{8.20}$$

where

$$\pi(w) \equiv F(L(w), M(w), \overline{K} - K_F(w))$$
$$- \{wL(w) + w^{e^*}(w)M(w) + r(w)(\overline{K} - K_F))\}.$$

The first-order condition for rent maximization by the domestic labor union is:

$$R_w = L + (w - \overline{w})dL / dw$$
$$- \theta\{(L + \overline{w}^* M de / dw + (\overline{K} - K_F)dr / dw\} = 0. \tag{8.21}$$

By totally differentiating (8.21), we immediately obtain:

$$dw / d\theta = -R_{w\theta} / R_{ww} < 0, \tag{8.22}$$

where $R_{w\theta} = -\{L + \overline{w}^* M de / dw + (\overline{K} - K_F)dr / dw\}$. The sign of $R_{w\theta}$ is negative from (8.18) and (8.19). Since $R_{ww} < 0$ from the second-order condition for rent maximization, the sign of $dw / d\theta$ is negative. A profit-sharing scheme by the host country's government causes the wage of domestic labor, w, to fall.

From (8.18) and (8.22), the effects of θ on L, M, r, L^*, r^* and K_F are derived using the chain rule:

$$dL/d\theta > 0, \ dM/d\theta < 0, \ dr/d\theta < 0,$$
$$dL^*/d\theta < 0, \ dr^*/d\theta < 0, \ dK_F/d\theta > 0, \tag{8.23}$$

where $dL/d\theta = (dL/dw)\cdot(dw/d\theta)$, for example. From (8.19) and (8.23), the effect of θ on the employment rate of foreign labor in the foreign country, e, is:

$$de/d\theta < 0. \tag{8.24}$$

Hence, the effect of θ on $w^{e^*}(=e\overline{w}^*)$ is:

$$dw^{e^*}/d\theta < 0. \tag{8.25}$$

From (8.23), (8.24) and (8.25), we can establish the following proposition:

Proposition 8.3 [Yoshida and Ohta (1994)]
A profit-sharing scheme introduced by the domestic government has the following effects. Employment of domestic labor rises; the number of immigrants falls; the employment of foreign labor in the foreign country decreases; the expected wage of foreign labor decreases; the rental rates of capital in both countries decrease; and domestic capital outflow to the foreign country increases.

8.3.2 Welfare effects

In this subsection, we examine the effects of a profit-sharing scheme on the host country's welfare, the foreign country's welfare, and on global welfare, defined as:

$$Y = F(L, M, \overline{K} - K_F) - w^{e^*}M + r^*K_F, \tag{8.26}$$

$$Y^* = F^*(L^*, \overline{K}^* + K_F) + w^{e^*}M - r^*K_F, \tag{8.27}$$

and

$$Y + Y^* = F(L, M, \overline{K} - K_F) + F^*(L^*, \overline{K}^* + K_F), \tag{8.28}$$

where r^*K_F are the rental revenues paid to domestic capital exports in the foreign country, K_F. By differentiating (8.26) through (8.28) with respect to θ, the effects of θ on Y, Y^* and $(Y + Y^*)$ are obtained from (8.23) through (8.25):

$$dY/d\theta = wdL/d\theta - \overline{w}^*Mde/d\theta + K_Fdr^*/d\theta, \tag{8.29}$$

$$dY^*/d\theta = \overline{w}^*dL^*/d\theta + w^{e^*}dM/d\theta + \overline{w}^*Mde/d\theta - K_Fdr^*/d\theta, \tag{8.30}$$

$$d(Y + Y^*)/d\theta = wdL/d\theta + \overline{w}^*dL^*/d\theta + w^{e^*}dM/d\theta \gtreqless 0. \tag{8.31}$$

We find from (8.23) and (8.24) that (8.29), (8.30) and (8.31) are indeterminate. However, evaluating (8.29) and (8.30) at the zero capital export level, $K_F = 0$, we know from (8.23) and (8.24) that introduction of a profit-sharing scheme increases (decreases) the host (foreign) country's welfare:

$$dY / d\theta\big|_{K_F=0} = wdL / d\theta - \overline{w}^* Mde / d\theta > 0 , \tag{8.29}'$$

$$dY^* / d\theta\big|_{K_F=0} = \overline{w}^* dL^* / d\theta + w^{e^*} dM / d\theta + \overline{w}^* Mde / d\theta < 0 . \tag{8.30}'$$

Even if (8.31) is evaluated at the zero capital export level, $K_F = 0$, the sign of $d(Y + Y^*) / d\theta$ can not be determined. The effect of a profit-sharing scheme introduced by the domestic government on global welfare, $(Y + Y^*)$ is ambiguous.

By summarizing the above argument, we obtain the following proposition:

Proposition 8.4 [Yoshida and Ohta (1994)]
In the presence of international capital mobility, a profit-sharing scheme introduced by the domestic government increases the host country's welfare, reduces the foreign country's welfare, and may or may not increase global welfare.

8.4 Concluding remarks

In this chapter, we examined the economic effects of a profit-sharing scheme introduced by the domestic government in the standard (two-country, one-good, two-factor) model of international factor movements, in which unemployment exists in both countries. First, it was shown that in the presence of international capital immobility, a profit-sharing scheme causes the following. (8.1.a) The unemployment rate of domestic workers falls; (8.1.b) immigration from the foreign country falls; (8.1.c) the host (foreign) country's welfare increases (decreases); and under certain conditions, (8.1.d) global welfare increases.

Secondly, we considered the economic effects of a profit-sharing scheme in the presence of international capital mobility. We found that profit-sharing causes the following. (8.2.a) Employment of domestic labor rises; (8.2.b) immigration from the foreign country falls; (8.2.c) domestic capital outflows to the foreign country increase; (8.2.d) the host country's welfare increases; (8.2.e) the foreign country's welfare decreases; and (8.2.f) global welfare may or may not increase.

In this chapter, we can see from our main results, (8.1.a), (8.1.b), (8.1.c), (8.2.a), (8.2.b) and (8.2.d), that the introduction of a profit-sharing plan by the domestic (US) government can alleviate problems present in the

US economy. These problems include the unemployment of domestic (US) labor and large-scale migration from low-wage countries, such as Mexico and the other Central and South American countries.

Appendix

In this appendix, we derive the effects of w on L, M, K_F, L^* and r^* by differentiating system (8A) with respect to w:

$$dL/dw = [F_{LL}^*(F_{KK}F_{MM} - F_{KM}^2) + F_{MM}(F_{LL}^*F_{KK}^* - F_{LK}^{*2})$$
$$- w^{e^*}\{F_{KK}F_{LL}^* + (F_{LL}^*F_{KK}^* - F_{LK}^{*2})\}$$
$$+ \overline{w}^* F_{KM}F_{LK}^*/(\overline{L}^* - M)]/\Delta_2 < 0. \tag{8A.1}$$

$$dM/dw = [-F_{ML}\{F_{KK}F_{LL}^* + (F_{LL}^*F_{KK}^* - F_{LK}^{*2})\}$$
$$- F_{KL}\{F_{LL}^*F_{MK} + (\overline{w}^* F_{LK}^*/(\overline{L}^* - M))\}]/\Delta_2 > 0, \tag{8A.2}[8]$$

$$dK_F/dw = F_{LL}^*[-F_{ML}F_{KM} + F_{KL}\{F_{MM} - (w^{e^*}/(\overline{L}^* - M))\}]/\Delta_2 < 0, \tag{8A.3}$$

$$dL^*/dw = F_{LK}^*[F_{ML}F_{KM} - F_{KL}\{F_{MM} - (w^{e^*}/(\overline{L}^* - M))\}]/\Delta_2 > 0, \tag{8A.4}$$

$$dr^*/dw = (F_{LL}^*F_{KK}^* - F_{LK}^{*2})[-F_{ML}F_{KM}$$
$$+ F_{KL}\{F_{MM} - (w^{e^*}/(\overline{L}^* - M))\}]/\Delta_2 > 0, \tag{8A.5}$$

where

$$\Delta_2 \equiv -[(F_{LK}^{*2} - F_{LL}^*F_{KK}^*)\{(F_{LL}F_{MM} - F_{ML}^2) - w^{e^*}F_{LL}\}$$

$$- F_{LL}^* \begin{vmatrix} F_{LL} & F_{LM} & F_{LK} \\ F_{ML} & F_{MM} & F_{MK} \\ F_{KL} & F_{KM} & F_{KK} \end{vmatrix} - \overline{w}^* F_{LK}^*(F_{LL}F_{KM} - F_{LM}F_{LK})/(\overline{L}^* - M)$$

$$+ \{F_{LL}^* w^{e^*}(F_{LL}F_{KK} - F_{KL}^2)/(\overline{L}^* - M)\}] > 0.$$

Notes

1 For specific explanations on profit-sharing, see Weitzman (1983, 1985 and 1987), Pohjola (1987), Jackman (1988), Wadhwani (1988) and Fung (1989a, b). Using models, which are *different from* our model, all authors except Wadhwani (1988) have concluded that profit-sharing can increase the employment of workers.

2 In our model, the foreign migrant workers in the host country are the workers that legally migrate to the host country from the foreign country. For the discussions on enforcement aspects of illegal migration, see Ethier (1986a), Bond and Chen (1987), Brecher and Choudhri (1987) and Yoshida (1993).

3 Our model assumes, for example, that the service domestic labor offers in the host country may qualitatively differ from that of foreign migrant labor.

4 For example, Batra and Seth (1977) have introduced a concave production function in the international trade model.

5   From the property of strictly concave production functions, the following relations are derived:

$$F_{LL} < 0, \ F_{MM} < 0, \ F_{KK} < 0, \ (F_{LL}F_{MM} - F_{ML}^2) > 0,$$

$$(F_{MM}F_{KK} - F_{MK}^2) > 0 \ \text{ and } \ \begin{vmatrix} F_{LL} & F_{LM} & F_{LK} \\ F_{ML} & F_{MM} & F_{MK} \\ F_{KL} & F_{KM} & F_{KK} \end{vmatrix} < 0,$$

where subscripts are partial derivatives. Throughout the chapter, we assume that $F_{LM} < 0$, $F_{LK} < 0$ and $F_{KM} > 0$. It can be seen, from this assumption, that domestic labor is a substitute for foreign migrant labor (or domestic capital), and domestic capital is a complement to foreign migrant labor (see Hicks (1956) and Bond (1989)). In general, it is said that domestic (US) labor is a substitute to foreign migrant labor in the US economy (see Killingsworth (1983)). Burgess (1974a) has shown that in 1929-1969, $F_{LM} < 0$, $F_{LK} < 0$ and $F_{KM} > 0$ in the US economy. However, M in his analysis is not explicitly foreign migrant labor but some imports utilized as productive factors. Also, Burgess (1975) has derived the same results for 1947-1968 in the US economy as Burgess (1974a).

6   The strictly concave production function, $F^*(L^*, K^*)$ has the following properties:

$$F_{LL}^* < 0, \ F_{KK}^* < 0 \ \text{ and } \ \begin{vmatrix} F_{LL}^* & F_{LK}^* \\ F_{KL}^* & F_{KK}^* \end{vmatrix} > 0,$$

where subscripts are partial derivatives. In this chapter, we assume that $F_{LK}^* < 0$, which implies that foreign labor is a substitute for foreign capital (see Hicks (1956) and Bond (1989)).

7   (8.8) can be simplified as $R = \bar{w}L + \theta\pi$ where $\bar{w}$ is the base wage, and R is an employee's total income (see Weitzman (1985), Anderson and Devereux (1989), Stewart (1989), Bensäid and Gary-Bobo (1991) and Sφrensen (1992))).

8   The sign of dM/dw is ambiguous, because the first term in the numerator on the right-hand side of (8A.2) is positive, and the second term is negative, by assumption (see footnotes 4 and 5). Here we assume that this sign is positive, which implies that domestic and foreign migrant workers are *Hicks-Allen substitutes* (cf. Hicks (1956), Sato and Koizumi (1973) and Takayama (1985)).

9

International Migration, Profit-Sharing and National Welfare

We develop a two-country model of international migration with unemployment in order to examine the welfare effects of a profit-sharing scheme implemented in the host country. Assuming the absence of international capital mobility, our results show that an increase in the rate of profit-sharing has the following effects. (1) It reduces the wages of domestic and migrant workers who compete with each other for employment; (2) it increases the number of immigrants in the host country; (3) it lowers unemployment rates in both countries; (4) it raises the profits of domestic firms; and (5) it increases domestic and foreign welfare.

9.1 Introduction

Over the past decade the number of temporary migrant workers in Japan has greatly increased. The number of short-term migrant workers is believed to have reached half a million. Legal and illegal migrants alike, most of these workers are from countries that suffer from chronic unemployment. In addition to the general low per capita incomes in their countries of origin, unemployment certainly constitutes a motivating factor in their migration decisions. In so far as wages are expected to be higher and job opportunities more secure abroad, these workers face great motivation to migrate to wealthier neighboring countries.

There are, in addition, factors that motivate developed countries to welcome migrant workers. Along the path of economic growth, the industrial structure shifts its weight from labor-intensive sectors using less skilled manual workers to service-intensive tertiary sectors that use more highly skilled workers. More importantly, the wages in the latter sector tend to be higher than wages in the former sector. High wages in the tertiary service industry attract most of the newcomers to the labor market, while the traditional manual labor sector is left with substantial labor shortages. It has been pointed out for several years now that the younger generation dislikes physically demanding work, which aggravates the wage gap between skilled and unskilled workers in Japan. This sectoral imbalance in the labor supply-demand equation is often called "miss-matching".

Thus, the movement of unskilled labor between countries has implications for the future of both the labor importing and the labor exporting economies, and we need to be able to assess whether this migration should be encouraged. Although there have been some policy debates, as a matter of formality, Japan has not allowed the immigration of unskilled workers.

Those who support an open-door policy emphasize, among other things, the international responsibility of developed countries to accept migrant workers. Those who are against this policy argue that their (host) country could be better off without migrant workers if their domestic labor was appropriately reallocated within the domestic market. The purpose of the present chapter is to add insight into these arguments by presenting a model of profit-sharing between domestic workers and the domestic firm, and to show that the profit-sharing scheme works well in reducing unemployment and in raising national welfare. It should be noted that we have tried to find a mechanism to tackle this issue taking into account the welfare of both the host and foreign country, and assessing effects on global welfare as well.

Some authors have regarded profit-sharing as one of the characteristics of the Japanese style of corporate management (Fung (1989a), Weitzman (1985)). Using a simple one sector, two-country model, we conclude that a rise in the rate of profit-sharing given to domestic labor increases incomes and reduces rates of unemployment in both countries. Wages are lowered, demand for labor increases and more unskilled workers migrate from the foreign country to the host country. It is interesting to note that these results are obtained even if migrant workers are ineligible to participate in profit-sharing with the firm.

Complementarity between the services of domestic and migrant workers in the production process and in their strategic rent-seeking activities plays the largest role in the derivation of these results. Capital and the two types of labor - domestic and migrant - are assumed to be substitutes in the model. If we dispense with these conditions, the welfare effects of raising the rate of profit-sharing are ambiguous and it is most likely that the foreign country becomes worse off.

The importance of factor substitution and complementarity has been noted by Ethier (1985). Observing the guest-worker system, especially in Europe, he argues that the two types of labor are both substitutes and complements. They are substitutes in times of recession, as domestic workers compete with migrant workers for even low wage jobs. They are complements at other times, in that they preserve jobs for domestic workers by maintaining the international competitiveness of firms that utilize low-skilled workers. However, Ethier's model is presented from a host country perspective, while we believe, as he notes (Ethier (1985), p.705), that analysis for the labor exporting (foreign) country should also be included. To that end, Kenen (1971) has examined the economic welfare of the source country of migrants with models of one-product closed economies, two-product closed economies and two-product open economies, respectively. Although labor migration is analyzed, there is a basic symmetry between emigration and immigration in Kenen (1971); what is good for the source country turns out to be bad for the host country, and *vice versa*. We believe that his model is limited since it assumes that migration is exogenous and migrants and their families migrate permanently to the host country. We do not adopt these assumptions in the present chapter but rather try to endogenise the increments to migration, and we assume that migrant workers remit earnings to their families, who remain in the foreign country.

Although nearly half of the migrant workers presently in Japan are believed to be illegal migrants, our model is not explicitly an illegal migration analysis. Bond and Chen (1987) extend the crime-theoretic model of illegal migration introduced by Ethier (1986a) to a two-country model and provide the condition for welfare improvements in the host country. Yoshida (1993) complements Bond and Chen (1987) by showing that the introduction of an enforcement policy against illegal migrants within the host country makes the source country and world as a whole unambiguously worse off. While the present chapter follows Bond and Chen (1987) in providing a single good, two-country model, it departs from their analysis by introducing unemployment in both the host and source countries.

Confining themselves to a single good model, as in the present case, Brecher and Choudhri (1987) emphasized the implications of unemployment in the analysis of labor imports versus capital exports. They show that the policy ranking among factor movements in the presence of unemployment are the reverse of that under full employment, as seen in Ramaswami (1968), Bhagwati and Srinivasan (1983), Calvo and Wellisz (1983) and Jones, Coelho and Easton (1986). All but Brecher and

Choudhri (1987) assume full employment in the labor-exporting country. As we emphasize above, we assume unemployment everywhere, since it constitutes an important part of the motivation for international labor movements.

This chapter is organized as follows. Section 9.2 presents our basic model. A host country produces a single commodity with labor and capital using a concave production function. Specifically, we consider the case where domestic labor is distinguishable from unskilled migrant labor migrating from a neighboring country, which is presumably abundant in unskilled labor. As in Brecher and Choudhri (1987), we assume that the host country provides its own workers with unemployment insurance and/or welfare payments that effectively function as a minimum-income guarantee. The source country of migrant labor is modeled with an expected wage - minimum wage combination of the Harris and Todaro (1970) type.

Domestic and migrant workers are complements in production and at the same time their services are strategic complements in their rent-seeking activities, but capital and both types of labor are either independent or substitutes in the production process. An increment in the rate of profit-sharing has the following effects: (1) wages for both types of labor decrease, (2) the number of migrants increases, (3) unemployment rates in both countries decrease, (4) the profit of domestic firms increases, and (5) the welfare levels of both countries increase.

Section 9.3 extends the analysis by allowing international capital mobility. The desirable results obtained in section 9.2 no longer hold, except in the case when the initial equilibrium is such that the level of capital exports was exactly zero. Section 9.4 offers some concluding remarks.

9.2 The basic model

We present a simple model of profit-sharing, to examine its effects on international migration and national welfare. There are two countries, a host country and a foreign country, having fixed amounts of capital and labor, respectively, and producing a commodity with concave production technologies.[1] Firms in the host country utilize two types of labor, domestic and foreign, in conjunction with domestic capital to produce a single commodity. We consider that domestic labor in the host country represents skilled labor and foreign migrant labor represents unskilled labor.

Like Brecher and Choudhri (1987), we assume that the host country uses lump-sum taxes to provide domestic workers with a package of unemployment insurance and welfare benefits. It implies that domestic workers would not accept employment if facing wage offers less than w^0, the real value of the package per worker. In other words, w^0 effectively works as a minimum wage for domestic workers. If this minimum is higher than the level of marginal product of the domestic workers under full employment, as we assume, then the host country suffers from unemployment, which constitutes a social cost.

The portion of the production process utilizing unskilled labor is satisfied by foreign migrant labor. These workers migrate from their native country, which suffers from unemployment. Their wages in the host country are higher than the expected wage they would have earned in their native country, so incentives for migration continue to exist and wages earned in the host country are remitted back to the native country. The labor inflow ceases when migrant labor faces the same expected wage in both countries.

The production function of the host country is written as $F(L,M,K)$ with inputs of domestic labor, L, migrant labor, M, and domestic capital, K, and is assumed to be concave with respect to its arguments. Given the wage levels that domestic and migrant workers obtain within the host country, w and v, respectively, and the rate of returns to capital, r, the firm's profit maximization ensures that $w = F_L(L,M,K)$, $v = F_M(L,M,K)$ and $r = F_K(L,M,K)$ where subscripts indicate partial derivatives of the function with respect to its arguments, and commodity prices are normalized at unity everywhere. In the present section, we rule out the possibility of international capital mobility and we assume that K is fixed at $\bar{K}$, the endowment level of domestic capital. Employment levels of domestic and migrant labor are readily determined by their wages, w and v.

Total differentiation summarizes these relations by

$$dw = F_{LL}dL + F_{LM}dM,$$
$$dv = F_{ML}dL + F_{MM}dM, \tag{9.1}$$

and effects of wage changes on the employment levels are thus written as

$$L_w \equiv \partial L / \partial w = F_{MM} / \Delta_1,$$
$$L_v \equiv \partial L / \partial v = -F_{LM} / \Delta_1, \tag{9.2}$$
$$M_w \equiv \partial M / \partial w = -F_{ML} / \Delta_1,$$
$$M_v \equiv \partial M / \partial v = F_{LL} / \Delta_1,$$

where $\Delta_1 \equiv F_{LL}F_{MM} - F_{LM}{}^2$ and $F_{MM} \equiv \partial^2 F / \partial M^2$.

Now, the strict concavity of the production function immediately guarantees that $\Delta_1 > 0$, $L_w < 0$ and $M_v < 0$. Further, we assume that $F_{LM} = F_{ML} > 0$. This implies that domestic and migrant workers are quantity-complements, or, that an increase in the quantity of a factor raises the marginal valuation of the other factor.[2] Then, the second and third equations in (9.2) indicate that $L_v < 0$ and $M_w < 0$, and that the two types of labor are also regarded as price-complements. Ethier (1985) noticed the importance of the complementarity between migrant and native labor, in the sense that cheap migrant workers can help domestic firms survive in an environment of severe international competition. He also suggests that the two types of labor become substitutes once the domestic economy faces a downturn. In modeling his ideas, Ethier (1985) regards migrant labor as an imperfect substitute, on balance, for domestic labor in the production process. The present chapter goes beyond this type of factor substitutes/complements definition by precisely defining these terms with signs of the cross derivatives of the production function, since we believe that the arguments endorsed by Ethier are already embodied in a production function having both types of labor as its arguments.

The rate of returns to capital in turn receives the effects of wage changes so as to clear the capital market.

$$r_w \equiv \partial r / \partial w = F_{KL} L_w + F_{KM} M_w \geq 0,$$
$$r_v \equiv \partial r / \partial v = F_{KL} L_v + F_{KM} M_v \geq 0, \tag{9.3}$$

where we assume that $F_{KL} \leq 0$ and $F_{KM} \leq 0$.[3] Our technological assumptions are now clear. While migrants and native workers are complements, they are both weak substitutes for capital in production. Labor complementarity and substitutability with capital are easier to understand if we contrast domestic workers with skilled labor and migrant workers with unskilled labor, and if we notice the possibility of increasing dependency on highly advanced capital-intensive technologies in the face of labor shortages. Indeed, several authors have presented empirical results suggesting the substitutability between capital and labor as productive factors. Burgess (1974b), for example, has shown that $F_{KM} < 0$ for certain sample periods as well as $F_{LM} > 0$, although M in the analysis is not explicitly migrant labor but some imports utilized as productive factors. For further empirical discussion, refer to Mohabbat and Dalal (1983) among others.

Turning to the foreign country, we write its production as $F^*(L^*, K^*)$ where L^* and K^* are levels of employment and capital services, respectively. As in the host country, capital is fully employed and thus equal to its endowment throughout the present section: $K^* = \overline{K}^*$. Notice that the foreign country uses a single type of labor, although it is not necessarily confined to unskilled labor. It has been pointed out that some of the recent migrants to Japan had previously been working as skilled labor in their native countries, yet they find only unskilled jobs in the host country to which they migrate.

Again, we introduce unemployment in the foreign country. As in the Philippines, it is sufficient to consider minimum wage legislation, at least for urban labor. The minimum level, $\overline{w}^*$, requires profit-maximizing firms to employ workers, L^*, at wages $\overline{w}^* = F_L^*(L^*, K^*)$. We assume $\overline{w}^*$ is not sufficiently low as to create full employment. Following Harris and Todaro (1970) and Ethier (1986a), we regard the expected wage for workers in the foreign country, w^e, as being equal to the minimum wage multiplied by the rate of employment in the country, e. A part of the foreign labor force migrates to the host country seeking better jobs, and the labor market in the foreign country is characterized by

$$w^e = e\overline{w}^*,$$
$$e = L^*/(\overline{L}^* - \underline{M}), \tag{9.4}$$

where $\overline{L}^*$ is labor endowment in the foreign country and $\underline{M}$ is the number of migrants in the host country.

Finally, international migration ceases at the point where migrants can expect the same level of wages wherever they go. Observing that the domestic firm employs only M immigrants, the expected wage for migrant workers becomes $vM/\underline{M}$ and thus equilibrium requires that

$$vM/\underline{M} = e\overline{w}^*. \tag{9.5}$$

Domestic and migrant workers try to behave optimally in establishing their own equilibrium wages. Suppose that they are obtaining economic rents by forming their own labor unions. Once we notice that migrant workers are indispensable in the production process of the host country, it is not absurd to assume certain bargaining power in the hands of migrant labor. However, they are by no means eligible to a profit share from their employer. It is solely to domestic labor that the firm grants a profit share.

Thus, the economic rents for domestic and migrant workers to maximize are expressed, respectively, by

$$R \equiv (w - w^0)L + \theta\pi,$$
$$R^* \equiv (v - w^e)M, \tag{9.6}$$

where θ is the rate of profit-sharing granted to domestic workers, with $0 < \theta < 1$, and $\pi \equiv F(L,M,K) - (wL + vM + rK)$ is the firm's profit.

Fung (1989a, b) has examined unemployment problems in Europe, and suggested that Japanese economic success is partly attributable to their profit-sharing schemes, which take the form of a bonus system. As θ increases, workers have greater access to a share of the firm's profit, thereby improving their own well being. We follow this line of argument in forming (9.6) as the worker's objective, although Fung (1989a, b) did not assume two different types of labor simultaneously working in an industry, contrary to our assumption here.[4]

Domestic and migrant workers, respectively, maximize R and R^* by choosing appropriate levels of w and v, given the firm's factor demand curves, $L(w,v)$ and $M(w,v)$. The first terms in (9.6) are total rents other than the profit-share for workers behaving like labor unions.[5] Domestic workers do not want employment with wages less than w^0, the effective level as a minimum wage, and migrants set their minimum wage requirement as per the wage, w^e. In their wage claims, we do not assume that the two types of labor manifestly cooperate with each other.[6] Rather, they behave as Bertrand-Nash players.

The first order conditions are written as

$$R_w \equiv \partial R / \partial w = L + (w - w^0)L_w + \theta\pi_w = 0,$$
$$R_v^* \equiv \partial R^* / \partial v = (1 - w_v^e)M + (v - w^e)M_v = 0, \tag{9.7}$$

where π_w is the partial derivative of the firm's profit with respect to the wage of domestic workers.

The second order conditions are assumed to be satisfied, namely

$$R_{ww} \equiv \partial^2 R / \partial w^2 = 2L_w + (w - w^0)L_{ww} + \theta\pi_{ww} < 0,$$
$$R_{vv}^* \equiv \partial^2 R / \partial v^2 = 2(1 - w_v^e)M_v - Mw_{vv}^e + (v - w^e)M_{vv} < 0. \tag{9.8}$$

Noting that capital mobility is absent in the analysis of the present section and that the rate of returns to capital is a function of the two types of wages, we have

$$\pi_w \equiv \partial\pi / \partial w = -L - r_w\overline{K} < 0, \tag{9.9}$$

from the first equation of (9.3).

We examine the effects of an increase in the rate of profit-sharing on labor's wage determination.[7] Total differentiation of the first order conditions (9.7) shows us that

$$R_{ww}dw + R_{wv}dv + R_{w\vartheta}d\theta = 0,$$
$$R_{vw}^*dw + R_{vv}^*dv = 0. \tag{9.10}$$

For any given level of θ, slopes of the reaction functions for domestic and migrant workers are expressed by, respectively,

$$dv/dw\big|_{R_w=0} = -R_{ww}/R_{wv} \gtrless 0 \quad \text{as} \quad R_{wv} \lessgtr 0, \tag{9.11a}$$

$$dv/dw\big|_{R_v^*=0} = -R_{vw}^*/R_{vv}^* \gtrless 0 \quad \text{as} \quad R_{vw}^* \lessgtr 0, \tag{9.11b}$$

where the second order conditions (9.8) are taken into account.

Signs $R_{wv} > 0$ and $R_{vw}^* > 0$ represent the strategic effects of a change in one player's equilibrium strategy on the other player's economic rent, and positive (negative) signs here indicate that a more (less) aggressive strategy taken by one type of labor also raises the marginal welfare of the other type of labor.

To examine the effects of profit-sharing, let us assume $R_{wv} > 0$ and $R_{vw}^* > 0$. Based on the definitions by Bulow, Geanakoplos and Klemperer (1985), this means that the services of the two types of labor are strategic complements. At the end of the present section, in order to complete the discussion, we briefly mention the implications if the two types of labor were strategic substitutes.

In addition to the strategic complementarity, we need conditions for the stability of the Bertrand behavior. The reaction function of domestic workers should be steeper than that of migrant workers. Thus, we have

$$D \equiv R_{ww}R_{vv}^* - R_{wv}R_{vw}^* > 0. \tag{9.12}$$

Then, from (9.10) we see the effects of a change in the rate of profit-sharing on wages as

$$dw/d\theta = -R_{vv}^* R_{w\theta}/D < 0,$$
$$dv/d\vartheta = R_{vw}^* R_{w\theta}/D < 0. \tag{9.13}$$

since $R_{w\theta} = \pi_w < 0$ from (9.7).

Wages to both types of labor are reduced as a result of any increment to the rate of profit-sharing. It is not, of course, surprising to see that domestic workers would lower their wage claims in order to increase the firm's profit, since they are eligible to acquire a part of the increased profit. What is more important is that migrant workers also lower their wages in order to remain competitive in the labor market. From the third and fourth equations in (9.2), we know that M increases if w falls when $F_{ML} > 0$, while it decreases if v rises. However, it is natural to suppose that the former effect (cross effect) is outweighed by the latter (own effect) in absolute terms, namely $|M_w| < |M_v|$, and thus migrants find it disadvantageous to raise their wage, v, in the face of domestic wage reduction.

Equipped with (9.13), it is easy to find that the employment levels of both types of labor increase and hence domestic production rises.

$$dL/d\theta = L_w dw/d\theta + L_v dv/d\theta > 0, \tag{9.14}$$

$$dM/d\theta = M_w dw/d\theta + M_v dv/d\theta > 0, \tag{9.15}$$

$$dF/d\theta = F_L dL/d\theta + F_M dM/d\theta > 0. \tag{9.16}$$

Also, the firm's profit is shown to increase, since using (9.3) we obtain

$$d\pi/d\theta = -Ldw/d\theta - Mdv/d\theta$$
$$- \overline{K}(r_w dw/d\theta + r_v dv/d\theta) > 0. \tag{9.17}$$

These results are summarized by the following proposition.

Proposition 9.1 [Ohta and Yoshida (1995)]
*Consider two types of labor, domestic and migrant, competing for wage deter-
mination in a Bertrand-Nash fashion in a world with no international capital
mobility. Suppose that these two types of labor are quantity complements in
production and strategic complements in rent-seeking activities, but both are
either substitutes to capital or independent of capital. Then an increase in the
rate of profit-sharing granted to domestic labor, (i) decreases the wages of both
types of labor, (ii) increases levels of employment for both types of labor, and
(iii) increases the profits of domestic firms.*

Result (ii) in proposition 9.1 implies that the unemployment rate in the host country decreases and that the domestic firm hires more immigrants. We should be interested in the implication this has for the national welfare of both the host country and the foreign country. If both countries are better off, a fortification of the profit-sharing program is recommended as an immediate remedy for the backlog of would-be international migrants. The Japanese bonus system, for instance, would not only reduce unemployment, as discussed in Fung (1989a, b), but would be firmly lauded from a global point of view. We may not need to linger on the crime-theoretic analysis of illegal migration, as Ethier (1985) and Bond and Chen (1987) have done, to tackle existing immigration conflicts.

As in Brecher and Choudhri (1987), domestic welfare is represented by national income, Y :

$$Y = F(L, M, \overline{K}) - vM. \tag{9.18}$$

For simplicity, migrants are assumed to remit all earnings to their native country. From the condition of profit maximization facing the domestic firm, and with the second equation of (9.13) and (9.14), we have

$$dY/d\theta = F_L dL/d\theta - M dv/d\theta > 0. \tag{9.19}$$

In the foreign country, the minimum wage, $\overline{w}^*$, is crucial in deriving its local employment, L^*. As $\overline{w}^*$ is fixed, L^* is also constant from profit maximization conditions, since capital is assumed to be fully employed. Thus, from the second equation of (9.4) and (9.5) we have:

$$e_v = (M + vM_v)/\overline{w}^* \overline{L}^*. \tag{9.20}$$

From the second equation in (9.7), we have that $M + vM_v = w_v^e M + w^e M_v$, which in turn, using (9.4), becomes

$$M + vM_v = \overline{w}^* Me_v + \overline{w}^* eM_v. \tag{9.21}$$

Substituting (9.20) and (9.21), and using the fourth equation of (9.2) and the concavity of the production function, we find

$$e_v = eM_v/(\overline{L}^* - M) < 0. \tag{9.22}$$

Thus, again with the first equation of (9.4), we have that $w_v^e = \overline{w}^* e_v < 0$ and

$$M + vM_v < 0. \tag{9.23}$$

Therefore, from (9.4) and (9.5), we obtain that

$$de/d\theta = [vM_w dw/d\theta + (M + vM_v)dv/d\theta]/\overline{w}^* \overline{L}^* > 0. \tag{9.24}$$

Also, from (9.4) and (9.5), it is known that

$$d\underline{M}/d\theta = (\overline{L}^* - \underline{M}) \cdot (1/e^2)de/d\theta > 0. \tag{9.25}$$

An increase in the rate of profit-sharing in the host country raises the rate of employment within the foreign country and at the same time, increases migration into the host country.

Using the second equation in (9.4), we define foreign country income, Y^*, by

$$Y^* = F^*(e(\overline{L}^* - \underline{M}), \overline{K}^*) + vM. \tag{9.26}$$

This leads to the impact of profit-sharing as

$$dY^*/d\theta = (M + vM_v)dv/d\theta + vM_w dw/d\theta > 0, \tag{9.27}$$

where (9.23) is taken into account. Together with the third equation in (9.2), (9.13) and (9.23), we have $dY^*/d\theta > 0$.

To see the effects on the rate of employment among foreign workers staying in the host country, let us use (9.5) to obtain

$$d(M/\underline{M})/d\theta = (\overline{w}^* e_v - M/\underline{M})dv/d\theta + \overline{w}^* e_w dw/d\theta. \qquad (9.28)$$

Now, the first order conditions for the foreign firm and migrant workers guarantee that

$$e_w = vM_w/\overline{w}^*\overline{L}^* < 0, \qquad (9.29)$$

and thus that the second term in (9.28) is positive.

The remaining term is also proved to be positive by noting that

$$\overline{w}^* e_v - (M/\underline{M}) = (M/\underline{M})(M + vM_v - \overline{L}^*)/(\overline{L}^* - M) < 0,$$

with the aid of (9.5), the second equation of (9.13), and (9.23). Therefore, an increment in the rate of profit-sharing gives rise to favorable opportunities for immigrants as well as for those who remain in their source country.

Finally, the profits of foreign firms are invariant, since both $\overline{L}^*$ and $\overline{K}^*$ are constant and thus r^* is fixed as long as $\overline{w}^*$ is fixed.

Therefore, under the technological and behavioral assumption in the present section, we have as our main result,

Proposition 9.2 [Ohta and Yoshida (1995)]
Complementarity among the two types of labor and their weak substitutability with capital ensure that an increase in the rate of profit-sharing causes an increase in (i) domestic welfare, (ii) foreign welfare and (iii) the rate of employment everywhere.

As has already been emphasized, the directions of the complementarity- substitutability relations are critical in the proposition. Let us briefly summarize our results under the remaining scenarios.

The general conclusion is that unless the assumptions in the above propositions are satisfied, an increase in the rate of profit-sharing has an ambiguous effect on the host country's welfare while the foreign country tends to be worse off. When the services of migrants and domestic workers are strategic complements, the above two propositions provide us with the only definitive results.

When the two types of labor are strategic substitutes in rent-seeking, but continue to be complements in production, then an increase in profit-sharing reduces foreign welfare given the additional conditions $F_{KL} < 0$, $F_{KM} \geq 0$ and $|F_{KL}| > F_{KM}$.

If the services of labor are strategic substitutes as well as quantity substitutes, profit-sharing causes the foreign country to become unambiguously worse off, with either (i) $F_{KL} \leq 0$, $F_{KM} \geq 0$ or (ii) $F_{KL} < 0$, $F_{KM} \leq 0$ and $|F_{KL}| > |F_{KM}|$.[8]

Although substitutabilities complicate the analysis, we need not be deterred. We believe that the assumptions in Proposition 9.1 are the most probable combinations applicable to the current industrialized economies, and applicable at least to Japan as long as a single sector model is concerned. What is of greater concern is the effect of capital mobility, which we examine in the next section.

9.3 Capital mobility

With quantity substitutability between capital and both types of labor, the rate of return to domestic capital, r, is reduced by an increase in the rate of profit-sharing if the possibility of capital mobility is absent. Since the foreign rental rate, r^*, is kept constant, as mentioned in the previous section, this creates pressure for capital to migrate from the host country to the foreign country. Let us ask if the above propositions carry over to a world with free capital movements across countries.

To keep the arguments simple, we begin by listing all of the equilibrium equations.

$$w = F_L(L, M, K), \tag{9.30a}$$

$$v = F_M(L, M, K), \tag{9.30b}$$

$$r = F_K(L, M, K), \tag{9.30c}$$

$$w^* = F_L^*(L^*, K^*), \tag{9.30d}$$

$$r^* = F_K^*(L^*, K^*), \tag{9.30e}$$

$$r = r^*, \tag{9.30f}$$

$$\overline{K} - K = K_F = K^* - \overline{K}^*, \tag{9.30g}$$

$$L^* = e(\overline{L}^* - \underline{M}), \tag{9.30h}$$

$$vM / \underline{M} = e\overline{w}^*. \tag{9.30i}$$

The notation is the same as in the previous section, except for K_F, which is the amount of capital exports from the host country as defined in (9.30g). The endogenous variables are L, M, K, r, K_F, r^*, L^*, K^*, e and $\underline{M}$, while w and v are determined by rent-seeking labor as before, with the following variables being exogenous: $\overline{w}^*$, $\overline{K}$, $\overline{K}^*$ and $\overline{L}^*$. Because of free mobility, rates of returns to capital in the two countries are equalized in equilibrium as shown in (9.30f).

Assuming quantity and strategic complementarities among the services of labor and their substitutability with capital, as in section 9.2, we reproduce (9.13) as the effects of an increase in the rate of profit-sharing on wages. The only modification we need is to regard the amount of capital used in the host country, K, as a function of w and v now, instead of as a constant $\overline{K}$. To see the welfare effects of profit-sharing, let us firstly differentiate system (9.30) totally with respect to w and v. Leaving the algebraic details to the Appendix, we have the following partial impacts of wages, w and v, respectively.

$$L_w < 0, \ M_w < 0, \ K_{Fw} < 0, \ r_w = r_w^* > 0, \ e_w \gtreqless 0, \ \underline{M}_w < 0, \quad (9.31a)$$

$$L_v < 0, \ M_v < 0, \ K_{Fv} < 0, \ r_v = r_v^* > 0, \ e_v \gtreqless 0, \ \underline{M}_v \gtreqless 0, \quad (9.31b)$$

where, as before, subscripts indicate variables used in taking the derivatives. It is also clear from (9.31) that $K_w > 0$, $K_w^* > 0$, $K_v > 0$, $K_v^* < 0$, $L_w^* \gtreqless 0$ and $L_v^* \gtreqless 0$.

Therefore, combined with the effects on wages of the profit-sharing program, (9.31), movements in the levels of employment and capital flows are derived as:

$$dL / d\theta = L_w dw / d\theta + L_v dv / d\theta > 0, \quad (9.32a)$$

$$dM / d\theta = M_w dw / d\theta + M_v dv / d\theta > 0, \quad (9.32b)$$

$$dK_F / d\theta = K_{Fw} dw / d\theta + K_{Fv} dv / d\theta > 0. \quad (9.32c)$$

Notice that (9.32a) and (9.32b) are the same in (9.14) and (9.15) for the capital immobility case. An increase in the rate of profit-sharing granted to domestic workers reduces unemployment of domestic skilled labor and increases employment of migrant workers, while it encourages capital exports to the migrants' native country. Unfortunately, with capital mobility, we do not know the impact on the level of immigration into the host country. Interestingly, profit-sharing reduces rates of returns to capital:

$$dr^* / d\theta = dr / d\theta = r_w dw / d\theta + r_v dv / d\theta < 0. \quad (9.33)$$

This is the direct consequence of the assumption that capital and the two types of labor are quantity substitutes, rather than complements. In the host country, capital outflows naturally put upward pressure on the rate of return. However, as we see with (9.30c), substitutability imposes downward pressure and this effect outweighs that of capital exports. Owners of capital suffer from the unfavorable impact of profit-sharing, even in the presence of capital mobility.

The labor market in the foreign country, on the other hand, does not demonstrate definitive effects:

$$de / d\theta \gtreqless 0, \ dL^* / d\theta \gtreqless 0. \quad (9.34)$$

Capital mobility obscures the profit-sharing effects on the employment opportunities for immigrant labor in the host country. Likewise, output levels in both countries are now ambiguous:

$$dF/d\theta = F_L dL/d\theta + F_M dM/d\theta + F_K dK/d\theta \gtreqless 0, \qquad (9.35a)$$

$$dF^*/d\theta = F_L^* dL^*/d\theta + F_K^* dK^*/d\theta \gtreqless 0. \qquad (9.35b)$$

Finally, we ask whether the favorable welfare effects on domestic labor from an increase in the rate of profit-sharing survive the introduction of international capital mobility. Domestic income is modified to

$$Y \equiv F(L,M,K) - vM + r^* K_F. \qquad (9.36)$$

With the aid of the firm's profit maximizing conditions, we derive

$$dY/d\theta = wdL/d\theta - Mdv/d\theta + K_F dr^*/d\theta, \qquad (9.37)$$

and the first equation of (9.13), (9.32a) and (9.33) reveal the sign to be indeterminate. Profit-sharing makes the host country better off only when the amount of free capital movement equals zero, $K_F = 0$, at the initial equilibrium:

$$dY/d\theta\big|_{K_F=0} > 0. \qquad (9.38)$$

It is even more difficult to see the welfare impact on the foreign country. Its income is written as

$$Y^* = F^*(L^*, K^*) + vM - r^* K_F, \qquad (9.39)$$

and a similar manipulation as above shows that

$$dY^*/d\theta = w^* dL^*/d\theta + (M + vM_v)dv/d\theta$$
$$+ vM_w dw/d\theta - K_F dr^*/d\theta, \qquad (9.40)$$

the sign of which is indeterminate.

Thus, we summarize the arguments in this section with the following proposition.

Proposition 9.3 [Ohta and Yoshida (1995)]

Consider a two-country model of factor movements under unemployment, in which a proportion of labor migrates from the foreign country to the host country and capital is freely mobile across countries. Suppose that domestic and migrant workers are complements in the sense of quantity usage in production and in terms of strategies in rent-seeking. Suppose further that they are both substitutes to capital in the production process. Then, an increase in the rate of profit-sharing granted solely to domestic labor (i) decreases both wages as de-

*termined in a Bertrand-Nash competition among two types of labor, (ii) in-
creases the employment levels of both types of labor in the host country, (iii)
increases the amount of domestic capital exports, but (iv) may decrease the
welfare levels of both countries.*

9.4 Concluding remarks

International migration has increasingly attracted economists' attention.
European and North American experiences are already well known and
often used to analyze the impact of immigration on the welfare of host
countries. Using standard models of factor mobility, authors have extended the much-famed Ramaswami (1968) proposition to argue whether
an optimal policy should be more labor-import inclined, more capi-
tal-export inclined or, instead, buy-out oriented. Under full employment,
it has been ascertained, given certain restrictions, that national welfare is
increased by labor imports rather than by capital trade. When the host
country is suffering from unemployment, however, it should be noted
that the policy ranking is reversed, and labor imports may not constitute
an optimal economic policy at all. Furthermore, if we regard migrants as
illegal, a crime-theoretic analysis is useful in examining the implication
of enforcement policies by the host country's government.

We believe that most of these important discussions have been presented only from the host country's perspective. Exceptions include
Brecher and Choudhri (1987), who claim that in their world of unemployment, what is better for the host country also happens to be better
for the world as a whole, and Yoshida (1993), who explicitly considers
foreign and global welfare as well as that of the host country. When we
examine the possibility of opening our border to foreign labor, we should
not restrict ourselves to analyzing only the host country's welfare.

In the present chapter, we have presented a model of international
migration under unemployment in both the foreign country and the
host country, where unemployment in the former constitutes an important migration incentive. The mechanism we consider for the mutual
benefit of the two countries is a profit-sharing plan, implemented by
domestic firms within the host country. Because of the difference in
their bargaining positions with the firm, the profit-sharing scheme is
extended only to domestic labor. Nevertheless, it operates favorably for
both countries, although immigrants themselves have to endure lowered
wages because of the increased profit-sharing. The key assumptions we
use are complementarity between domestic and foreign labor and their
substitutability with capital. If these conditions accurately describe an

economy that utilizes skilled and unskilled workers, together with its own capital, to produce a commodity, then a policy that increases profit-sharing is recommended. Such a policy will simultaneously solve unemployment problems and address the international responsibility of the host country to open its doors to migrant workers from neighboring countries. Unfortunately, however, the same policy is not recommended in the case of free international capital mobility.

Appendix

The results of section 9.3 in this chapter are presented below in algebraic detail. Throughout the derivation it is assumed that $F_{LM} > 0$, $F_{KL} < 0$ and $F_{KM} < 0$, and that $F(\cdot)$ and $F^*(\cdot)$ are both strictly concave.

9.A Effects of changes in wages:

Differentiate system (9.30) with respect to w and v, and find the directions of change in the endogenous variables as follows.

$$\Delta \equiv e\overline{w}^* \overline{L}^* [F^*_{LL} \begin{vmatrix} F_{LL} & F_{LM} & F_{LK} \\ F_{ML} & F_{MM} & F_{MK} \\ F_{KL} & F_{KM} & F_{KK} \end{vmatrix} + \{F^*_{LL}F^*_{KK} - (F^*_{LK})^2\} \begin{vmatrix} F_{LL} & F_{LM} \\ F_{ML} & F_{MM} \end{vmatrix}] > 0. \quad (9A.1)$$

$$L_w = e\overline{w}^* \overline{L}^* [F^*_{LL}\{F_{MM}F_{KK} - (F_{MK})^2\} + F_{MM}\{F^*_{LL}F^*_{KK} - (F^*_{LK})^2\}]/\Delta < 0. \quad (9A.2)$$

$$M_w = -e\overline{w}^*\overline{L}^*[F_{ML}\{F^*_{KK}F^*_{LL} - (F^*_{LK})^2\} + F^*_{LL}(F_{KK}F_{ML} - F_{MK}F_{KL})]/\Delta < 0. \quad (9A.3)$$

$$K_{F_w} = e\overline{w}^*\overline{L}^* F^*_{LL}(F_{MM}F_{KL} - F_{ML}F_{KM})/\Delta < 0. \quad (9A.4)$$

$$r^*_w = -e\overline{w}^*\overline{L}^* \{F^*_{LL}F^*_{KK} - (F^*_{LK})^2\} \times (F_{ML}F_{KM} - F_{KL}F_{MM})/\Delta > 0. \quad (9A.5)$$

$$e_w = e[\overline{w}^* F^*_{LK}(F_{ML}F_{KM} - F_{MM}F_{KL}) - v\{F_{ML}(F^*_{LL}F^*_{KK} - (F^*_{KL})^2) + F^*_{LL}(F_{KK}F_{ML} - F_{MK}F_{KL})\}]/\Delta \gtreqless 0. \quad (9A.6)$$

$$\underline{M}_w = [\overline{w}^* \underline{M} F^*_{LK}(F_{ML}F_{KM} - F_{MM}F_{KL}) - v(\overline{L}^* - \underline{M})\{F_{ML}(F^*_{KK}F^*_{LL} - (F^*_{LK})^2 + F^*_{LL}(F_{KK}F_{ML} - F_{MK}F_{KL})\}]/\Delta < 0. \quad (9A.7)$$

$$L_v = -e\overline{w}^*\overline{L}^*[F^*_{LL}(F_{LM}F_{KK} - F_{KM}F_{LK}) + F_{LM}\{F^*_{LL}F^*_{KK} - (F^*_{LK})^2\}]/\Delta < 0. \quad (9A.8)$$

$$M_v = e\overline{w}^*\overline{L}^*[F^*_{LL}\{F_{LL}F_{KK} - (F_{LK})^2\} + F_{LL}\{F^*_{LL}F^*_{KK} - (F^*_{LK})^2\}]/\Delta < 0. \quad (9A.9)$$

$$K_{F_v} = e\overline{w}^*\overline{L}^* F^*_{LL}(F_{LL}F_{KM} - F_{KL}F_{LM})/\Delta < 0. \quad (9A.10)$$

$$r^*_v = e\overline{w}^*(\overline{L}^* - \underline{M})\{F^*_{KK}F^*_{LL} - (F^*_{LK})^2\}(F_{LL}F_{KM} - F_{LM}F_{KL})/\Delta > 0. \quad (9A.11)$$

$$e_v = -e[\overline{w}^*\overline{L}^*F_{LK}^*(F_{KM}F_{LL} - F_{LM}F_{LK}) - v\{F_{LL}(F_{LL}^*F_{KK}^* - (F_{LK}^*)^2)$$
$$+ F_{LL}^*(F_{LL}F_{KK} - (F_{KL})^2)\} + M\{F_{LL}F_{MM}(F_{LK})^2$$
$$+ F_{LL}^*F_{KK}^*(F_{LM})^2 - \begin{vmatrix} F_{LL} & F_{LM} & F_{LK} \\ F_{ML} & F_{MM} & F_{MK} \\ F_{KL} & F_{KM} & F_{KK} \end{vmatrix}\}]/\Delta \gtreqless 0. \tag{9A.12}$$

$$M_v = [\overline{w}^*\overline{L}^*F_{LK}^*(F_{LL}F_{KM} - F_{LM}F_{KL}) + v(\overline{L}^* - \underline{M})$$
$$\times \{F_{LL}(F_{LL}^*F_{KK}^* - (F_{LK}^*)^2) + F_{LL}^*(F_{LL}F_{KK} - (F_{LK})^2)\}$$
$$+ M(\overline{L}^* - \underline{M})\{(F_{LL}F_{MM} - (F_{LM})^2)(F_{LL}^*F_{KK}^* - (F_{LK}^*)^2)$$
$$+ F_{LL}^*\begin{vmatrix} F_{LL} & F_{LM} & F_{LK} \\ F_{ML} & F_{MM} & F_{MK} \\ F_{KL} & F_{KM} & F_{KK} \end{vmatrix}\}]/\Delta \gtreqless 0. \tag{9A.13}$$

Notes

1   See, for example, Batra and Seth (1977) for the usage of strictly concave production functions in the theory of international trade.

2   Bond (1989) argues that the terminology is suggested by Hicks (1956). Bond (1989) also indicates that if production function is homogeneous of degree one in the arguments, at most one of the cross effects (F_{LK}, F_{ML}, F_{MK}) can be negative. In the present chapter, we need not be bound by the limitation. Indeed, Hicks (1970) has confessed that he tried to avoid the constant returns to scale assumption in the discussion of technical substitution and complementarity in his *Value and Capital*.

3   See note 2 above.

4   A case of two different types of labor within an industry is examined by Oswald (1979). However, he has not considered the effect of profit-sharing with his model. Other aspects of labor union in economic analysis are summarized in Oswald (1985) and Farber (1986). Also, see Weitzman (1983, 1985, 1987) for macroeconomic implications of profit-sharing and its related topics.

5   In Bensäid and Gary-Bobo (1991), Sørensen (1992) and Weitzman (1985) equation (9.6a) is simplified as $R = wL + \theta\pi$ where w and R are called base wage and contractual wage, respectively. In the present chapter, we consider economic rent rather than direct wage levels as labor objective.

6   Oswald (1979) examines wage determinations in Cournot, a leader-follower and collective equilibria among two unions in a firm. However, utilities of the unions are not explicitly of economic rents as discussed here.

7   We do not ask precisely what makes the change in the rate of profit-sharing. θ may have been an institutionally determined variable, set by government decree, or outcome of power struggle between labors and their employer. Bensäid and Gary-Bobo (1991) assume profit-sharing contracts between firms and labors in non-cooperative game. In the present chapter, we do not

examine it further, but simply assume that θ is raised by consent among workers and their employer.

8   We have utilized in addition the usual assumption of $|L_w| > M_w > 0$, that is, that own effect is greater than cross effect in absolute terms.

10

Can a Profit-Sharing Scheme Remedy Large Scale Unemployment in a Less Developed Country? [*]

In this chapter, we examine the effects of introducing a profit-sharing scheme in the urban sectors of a less developed country (LDC). We use a generalized Harris and Todaro (1970) model in which the LDC has a dual economy with urban-specific unemployment. We assume that the wage of urban labor is determined by a single labor union. We then introduce a profit-sharing scheme in the urban sector. We find that profit-sharing results in a decrease in wages and an increase in employment in the urban sector, an increase in employment and a decrease in wages in the rural sector, and an increase in the welfare of the LDC. We conclude that profit-sharing may remedy the large-scale urban unemployment problems of LDCs and improve the LDC's welfare.

10.1 Introduction

In most less developed countries, a wage differential between urban and rural sectors is believed to induce intersectoral migration from rural to urban areas, bringing about pervasive unemployment in cities. The wage mechanisms in the urban sectors of the LDCs may not operate so as to reduce such unemployment. We examine one policy designed to remedy large-scale urban unemployment, namely, a government imposed profit-sharing scheme.

There have been many recent studies on the effects of introducing a profit-sharing scheme, including those of Weitzman (1983, 1985), Pohjola (1987), Wadhwani (1988), Jackman (1988), and Fung (1989a, b). These papers analyzed the effects of a profit-sharing scheme on the unemployment rate, differing mainly in their assumptions about the goods market. The goods market was assumed to operate under perfect competition, monopolistic competition, monopoly, duopoly or oligopoly. Most authors, with the exception of Wadhwani (1988), showed that a conversion from a fixed-wage scheme to a profit-sharing scheme could reduce the rate of unemployment in the entire economy.

Given the dual economy inherent in LDCs and the resulting large scale urban unemployment, the extent to which a profit-sharing scheme could reduce this unemployment remains unclear. In this chapter, we use a generalized Harris and Todaro (1970) model to examine the impact of profit-sharing on wages and employment levels.[1]

The Harris and Todaro model assumes a dual economy, inherent in an LDC, with urban-specific unemployment. We extend their model with the assumption that urban sector wages are determined by a labor union. We then introduce profit-sharing in the urban sector and examine its impacts on urban workers' wages, urban employment, total employment (composed of the sum of both urban and rural sector employment), rural workers' wages, rural employment and the LDC's welfare. Although it is generally said that it is difficult for an industrialized country's government to implement a profit-sharing scheme, Blanchflower and Oswald (1987) have reported that profit-sharing schemes have been introduced in the United Kingdom, Germany, Japan, the United States and various other countries. Hence, it may be meaningful to examine the effects of a profit-sharing plan on an LDC's economy.

Our conclusions are that the introduction of profit-sharing causes the following effects. In the urban sector, labor wages fall and employment rises. In the rural sector, employment rises and labor wages fall. Total national employment may rise, and hence the LDC's welfare increases. Hence, a profit-sharing scheme may resolve the urban unemployment problems of an LDC and improve the country's welfare. Since LDCs often face large-scale urban unemployment, we believe it is worth while to examine the policy implications of profit-sharing schemes, if they do, in fact, reduce a serious unemployment problem and increase the country's welfare.

The remainder of this chapter is organized as follows. In subsection 10.2, we introduce a generalized Harris and Todaro (1970) model, in which the urban laborer's wage is determined by his labor union, and we then examine the comparative static effects of a profit-sharing scheme. In subsection 10.3, we examine the effects of a profit-sharing scheme on the welfare of LDC. The final section offers some concluding remarks.

10.2 The basic model

In this section, we consider a less developed country characterized by urban-specific unemployment, that is, a Harris and Todaro (1970) model. The original Harris and Todaro (1970) model is composed of urban and rural sectors: the urban sector produces the manufactured goods (X) and the rural sector produces the agricultural goods (Y); the urban sector faces unemployment while there is full employment in the rural sector.

Assumption (i): the Harris and Todaro (1970) model is extended by assuming that the urban wage, w_x, is determined by the urban labor union at a level above the fixed minimum urban wage, $\overline{w}$.[2,3]

Assumption (ii): goods X and Y are internationally traded at exogenously determined world prices. The LDC can maintain imperfectly specialization.

The production functions of the urban and rural sectors' firms are, respectively, as follows:

$$X = X(L_x, K_x),\tag{10.1}$$

$$Y = Y(L_Y, K_y),\tag{10.2}$$

where L_x and L_y are the labor employment in the urban and rural sectors, respectively, and K_x and K_y are the capital employment in the urban and rural sectors, respectively.

Assumption (iii): the production functions of the urban and rural firms, (10.1) and (10.2) are strictly concave production functions.

Assumption (iv): *in the short run*, the capital input is assumed to be *fixed* within each sector [see Chen and Choi (1994)]. Hence, L_x and L_y are the only variable factors in the urban and rural sectors and they exhibit positive but diminishing marginal productivity.

Assumption (v): capital is fully employed in each sector and the rental rates of capital in the urban and rural sectors, r_x and r_y, are exogenously given with $r_x \neq r_y$.

Given assumption (iv), (10.1) and (10.2) can be rewritten as:

$$X \equiv X(L_x), \tag{10.1}'$$

$$Y \equiv Y(L_y), \tag{10.2}'$$

Before considering labor market equilibrium, we make the following assumption.

Assumption (vi): labor can freely move between the urban and rural areas.

The urban wage is determined by unions in the urban sector and set at a level higher than the market-clearing wage. This results in urban sector unemployment. Following Harris and Todaro (1970), we adopt the hypothesis that at the labor market equilibrium, the rural wage, w_y, is equal to *expected urban labor income*.[4] Expected urban labor income is the product of the probability of gaining employment in the urban sector, $L_x/(L_x + L_u)$, and the sum of the urban wage, w_x, and the urban worker's share of a firm's profits, $\theta \pi_x / L_x$:

$$\{L_x/(L_x + L_u)\}\{w_x + (\theta \pi_x / L_x)\} = w_y. \tag{10.3}$$

In (10.3), L_u is the number of unemployed workers in the urban sector; π_x is the urban firms' profits; and θ is the share of an urban firm's profits going to its workers.[5]

The first order conditions for profit-maximization[6] of the firms in the urban and rural sectors are:

$$w_x = pdX/dL_x, \tag{10.4}$$

$$w_y = pdY/dL_y, \tag{10.5}$$

where p is the relative price of good X to good Y, and good Y is chosen as the numeraire. Given the small-country assumption (assumption (ii)), the price of the manufactured good, p, is exogenously determined.

Let total labor endowment be denoted by $\bar{L}$. $\bar{L}$ is expressed as

$$\bar{L} = L_x + L_y + L_u, \tag{10.6}$$

where the first term in the right hand side, L_x is the sum of permanent urban labor and migrant labor from the rural area to the urban area.

Equation system (A), which consists of equations (10.3) through (10.6), has four endogenous variables, L_x, L_y, w_y and L_u. We treat w_x as an exogenous variable, since it is assumed to be determined by the urban sector labor union. Let us examine the comparative static effects of w_x on L_x, L_y, w_y and L_u by differentiating the equations in system (A) with respect to w_x:

$$dL_x / dw_x \big|_{\theta=0} = 1/p(d^2X/dL_x^2) < 0, \tag{10.7}$$

$$dL_y / dw_x \big|_{\theta=0} = [-L_x p(d^2X/dL_x^2) - w_x]/\Delta \gtreqless 0, \tag{10.8}$$

$$dw_y / dw_x \big|_{\theta=0} = (d^2Y/dL_y^2)[-L_x p(d^2X/dL_x^2) - w_x]/\Delta \gtreqless 0, \tag{10.9}$$

$$dL_u / dw_x \big|_{\theta=0} = [L_x p(d^2X/dL_x^2) + w_x$$
$$+ (L_x + L_u)d^2Y/dL_y^2 - w_y] \gtreqless 0. \tag{10.10}$$

Note that (10.7) through (10.10) are evaluated at the zero enforcement level of the profit-sharing scheme, $\theta = 0$. The signs of d^2X/dL_x^2 and d^2Y/dL_y^2 are both negative due to the assumption (iii) of strict concavity of the strict production functions. Hence, $\Delta \equiv -p(d^2X/dL_x^2)\{-w_y + (L_x + L_u)d^2Y/dL_y^2\} < 0$. Given the concavity of the production functions (assumption (iii)), we find that the sign of (10.7) is negative, while the signs of (10.8), (10.9) and (10.10) are indeterminate. Substituting (10.7) into (10.8), (10.9) and (10.10), equations (10.8), (10.9) and (10.10) are, respectively, rewritten as:

$$dL_y / dw_x \big|_{\theta=0} = -w_x[(\varepsilon - 1)/\varepsilon]/\Delta, \tag{10.8$'$}$$

$$dw_y / dw_x \big|_{\theta=0} = -w_x(d^2Y/dL_y^2)[(\varepsilon - 1)/\varepsilon]/\Delta, \tag{10.9$'$}$$

$$dL_u / dw_x \big|_{\theta=0} = w_x[(\varepsilon - 1)/\varepsilon]/\Delta - pd^2X/dL_x^2, \tag{10.10$'$}$$

where $\varepsilon \equiv -(w_x/L_x) \cdot (dL_x/dw_x) > 0$, the wage elasticity of demand for urban labor. If ε exceeds one or does not, then the sign of (10.8)$'$ is positive or negative, and the sign of (10.9)$'$ is negative or positive, and the sign of (10.10)$'$ is indefinite or positive, since $\Delta < 0$, $d^2X/dL_x^2 < 0$ and $d^2Y/dL_y^2 < 0$ from the assumptions (iii) and (iv). From equations (10.7) through (10.10), we can define L_x, L_y, w_y and L_u as functions of w_x, respectively, $L_x \equiv L_x(w_x)$, $L_y \equiv L_y(w_x)$, $w_y \equiv w_y(w_x)$ and $L_u \equiv L_u(w_x)$.

Next, we consider how the wage of urban labor, w_x is determined. We assume that the urban labor union obtains an economic rent as well as a share of the profits of urban firms (which can be thought of as similar to the well-known bonus of the Japanese firm).[7] This urban labor union monopolistically sets the wage (see Jackman (1988)) (assumption (i)), and sets it at a rate higher than the minimum wage. Hence, the rent earned by the urban labor union, R, is composed of its economic rent, $(w_x - \overline{w})L_x$, and a share of the urban firms' profits, $\theta\pi_x$,

$$R \equiv (w_x - \overline{w})L_x(w_x) + \theta\pi_x(w_x), \tag{10.11}$$

where $\pi_x(w_x) \equiv pX(L_x(w_x), K_x) - (w_x L_x(w_x) + r_x K_x) > 0$. The urban labor union maximizes its rent with respect to w_x. The first-order condition for the labor union is:

$$dR/dw_x = L_x + (w_x - \overline{w})dL_x/dw_x + \theta d\pi_x/dw_x = 0, \qquad (10.12)$$

where $d\pi_x/dw_x$ is $-L_x$ from (10.4) and (10.7). The labor union chooses the optimal w_x such that (10.12) is satisfied.

We assume that the LDC's government can determine a share parameter, θ (see Fung (1989a,b)). From (10.12), we define $R_{w_x} (\equiv dR/dw_x)$ as

$$R_{w_x} = R_{w_x}(w_x; \theta). \qquad (10.13)$$

The total differential of (10.13) is

$$R_{w_x w_x} dw_x + R_{w_x \theta} d\theta = 0. \qquad (10.14)$$

From (10.14), the effect on w_x of introducing the profit-sharing scheme is obtained:

$$dw_x/d\theta \big|_{\theta=0} = -R_{w_x \theta}/R_{w_x w_x} < 0, \qquad (10.15)$$

where $R_{w_x \theta} = -L_x$ from (10.12). From the second-order condition for the rent maximization of the urban labor union, the sign of $R_{w_x w_x}$ is strictly negative. Hence, from (10.15) the effect of an increase in θ on w_x is negative. The introduction of a profit-sharing scheme by the LDC's government causes the urban worker's wages to fall.

The effects of the profit-sharing scheme on L_x, L_y, w_y and L_u are, by using the chain rule, derived from (10.7), (10.8)', (10.9)', (10.10)' and (10.15):

$$dL_x/d\theta \big|_{\theta=0} = (dL_x/dw_x)(dw_x/d\theta) > 0, \qquad (10.16a)$$

$$dL_y/d\theta \big|_{\theta=0} = (dL_y/dw_x)(dw_x/d\theta) \gtrless 0, \qquad (10.16b)$$

when $\varepsilon \gtrless 1$,

$$dw_y/d\theta \big|_{\theta=0} = (dw_y/dw_x)(dw_x/d\theta) \gtrless 0, \qquad (10.16c)$$

when $\varepsilon \gtrless 1$, and

$$dL_u/d\theta \big|_{\theta=0} = (dL_u/dw_x)(dw_x/d\theta) < 0, \qquad (10.16d)$$

when $\varepsilon < 1$.

We know the following two scenarios from (10.15) and (10.16a) through (10.16d). We find from (10.16a) that the effect of an increase in θ on L_x is positive, irrespective of the magnitude of ε. This causes the demand for urban labor to increase. Therefore, if $\varepsilon > 1$, then it promotes intersectoral migration from the rural area to the urban area, thereby raising the wage of rural labor, while it does not necessarily reduce the unemployment of urban labor. Next, if $\varepsilon < 1$, then an increase in the employment of urban labor due to a decline in the wage of urban labor reduces the unemployment of urban labor. A reduction in the urban labor's wage also partly causes the expected urban wage to decrease, thereby reducing the differential between the expected urban and rural earnings. This gives rise to reverse migration from the urban sector to the rural sector and an increase in the employment of rural labor, and hence reduces the wage of rural labor.

Moreover, from (10.7), (10.8)', (10.15), (10.16a) and (10.16b), we obtain the total employment effect of the profit-sharing scheme in this LDC:

$$d(L_x + L_y)/d\theta\big|_{\theta=0} = (dL_x/dw_x + dL_y/dw_x)(dw_x/d\theta)$$

$$= [\{1/(pd^2X/dL_x^2)\} - w_x\{(\varepsilon-1)/\varepsilon\}/\Delta]$$

$$\times(dw_x/d\theta) > 0, \tag{10.17}$$

when $\varepsilon < 1$.

The sign of the second term in the first bracket on the right-hand side is indeterminate, since we cannot know whether the sign of $(\varepsilon-1)$ is negative or not. Consequently, the effect of the profit-sharing scheme on $(L_x + L_y)$ is ambiguous. However, we find that if $\varepsilon < 1$, then the sign of (10.17) is positive from the assumptions (iii) and (iv), (10.15) and $\Delta < 0$. This implies that an introduction of the profit-sharing plan increases the overall employment in the LDC economy, when the wage elasticity of urban employment is less than unity.

10.3 Welfare effect

Let us turn to the examination of the welfare effect of introducing a profit-sharing scheme. A duality approach often used in trade literature is utilized. Let the demand side of the economy be denoted by an expenditure function:

$$E(p,1,u) = \min(pC_x + C_y) \text{ subject to } u(C_x, C_y) \geq u. \tag{10.18}$$

Expenditure is minimized with respect to the demand for the two final goods, C_x and C_y, subject to obtaining a utility level, u, with a strictly quasi-concave utility function $u(C_x, C_y)$.

The economy's budget constraint is given by

$$E(p,1,u) = pX + Y ,   \tag{10.19}$$

which implies that national expenditures equal the final gross revenues of sectors X and Y.[8]

Totally differentiating (10.19) and defining the welfare change by $dW \equiv E_u du$, we obtain

$$dW = p(dX / dL_x)dL_x + (dY / dL_y)dL_y .   \tag{10.20}$$

From (10.4), (10.5), (10.7), (10.8)', (10.15), (10.16a) and (10.16b), (10.20) is rewritten as

$$dW / d\theta\big|_{\theta=0} = (w_x dL_x / dw_x + w_y dL_y / dw_x)(dw_x / d\theta)$$
$$= [\{w_x w_y - w_x(L_x + L_y)(d^2Y / dL_y{}^2)$$
$$-w_x w_y((\varepsilon-1)/\varepsilon)\} / \Delta](dw_x / d\theta) .   \tag{10.21}$$

We can find from the assumptions (iii) and (iv), (10.15) and $\Delta < 0$ that if $\varepsilon < 1$, then the sign of (10.21) is positive. This means that an introduction of a profit-sharing scheme by the LDC's government makes the LDC's welfare higher, when ε is less than one. We obtain the following proposition.

Proposition [Yoshida (2000a)]
The introduction of a profit-sharing scheme improves the LDC's welfare, when the wage elasticity of urban employment is less than one.

10.4 Concluding remarks

In this chapter, we examine the effects of introducing a profit-sharing scheme in the urban sectors of a less developed country (LDC). We use a generalized Harris and Todaro (1970) model in which the LDC has a dual economy with urban-specific unemployment, and assume that the wage of urban labor is determined by a labor union. We introduce a profit-sharing scheme in the urban sector, which has the following interesting effects, *when the wage elasticity of demand for urban labor is less than unity.* In the urban sector, there are decreases in wages and the unemployment rate and an increase in employment. A reduction in urban wages reduces the expected urban-rural wages differential, and hence induces rural-migrant labor to return to the rural area. In the rural sector, there is an increase in employment, and hence wages decrease. The LDC's welfare may increase, since national employment increases. Hence, if a profit-sharing scheme is introduced in the urban sectors of the LDC, this scheme may reduce the large-scale urban unemployment problems of the LDC and improve the country's welfare under some circumstances.

Notes

* This chapter was first published in the Indian Journal of Applied Economics (2000a).
1 Calvo (1978) developed a model very similar to our model. However, he did not examine the economic effects of a profit-sharing scheme.
2 As the labor union is a monopoly union existing in an environment of perfectly competitive firms, the union can monopolistically determine its own wage rate. Therefore, it will set the wage rate at a level higher than the minimum wage (see Jackman (1988)).
3 We assume that the fixed minimum urban wage level is greater than the labor-market clearing level.
4 An employed urban worker is assumed to earn a wage income, w_x, and a share of the urban firm's profit, $\theta \pi_x / L_x$.
5 See footnote 6 on the definition of urban firms' profits.
6 The profit functions of the firms of the urban and rural sectors are, respectively, expressed as follows:

$$\pi_x = pX(L_x, K_x) - (w_x L_x + r_x K_x),$$

$$\pi_y = Y(L_y, K_y) - (w_y L_y + r_y K_y),$$

where r_x and r_y, respectively, are the rental rates of capital in the urban and rural areas. We assume in the short-run that both urban and rural firms can make positive profits *under perfect competition with barriers to entry* (see the comments below and equation (13) on p. 430 in Chen and Choi (1994)).
7 Twice a year, Japanese workers receive bonuses, which can amount to four months of their wages or more, depending upon their firms' performance [see Fung (1989a)].
8 We assume that the urban firms equally divide their net profits, $(1 - \theta)\pi_x$, among the workers in the urban area and that the rural firms equally divide their profits, π_y, among rural workers (see the comments below equation (9.13) on p. 430 in Chen and Choi (1994)).

Afterword

Immigration arise as a result of many factors. Some of those factors are (1) the large difference of income between an abundant country and a poor country, (2) internal disturbances caused by political, ethnic and religious frictions, (3) a reduction in the costs of international migration, (4) a formation of an underground economy in a migrant-receiving country, and (5) to gather a migrant's family from his native country. The labor-importing country characterized as the developed country is disposed to control such immigrations by making use of two main tools: border patrol and employer sanctions. Hence, it is inevitable for the above mentioned factors to generate illegal immigration.

First, we surveyed the society of developed countries and immigration in the Introduction. We explained not only why the immigration take place but also the negative effects that the irregular aliens bring about in the host country's labor market. We also outlined immigration laws of the labor-importing country.

We noticed that no one has examined the effects of the immigration laws on the migrant-source country's welfare as well as the two-country combined (global) welfare. Nor has anyone analyzed whether or not there is an optimal level of the internal inspection in terms of the host country's welfare. The aim of this book is to investigate such issues not considered in prior reseaches on illegal immigration.

Second, in Part I, we assessed immigration policies, i.e., employer sanctions and border patrol, from the viewpoint of a combined (global) income of two countries consisting of a labor-importing country and a labor-exporting country. When capital is immobile between the two countries, the enforcement of the immigration regulations is harmful in terms of global welfare. However, in the presence of capital mobility, each enforcement is globally beneficial if some conditions, (3C.1) in the Chapter 3 or (4C.1) in the Chapter 4, hold. The result is contrary to that in the presence of capital immobility. In a pre-enforcement equilibrium, there is a distortion of tax imposed on earnings of home capital employed in the foreign country. An intensification of a second distortion, the employer sanctions, may enhance the global income for the standard second-best reasons.

In Chapter 5, we also used the models of Chapters 2 and 3 and introduced a budget constraint on the host country's government. We examined the welfare effects of finance-constrained internal enforcement.

172

If the costs of internal enforcement are assumed to be directly financed by the penalties levied on domestic firms caught employing illegal foreign workers, then this is called the direct fiscal effect (*DFE*). If *DFE* = 0, no additional financing is needed. However, if *DFE* ≠ 0, other financing methods are required to ensure a balanced budget, such as income taxation of domestic workers.

Regardless of whether capital is internationally mobile or immobile, pre-enforcement equilibrium involves an income tax distortion (see equations (5.19) and (5.38)). Internal enforcement introduces a second distortion that may improve global welfare for standard second-best reasons, which is similar to Chapter 3. When the direct fiscal effect is positive and the indirect fiscal effect is negative, enforcement will improve global welfare under some circumstances.

When the direct fiscal effect is positive, it will cause the indirect fiscal effect to decrease. In short, the direct fiscal effect reduces the degree of the initial income tax distortion. A positive direct fiscal effect implies that enforcement brings about some welfare gain, since revenues from enforcement penalties are larger than the costs of enforcement. Thus, under certain conditions, internal enforcement improves global welfare.

Third, in Part II, we explored whether or not there is an optimal level of internal enforcement viewed in the light of the migrant-importing country's welfare. Chapter 6 re-introduced the Bond and Chen (1987) model, using a Cobb-Douglas production function. Our results were that the immigration bureau of the host country can optimally put the employer sanctions into force from the viewpoint of the country's welfare, irrespective of the presence or absence of capital mobility.

Chapter 7 incorporated a budget constraint of the home country's government into the model of Chapter 6. We also attempted to discover an optimal level of the enforcement in terms of the migrant-receiving country's income. We obtained that there was an optimal enforcement level of the interior inspection when the direct fiscal effect of the enforcement surpasses the indirect fiscal effect irrespective of the immobility or mobility of the capital. However, in order to optimally enforce internal scrutiny, the immigration authority must keep to several necessary conditions. Those are to make an effort to minimize expenditure on the enforcement of employer sanctions, to implement innovative techniques to detect and apprehend illegal foreign workers, to recover the cost of inspecting home firms and to minimize the cost of collecting income taxes from home workers.

Fourth, we analyzed the economic impacts of a profit-sharing scheme. It is well known that a profit-sharing policy is enforced to increase employment in an economy (Weitzman (1983, 1985, 1987), Pohjola (1987), Jackman (1988), Fung (1989a,b)). Chapters 8 and 9 developed a two-country, one-good, two-factor model of profit-sharing. A home capital abundant country absorbs large scale immigration from a foreign labor abundant country. The migrants compete with domestic unskilled labor in a home unskilled labor market. This causes a lot of unemployment of unskilled workers in the home market. We concluded that an introduction of the profit-sharing plan by the host country's government might increase employment of the home workers, decrease immigration, and improve the labor-receiving country's welfare.

Chapter 10 introduced a generalized Harris-Todaro (1970) model of profit-sharing. We assumed that a less developed country's (LDC's) government introduces the profit-sharing policy in an urban sector. The urban region receives many migrants from a rural region, which raises unemployment in the urban region. We inquired into the effects of the profit-sharing system on the unemployment and the country's welfare.

We obtained the following interesting outcomes, *when the wage elasticity of demand for urban labor is less than unity.* In the urban sector, there are decreases in wages and the unemployment rate and an increase in employment. A reduction in urban wages reduces the expected urban-rural wages differential, and hence obliges rural-migrant labor to move back to the rural area. In the rural region, there is an increase in employment due to returned rural-migrant labor, and hence wages decrease. The LDC's welfare may increase, since national employment increases. Hence, if a profit-sharing scheme is introduced in the urban sectors of the LDC, then this scheme may reduce the large-scale urban unemployment problems of the LDC and improve the country's welfare.

We recommend that the profit-sharing plan be commenced in the urban sector of the LDC. If the profit-sharing policy is well enforced, then the unemployment problem in the urban area may be resolved, and the LDC's economy may experience beneficial effects.

As described in the opening of this section, industrialized countries may receive more immigration mainly from LDCs hereafter. The migrations often bring about illegal immigration and unemployment of the host countries' workers. Most developed country's governments deal with foreign irregular workers by carrying out employer sanctions.

However, the average probability of detection on the irregular workers is in the neighborhood of 2-3 % (see Figure 1.1). Thus internal enforcement works poorly. The new immigration law, employer sanctions prescribed by IRCA has given the US INS more resources to enhance this agency's enforcement power. For fiscal year 1985, INS Commissioner

Alan C. Nelson had asked for 574.5 million dollars; by 1995, INS appropriations were nearly 1.15 billion dollars, a budgetary increase of roughly 200 percent (US House of Representatives; Salaries and expenses appropriations for fiscal years 1985-1995).

The objectives of the book are (1) to appraise border patrol and the employer sanctions in terms of two-country combined (global) income, and (2) to find out an optimal level of the interior enforcement in view of the migrant-importing country's welfare.

Illegal immigration is a problem to not only a labor importing country but also to a labor exporting country, since the implementation of strict immigration policies, i.e., border patrol and employer sanctions, affects both economies. We observe that the disparity in income levels between South and North countries gives rise to illegal immigrations to the North. If the reinforced internal enforcement leads to simultaneous increases in both countries' incomes, then it can diminish undocumented immigrations. Therefore, it is consequential to examine the effectiveness of the employer sanctions concerning the global welfare.

Because huge budgets on both border and internal enforcement are appropriated to the US DHS (formerly INS) each fiscal year, it follows from this that it is important to discover an optimal level of the internal inspection regarding the labor importing country's welfare. In order for stricter internal inspections to raise US welfare, the US DHS should try to minimize expenditure on the enforcement of employer sanctions, implement innovative techniques to detect and apprehend illegal foreign workers, recover the cost of inspecting home firms, and minimize the cost of collecting income taxes from home workers.

We propose from the gobal viewpoint that the optimal enforcement of the employer sanctions should make the migrant-source country's income higher. This may reduce illegal immigrations from the South to the North. We confirmed in Chapter 3 that tougher employer sanctions improve the labor exporting country's welfare, when capital is internationally mobile. Also, we showed in Chapters 6 and 7 that in the presence of capital mobility the immigration bureau of the host country can optimally put the interior enforcement into operation from the viewpoint of the country's welfare given some necessary conditions. Capital mobility between the North and the South actually occurs. Hence, in the real world, the optimal enforcement of the employer sanctions by the immigration authority of the host country can lessen irregular aliens to the North. Also, it need scarcely be said that capital exports to the South may also help induce a decline in clandestine immigration.

Bibliography

Acevedo, D. and T. J. Espenshade, 1992, Implications of a North American Free Trade Agreement for Mexican migration into the United States, Population and Development Review 18, 729-744.

Agiomirgianakis, G. and A. Zervoyianni, 2001, Macroeconomic equilibrium with illegal immigration, Economic Modelling 18, 181-202.

Alston, L. J. and J. P. Ferrie, 1993, The bracero program and farm labor legislation in World War II, in G. T. Mills and H. Rockoff eds., The sinews of war: Essays on the economic history of World War II (Iowa State University Press, Ames, Iowa), 129-149.

Altonji, J. G., and D. Card, 1991, The effects of immigration on the labor market outcomes of less-skilled natives, in J. M. Abowd and R. B. Freeman eds., Immigration, trade and the labor market (University of Chicago Press, Chicago).

Anderson, S., and M. Devereux, 1989, Profit-sharing and optimal labour contacts, Canadian Journal of Economics 22, 425-433.

Arreola, D. D. and J. R. Curtis, 1993, The Mexican border cities: Landscape anatomy and place personality (The University of Arizona Press, Tucson, Arizona), 201-208.

Asahi Shimbun, Oranda kain nanmin shinseisha ni kikoku semaru houan kaketsu (in Japanese), 18 Feburuary, 2004.

Baldacci, E., L. Inglese and S. Strozza, 1999, Determinants of foreign workers' wages in two Italian regions with high illegal immigration, Labour 13, 675-709.

Bandyopadhyay, S. and S. C. Bandyopadhyay, 1998, Illegal immigration: A supply side analysis, Journal of Development Economics 57, 343-360.

Bangfu, M., 1994, Snake-Head (in Japanese) (Soshisha, Tokyo).

Batra, R. N. and A. C. Seth, 1977, Unemployment, tariffs and the theory of international trade, Journal of International Economics 7, 295-306.

BBC News, EU sea patrols target illegal immigrants, 28 January, 2003.

BBC News, Illegal workers face deportation, 26 February, 2003.

BBC News, 'Illegal immigrants' search begins, 27 February, 2003.

BBC News, Iraqi asylum decisions 'on hold', 24 March, 2003.

BBC News, EU 'support' for asylum plan, 28 March, 2003.

Bean, F., B. Edmonston and J. S. Passel, 1990, Undocumented migration to the United States: IRCA and the experience of the 1980s (The Urban Institute Press, Washington, D.C.).

Bean, F. D., T. J. Espenshade, M. J. White and R. F. Dymowski, 1990, Post-IRCA changes in the volume and composition of undocumented migration to the United States: An assessment based on apprehensions data, in F. D. Bean, B. Edmonston and J. S. Passel eds., Undocumented migration to the United States: IRCA and the experience of the 1980s (The Urban Institute Press, Washington, D.C.), 111-158.

Bean, F. D., W. P. Frisbie, E. Telles and B. L. Lowell, 1992, The economic impact of undocumented workers in the Southwest of the United States, in J. R. Weeks and C. R. Ham, eds., Demographic dynamics of the US-Mexico border (Texas Western Press, El Paso), 219-237.

Bean, F. D., B. L. Lowell and L. J. Taylor, 1988, Undocumented Mexican immigrants and the earnings of other workers in the United States, Demography 25, 35-52.

Bean, F. D., E. E. Tells and B. L. Lowell, 1987, Undocumented migration to the United States: Perceptions and evidence, Population and Development Review 13, 671-690.

Becker, G., 1968, Crime and punishment: An economic approach, Journal of Political Economy 76, 169-217.

Bensäid, B. and R. J. Gary-Bobo, 1991, Negotiation of profit-sharing contracts in industry, European Economic Review 35, 1069-1085.

Beranek, W., 1982, The illegal alien work force, demand for unskilled labor, and the minimum wage, Journal of Labor Research 3, 89-99.

Bhagwati, J. N. and T. N. Srinivasan, 1983, On the choice between capital and labour mobility, Journal of International Economics 14, 209-221.

Birchard, K., 1997, Dublin Convention on handling of EU asylum seekers becomes law, The Lancet 350, No. 9079.

Blanchflower, D. G. and A. J. Oswald, 1987, Profit-sharing – Can it work?, Oxford Economic Papers 39, 1-19.

Bond, E., 1989, Optimal policy towards international factor movements with a country specific factor, European Economic Review 33, 1329-1344.

Bond, E. and Tain-Jy Chen, 1987, The welfare effects of illegal migration, Journal of International Economics 23, 315-328.

Borjas, G. J., 1984, The impact of immigrants on the earnings of the native-born, in V. M. Briggs, Jr. and M. Tienda eds., Immigration: Issues and policies (Olympus Publishing, Salt Lake City, Utah), 83-126.

Borjas, G. J., 1986a, Immigrants and the US labor market, in S. Pozo ed., Essays on legal and illegal immigration (W. E. Upjohn Institute for Employment Research, Kalamazoo, Michigan), 7-20.

Borjas, G. J., 1986b, The sensitivity of labor demand functions to the choice of dependent variable, Review of Economics and Statistics 68, 56-66.

Borjas, G. J., 1987, Immigrants, minorities, and labor market competition, Industrial and Labor Relations Review 40, 382-392.

Borjas, G. J., 1990, Friends or strangers (Basic Books, Inc., Publishers, New York).

Borjas, G. J., 1994, The economics of immigration, Journal of Economic Literature 32, 1667-1717.

Borjas, G. J., 1996, The earnings of Mexican immigrants in the United States, Journal of Development Economics 51, 69-98.

Borjas, G. J., R. Freeman and L. Katz, 1992, On the labor market effects of immigration and trade, in G. Borjas and R. Freeman eds., Immigration and the work force (University of Chicago Press, Chicago).

Borjas, G. J., R. Freeman and K. Lang, 1991, Undocumented Mexican-born workers in the United States: How many, how permanent?, in M. Abowd and R. B. Freeman eds., Immigration, trade, and the labor market (University of Chicago Press, Chicago, IL), 77-100.

Borjas, G. J. and V. Ramey, 1993, Foreign competition, market power and wage inequality: Theory and evidence, NBER Working Paper 4556.

Bratsberg, B., 1995, Legal versus illegal US immigration and source country characteristics, Southern Economic Journal 61, 715-727.

Brecher, R. A. and E. U. Choudhri, 1987, International migration versus foreign investment in the presence of unemployment, Journal of International Economics 23, 329-342.

Briggs, V. M., 1975, Illegal aliens: The need for a more restrictive border policy, Social Science Quarterly 56, 477-484.

Briggs, Jr. V. M., 1991, The Immigration Act of 1990: Retreat from reform, Population and Environment: A Journal of Interdisciplinary Studies 13, 89-93.

Brochmann, G. and T. Hammar, 1999, Mechanisms of immigration control: A comparative analysis of European regulation policies (Berg, Oxford).

Bucci, G. A. and R. Tenorio, 1996, On financing the internal enforcement of illegal immigration policies, Journal of Population Economics 9, 65-81.

Bulow, J. I., J. D. Geanakoplos and P. D. Klemperer, 1985, Multimarket oligopoly: Strategic substitutes and complements, Journal of Political Economy 93, 485-511.

Burgess, D. F., 1974a, A cost minimization approach to import demand equations, Review of Economics and Statistics 57, 225-234.

Burgess, D. F., 1974b, Production theory and the derived demand for imports, Journal of International Economics 4, 103-117.

Burgess, D. F., 1975, Duality theory and pitfalls in the specification of technologies, Journal of Econometrics 3, 105-121.

Bustamante, J. A., 1990, Undocumented migration from Mexico to the United States: Preliminary findings of the Zapata Canyon Project, in F. D. Bean, B. Edmonston and J. S. Passel, eds., Undocumented migration to the United States: IRCA and the experience of the 1980s (Rand Corporation, Santa Monica; Urban Institute, Washington, D.C.; distributed by University Press of America, Lanham, Md.), 211-226.

Calavita, K., 1998, Gaps and contradictions in US immigration policy: An analysis of recent reform efforts, in D. Jacobson ed., The immigration reader – America in a multidisciplinary perspective (Blackwell Publishers, Oxford, UK), 92-110.

California Department of Justice, 1989, Apprehension recidivism in the San Diego sector, Western region, US Border Patrol, INS.

Calvo, G. A., 1978, Urban unemployment and wage determination in LDC's: Trade unions in the Harris-Todaro model, International Economic Review 19, pp.65-81.

Calvo, G. and S. Wellisz, 1983, International factor mobility and national advantage, Journal of International Economics 14, 103-114.

Campos, J. E. and D. Lien, 1995, Political instability and illegal immigration, Journal of Population Economics 8, 23-33.

Carter, T. J., 1993, Efficiency wages and international factor mobility, International Economic Journal 7, 13-29.

Carter, T. J., 1999, Illegal immigration in an efficiency wage model, Journal of International Economics 49, 385-401.

Chang, W. W., 1981, Production externalities, variable returns to scale, and the theory of trade, International Economic Review 22, 511-525.

Chavez, L. R., 1992, Paradise at a cost: The incorporation of undocumented Mexican immigrants into a local-level labor market, in J. A. Bustamante, C. W. Reynolds, and R. A. Hinojosa-Ojeda eds., US-Mexico relations: Labor market interdependence (Stanford University Press, Stanford), 271-301.

Chen, J. and E. K. Choi, 1994, Trade policies and welfare in a Harris-Todaro Economy, Southern Economic Journal, 61, 426-434.

Chiswick, B. R., 1978, The effects of Americanization on the earnings of foreign-born men, Journal of Political Economy 85, 897-922.

Chiswick, B. R., 1982, The impact of immigration on the level and distribution of economic well-being, in B. R. Chiswick, ed., The Gateway: US Immigration Issues and Policies (American Enterprise Institute, Washington, D.C.), 289-313.

Chiswick, B. R., 1986a, Illegal aliens: A preliminary report on an employee-employer survey, American Economic Review Proceedings 72, 253-257.

Chiswick, B. R., 1986b, The illegal alien policy dilemma, in S. Pozo, ed., Essays on legal and illegal immigration (W. E. Upjohn Institute for Employment Research, Kalamazoo, Michigan), 73-87.

Chiswick, B. R., 1988a, Illegal immigration and immigration control, Journal of Economic Perspective 2, 101-115.

Chiswick, B. R., 1988b, Illegal aliens: Their employment and employers, (W. E. Upjohn Institute for Employment Research, Kalamazoo, Michigan).

Chiswick, B. R., 1992, Immigration, language, and ethnicity: Canada and the United States (AEI Press, Washington, D.C.).

Cline, W. R., 1997, Trade and income distribution (Institute for International Economics, Washington).

CNN News, EU seeks to curb illegal immigration, 8 February, 2001.

CNN News, Amnesty: Iraq war cover for human rights abuses, 29 March, 2003.

Cobb-Clark, D. A., C. R. Shiells and B. L. Lowell, 1995, Immigration reform: The effects of employer sanctions and legalization on wages, Journal of Labor Economics 13, 472-498.

Contini, B., 1982, The second economy in Italy, in V. Tanzi ed., The underground economy in the United States and abroad (D. C. Heath and Company, Lexington, Massachusetts), 199-208.

Contini, B., 1989, The irregular economy of Italy: A survey of contributions, in A. Portes, M. Castells, and L. Benton, eds., The informal economy: Studies in advanced and less developed countries (Johns Hopkins University Press, Baltimore).

Cornelius, W. A., 1989, Impacts of the 1986 US immigration law on emigration from rural Mexican sending communities, Population and Development Review 15, 689-705.

Cornelius, W. A., 1990, Impacts of the 1986 US immigration law on emigration from rural Mexican sending communities, in F. D. Bean, B. Edmonston and J. S. Passel eds., Undocumented migration to the United States: IRCA and the experience of the 1980s (The Urban Institute Press, Washington, D.C.), 227-249.

Corwin, A. F., 1983, The numbers game: Estimates of illegal aliens in the United States, 1970-1981, Law and Contemporary Problems 45, 223-297.

Crane, K., J. Asch, J. Zorn Heilbrunn and C. Cullinane, 1990, The effect of employment sanctions on the flow of undocumented immigrants to the United States (Program for Research on Immigration Policy, The RAND Corporation (Report JRI-03), Santa Monica, California, and The Urban Institute (UI Report 90-8), Washington, D.C.).

Davila, A., A. K. Bohara and R. Saenz, 1993, Accent penalties and the earnings of Mexican Americans, Social Science Quarterly 74, 902-916.

Davila, A, J. A. Pagan and M. V. Grau, 1999, Immigration reform, the INS and the distribution of interior and border enforcement resources, Public Choice 99, 327-345.

DeFreitas, G. and A. Marshall, 1984, Immigration and wage growth in US manufacturing in the 1970's, in B. D. Dennis ed., Proceedings of the thirty-sixth annual meeting, Dec. 28-30, 1983, San Francisco (Industrial Relations Research Association), 148-156.

Del Boca, D. and F. Forte, 1982, Recent empirical surveys and theoretical interpretations of the parallel economy in Italy, in V. Tanzi ed., The underground economy in the United States and abroad (D.C. Heath and Company, Lexington, Massachusetts), 181-197.

Dell'Aringa, C. and F. Neri, 1987, Illegal immigration and the informal economy in Italy, Labour, Review of Economics and Industrial Relations 1, 107-126.

Dillin, J., 1986, Illegal aliens flood across US Border, Christian Science Monitor 21.

Djajic, S., 1987, Illegal aliens, unemployment and immigration policy, Journal of Development Economics 25, 235-249.

Djajic, S., 1997, Illegal immigration and resource allocation, International Economic Review 38, 97-117.

Donato, K. M., J. Durand and D. S. Massey, 1992, Stemming the tide? Assessing the deterrent effects of the immigration reform and control act, Demography 29, 139-157.

Donato, K. M. and D. S. Massey, 1993, Effects of the Immigration Reform and Control Act on the wages of Mexican migrants, Social Science Quarterly 74, 523-541.

Dorantes, C. A. and Wei-Chiao Huang, 1997, Unemployment, immigration, and NAFTA: A panel study of ten major US industries, Journal of Labor Research 18, 613-619.

Durand, J., D. S. Massey and E. A. Parrado, 1999, The new era of Mexican migration to the United States, Journal of American History 86, No. 2, 518-536.

Epstein, G. S., 2003, Labor market interactions between legal and illegal immigrants, Review of Development Economics 7, 30-43.

Espenshade, T. J., 1990, Undocumented migration to the United States: Evidence from a repeated trials model, in F. D. Bean, B. Edmonston and J. S. Passel eds., Undocumented migration to the United States: IRCA and the experience of the 1980s (The Urban Institute Press, Washington, D.C.), 159-181.

Espenshade, T. J., 1994, Does the threat of border apprehension deter undocumented US immigration?, Population and Development Review 20, 871-892.

Espenshade, T. J. and D. Acevedo, 1995, Migrant cohort size, enforcement effort, and the apprehension of undocumented aliens, Population Research and Policy Review 14, 145-172.

Ethier, W. J., 1985, International trade and labor migration, American Economic Review 75, 691-707.

Ethier, W. J., 1986a, Illegal immigration: The host-country problem, American Economic Review 76, 56-71.

Ethier, W. J., 1986b, Illegal immigration, American Economic Review 76, 258-262.

EUROPA – Gateway to the European Union, 2004, EUROPA – Justice and Home Affairs – Freedom Security and Justice – Illegal immigration European Commission (http://europa.eu.int/index_en.htm).

European Report, Justice and home affairs: Green light for UK to take on some aspects of the Schengen Agreement, 28 July, 1999.

Faini, R. and A. Venturini, 1993, Trade, aid and migrations – Some basic policy issues, European Economic Review 37, 435-442.

FAIR, Federation for American Immigration Reform, 1989, Tens steps to securing America's borders, Washington, D.C.

Farber, H. S., 1986, The analysis of union behaviour, in O. C. Ashenfelter and R. Layard eds., Handbook of labor economics, Vol. 2 (North-Holland, Amsterdam), 1039-1089.

Fogel, W., 1977, Illegal aliens workers in the United States, Industrial Relations 16, 243-263.

Fogel, W., 1982, Twentieth-century Mexican migration to the United States, in B. R. Chiswick ed., The gateway: US immigration issues and policies (American Enterprise Institute for Public Policy Research, Washington, D.C.), 193-221.

Friedberg, R. M., 2000, You can't take it with you? – Immigrant assimilation and the portability of human capital, Journal of Labor Economics 18, 221-251.

Fung, K. C., 1989a, Unemployment, profit-sharing and Japan's economic success, European Economic Review 33, 783-796.

Fung, K. C., 1989b, Profit-sharing and European unemployment, European Economic Review 33, 1789-1798.

Garcia y Griego, M., 1979, El volumen de la migracion de Mexicanos no documentados a los Estados Unidos: Nuevas hipotesis (Ceniet, Mexico City).

Garcia y Griego, M. and F. Giner de los Rios, 1985, Es vulnerable la economia Mexicana a la applicacion de politicas migratorias estadounidenses?, in M. Garcia y Griego and G. Vega eds., Mexico-Estados Unidos: 1984 (Colegio de Mexico, Mexico City), 221-272.

Gatsios, K., P. Hatzipanayotou and M. S. Michael, 1999, International migration, the provision of public goods, and welfare, Journal of Development Economics 60, 559-575.

Gaytan-Fregoso, H. and S. Lahiri, 2000, Foreign aid and illegal immigration, Journal of Development Economics 63, 515-527.

Gaytan-Fregoso, H. and S. Lahiri, 2001, Regionalism and illegal immigration in North America – A theoretical analysis, in Sajal Lahiri ed., Regionalism and globalization – Theory and practice (Routledge, London and New York), 92-109.

Gerking, S. D. and J. H. Mutti, 1980, Costs and benefits of illegal immigration: Key issues for government policy, Social Science Quarterly 61, 71-85.

Gianaris, N. V., 1998, The North American Free Trade Agreement and the European Union (Praeger, London).

Gill, A. and S. Long, 1989, Is there an immigration status wage differential between legal and undocumented workers?: Evidence from the Los Angeles garment industry, Social Science Quarterly 70, 164-173.

Gimpel, J. G. and J. R. Edwards, Jr., 1999, The congressional politics of immigration reform (Allyn and Bacon, MA), 93-99.

Global Finance, Fighting to recover, November 1996.

Gonzalez, J. G., 1994, Illegal immigration in the presence of labor unions, International Economic Journal 8, 57-70.

Gonzalez-Arechiga, B., 1992, Undocumented Mexicans on the Mexican northern border: Their identity and role in regional development, in Jorge-A. Bustamante, Clark-W. Reynolds, and Raul-A. Hinojosa-Ojeda eds., US-Mexico relations: Labor market interdependence (Stanford University Press, Stanford, CA), 319-352.

Goto, J., 1998, The impact of migrant workers on the Japanese economy: Trickle vs. flood, Japan and the World Economy 10, 63-83.

Grazia, R. D., 1982, Clandestine employment: A problem of our times, in V. Tanzi ed., The underground economy in the United States and abroad (D.C. Heath and Company, Lexington, Massachusetts), 29-43.

Greenwood, M. J. and G. L. Hunt, 1995, Economic effects of immigrants on native and foreign-born workers: Complementarity, substitutability, and other channels of influence, Southern Economic Journal 61, 1076-1097.

Greenwood, M. J., G. L. Hunt and U. Kohli, 1997, The factor-market consequences of unskilled immigration to the United States, Labour Economics 4, 1-28.

Greenwood, M. J. and J. M. McDowell, 1986, The factor market consequences of US immigration, Journal of Economic Literature 24, 1738-1772.

Grossman, J. B., 1982, The substitutability of natives and immigrants in production, Review of Economics and Statistics 64, 596-603.

Grossman, J. B., 1984, Illegal immigrants and domestic employment, Industrial and Labor Relations Review 37, 240-251.

Hanami, C. and Y. Kuwahara, 1993, Anatano rinjin gaikokujin rodosha (in Japanese) (Toyo-Keizai Shinposha, Tokyo).

Hanami, C., 1997, Boeki to kokusai-rodokijun (in Japanese) (Nippon Rodo Kenkyu Kiko, Tokyo).

Hanson, G. H., 1996a, Economic integration, intraindustry trade, and frontier regions, European Economic Review 40, 941-949.

Hanson, G. H., 1996b, Localization economies, vertical organization, and trade, American Economic Review 86, 1266-1278.

Hanson, G. H. and A. Spilimbergo, 1996, Illegal immigration, border enforcement, and relative wages: Evidence from apprehensions at the US-Mexico border, National Bureau of Economic Research Working Paper No. 5592.

Hanson, G. H. and A. Spilimbergo, 1999, Illegal immigration, border enforcement, and relative wages: Evidence from apprehensions at the US-Mexico border, American Economic Review 89, No.5, 1337-1357.

Harper, D., 1995, How will NAFTA affect you?, Industrial Distribution 84.

Harris, J. R. and M. P. Todaro, 1970, Migration, unemployment and development: A two-sector analysis, American Economic Review 60, 126-142.

Hess, K., 1994, Personal communication, US Border Patrol 9.

Heyman, J. M., 1991, Life and labor on the border – Working people of Northeastern Sonora, Mexico, 1886-1986 (The University of Arizona Press, Tucson) 41-45.

Hicks, J. R., 1956, A revision of demand theory (Clarendon Press, Oxford).

Hicks, J. R., 1970, Elasticity of substitution again: Substitutes and complements, Oxford Economic Papers 22, 289-296.

Hill, J. K. and J. E. Pearce, 1987, Enforcing sanctions against employers of illegal aliens, Economic Review, Federal Reserve Bank of Dallas, 1-15.

Hill, J. K. and J. E. Pearce, 1990, The incidence of sanctions against employers of illegal aliens, Journal of Political Economy 98, 28-44.

Hillman, A. L. and A. Weiss, 1999, A theory of permissible illegal immigration, European Journal of Political Economy 15, 585-604.

Hondagneu-Sotelo, P., 1994, Gendered transitions: Mexican experiences of immigration (University of California Press, Berkeley and Los Angeles, California).

Jackman, R., 1988, Profit-sharing in a unionized economy with imperfect competition, International Journal of Industrial Organization 6, 47-57.

Jones, R. W., 1971, Distortions in factor markets and the general equilibrium model of production, Journal of Political Economy 79, 437-459.

Jones, R. W., I. Coelho and S. T. Easton, 1986, The theory of international factor flows; The basic model, Journal of International Economics 20, 313-327.

Kenen, P. B., 1971, Migration, the terms of trade, economic welfare in the source country, in J. N. Bhagwati et. al., ed., Trade, balance of payments and growth (North Holland, Amsterdam), 238-260.

Killingsworth, M. R., 1983, Effects of immigration into the United States on the US labor market: Analytical and policy issues, in M. M. Kritz, ed., US immigration and refugee policy: Global and domestic issues (D.C. Heath and Company, Lexington, Massachusetts), 249-268.

King, A. G., L. Lowell and F. D. Bean, 1986, The effects of Hispanic immigrants on the earnings of native Hispanic Americans, Social Science Quarterly 67, 673-689.

Kossoudji, S. A., 1992, Playing cat and mouse at the US-Mexican border, Demography 29, 159-180.

Kudrle, R. T., 2003, Hegemony strikes out: The US global role in antitrust, tax evasion, and illegal immigration, International Studies Perspectives 4, 52-71.

Levine, P., 1999, The welfare economics of immigration control, Journal of Population Economics 12, 23-43.

Lowell, B. L., 1996, Skilled and family-based immigration: Principles and labor markets, in H. Duleep and P. Wunnava eds., Immigrants and immigration policy: Individual skills, family ties, and group identities (JAI Press Greenwich, CT).

Markusen, J. R. and S. Zahniser, 1999, Liberalisation and incentives for labour migration: Theory with applications to NAFTA, in R. Faini, J. D. Melo and K. F. Zimmermann eds., Migration – The controversies and the evidence (Cambridge University Press, Cambridge, UK) 263-293.

Martin, P. L. and E. B. Sehgal, 1980, Illegal immigration: The guestworker option, Public Policy 28, 207-229.

Massey, D. S., J. Arango, G. Hugo, A. Kouauoci, A. Pellegrino and E. J. Taylor, 1998, Worlds in motion: Understanding international migration at the end of the millennium (Clarendon Press, Oxford), 62-68.

Massey, D. S., K. M. Donato and Z. Liang, 1990, Effects of the immigration reform and control act of 1986: Preliminary data from Mexico, in F. D. Bean, B. Edmonston and J. S. Passel eds., Undocumented migration to the United States: IRCA and the experience of the 1980s (The Urban Institute Press, Washington, D.C.), 183-210.

Massey, D. S. and A. Singer, 1995, New estimates of undocumented Mexican migration and the probability of apprehension, Demography 32, 203-213.

McCarthy, K. F. and R. B. Valdez, 1986, Current and future effects of Mexican immigration in California (Rand Corporation, Santa Monica, California).

Mills, G. T. and H. Rockoff, 1993, The sinews of war: Essays on the economic history of World War II (Iowa State University Press, Ames, Iowa).

Moehring, H. B., 1988, Symbol versus substance in legislative activity: The case of illegal immigration, Public Choice 57, 287-294.

Mohabbat, K. A. and A. J. Dalal, 1983, Factor substitution and import demand for South Korea: A translog analysis, Weltwirtshaftliches Archiv 119, 709-723.

Munoz, C. and P. Gottfried, 1995, Should citizens, legal immigrants, and illegal aliens receive different benefits?, American Enterprise 6, 21-22.

Mühleisen, M and K. F. Zimmermann, 1994, A panel analysis of job changes and unemployment, European Economic Review 38, 793-801.

Muller, T. and T. J. Espenshade, 1985, The fourth wave: California's newest immigrants (The Urban Institute Press, Washington, D.C.).

Neary, P. J, 1978, Dynamic stability and the theory of factor market distortions, American Economic Review 68, 671-682.

Nguyen, T. T., 1989, The parallel market of illegal aliens: A computational approach, World Development 17, 1965-1978.

Nguyen, T. T., 1991, The parallel labor market for illegal aliens, in R. Michael and J. Christine eds., Markets in developing countries: Parallel, fragmented, and black (ICS Press, San Francisco), 89-109.

Nihon Keizai Shimbun, Oushu – Yuragu seijuku shakai (in Japanese), 27 February 2004.

North, D. S. and M. F. Houstoun, 1976, The characteristics and role of illegal aliens in the US labor market: An exploratory study (Linton and Co., Washington, D.C.).

OECD, 1997, Economic survey of the United States 1997, Paris, France.

Ohta, H. and C. Yoshida, 1995, International migration, profit-sharing and national welfare, Discussion Paper no. 439 (University of Essex, Essex).

O'Meara, K. P., Breaking the law makes you legal, Insight on the News, November 29, 1999.

Oswald, A. J., 1979, Wage determination in an economy with many trade unions, Oxford Economic Papers 31, 369-385.

Oswald, A. J., 1985, The economic theory of trade unions: An introductory survey, Scandinavian Journal of Economics 87, 160-193.

Palmer, R. W., 1995, Pilgrims from the sun: West Indian migration to America (Twayne Publishers, New York).

Papademetriou, D. G., B. Lindsay Lowell and D. A. Cobb Clark, 1991, Employer sanctions: Expectations and early outcomes, in M. Fix ed., The paper curtain: Employer sanction's implementation, impact, and reform (The Urban Institute Press, Washington, D.C.), 215-237.

Passel, J. S., 1986, Undocumented immigration, The Annals of the American Academy 487, 181-200.

Pearce, J. E. and J. W. Gunther, 1985, Illegal immigration from Mexico: Effects on the Texas economy, Economic Review/ Federal Reserve Bank of Dallas, 1-14.

Perlmutter, T., 1996, Bringing parties back in: Comments on 'Modes of immigration politics in liberal democratic societies', International Migration Review 30, No. 1.

Phillips, J. A. and D. S. Massey, 1999, The new labor market: Immigrants and wages after IRCA, Demography 36, No. 2, 233-246.

Piore, M. J., 1986, Can international migration be controlled?, in S. Pozo, ed., Essays on legal and illegal immigration (W. E. Upjohn Institute for Employment Research, Kalamazoo, Michigan), 21-42.

Pohjola, M., 1987, Profit-sharing, collective bargaining and employment, Journal of Institutional and Theoretical Economics 143, 334-342.

Portes, A., 1987, Illegal immigration and the international system, lessons from recent legal Mexican immigrants to the United States, in S. W. Menard and E. W. Moen, eds., Perspectives on population: An introduction to concepts and issues (Oxford University Press, New York; Oxford; Toronto and Melbourne), 300-311.

Quirk, J. and R. Saposnik, 1968, Introduction to general equilibrium theory and welfare economics (Mcgraw-Hill, New-York).

Ramaswami, V. K., 1968, International factor movement and the national advantage, Economica 55, 151-167.

Razin, A. and E. Sadka, 1995, Population economics (The MIT Press, Cambridge, Massachusetts), 215-232.

Razin, A. and E. Sadka, 1999, Migration and pension with international capital mobility, Journal of Public Economics 74, 141-150.

Robert, S., 1996, Watching America's door: The immigration backlash and the new policy debate (Twentieth Century Fund Press, New York).

Robinson, J. G., 1980, Estimating the approximate size of the illegal alien population in the United States by the comparative trend analysis of age-specific death rates, Demography 17, 159-176.

Sain, G. E., P. Martin and Q. Paris, 1983, A regional analysis of illegal aliens, Growth and Change 14, 27-31.

Salgado, S., 1998, The border, Rolling Stone 776/777, 129-137.

Sato, R. and T. Koizumi, 1973, On the elasticities of substitution and complementarity, Oxford Economic Papers 25, 44-56.

Schuck, P. H., 1995, The message of 187: Facing up to illegal immigration, American Prospect, No. 21, 85-92.

Sehgal, E. and J. Vialet, 1980, Documenting the undocumented: data, like aliens, are elusive, Monthly Labor Review 103, 18-21.

Simon, J. L. and S. Moore, 1984, The effect of immigration upon unemployment: An across city estimation, unpublished manuscript.

Simpson, A., Would employer sanctions stem the illegal tide?, Denver Post, 8 March, 1998.

Smith, B. and R. Newman, 1977, Depressed wages along the US-Mexico border: An empirical analysis, Economic Inquiry 15, 51-56.

Sørensen, J. R., 1992, Profit-sharing in a unionized Cournot duopoly, Journal of Economics 55, 1992.

Sorensen, E., F. D. Bean, L. Ku and W. Zimmerman, 1992, Immigrant categories and the US job market – Do they make a difference? (The Urban Institute Press, Washington, D.C.).

Staring, R., 2000, International migration, undocumented immigrants and immigrant entrepreneurship, in J. Rath ed., Immigrant business – The economic, political and social environment (Macmillan Press Ltd, Great Britain).

Steineck, A., 1995, Der europäische schwarzmarkt für zuwanderer: Effektivität und effizienz von kontrollinstrumenten, Aussenwirtschaft 50, 571-592.

Stewart, G., 1989, Profit-sharing in Cournot oligopoly, Economics Letters 31, 221-224.

Stewart, J. B. and T. J. Hyclak, 1986, The effects of immigrants, women, and teenagers on the relative earnings of black males, The Review of Black Political Economy 15, 93-102.

Sydney Morning Herald, Migrants: Britain seeks refuge in Albania, 10 March, 2003.

Takayama, A., 1985, Mathematical Economics, 2nd ed., (Cambridge University Press, New York).

The Economist, Melting, 24 August, 1996.

The Economist, Europe: Modest rule, 14 August, 1999.

Thelen, D., 1999, Mexico, the Latin North American Nation: Conversation with Carlos Rico Ferrat, Journal of American History 86, No. 2, 467-480.

The Ministry of Welfare, 1993, Kokusai jinko ido no jittai (in Japanese) (Toyo-Keizai Shinpo Sha, Tokyo).

Todaro, M. P., 1969, A model of labor migration and urban unemployment in the less developed countries, American Economic Review 59, 138-148.

Todaro, M. P. and L. Maruszko, 1987, Illegal migration and US Immigration Reform: A conceptual framework, Population and Development Review 13, 101-114.

Torok, S. J. and W. E. Huffman, 1986, US- Mexican trade in winter vegetables and illegal immigration, American Journal of Agricultural Economics 68, 246-60.

US Department of Homeland Security, 2003, Yearbook of immigration statistics, 2002 (US Government Printing Office, Washington, D.C.). (http://uscis.gov/graphics/index.htm).

US Congress. House Committee on the Judiciary, 1986, The Immigration Reform and Control Act of 1986: A Summary and Explanation, 99th Congress, 2d sess (Government Printing Office, Washington).

US House of Representatives. Department of Commerce, Justice, and State, the judiciary, and related agencies appropriations for 1985-1995: Hearings before a subcommittee of the Committee on appropriations. Various years.

US Immigration and Naturalization Service, 1991, Statistical yearbook of the Immigration and Naturalization Service (US Government Printing Office, Washington, D.C.).

US Immigration and Naturalization Service, 1992, Immigration Reform and Control Act: Report on the legalized alien population, No. M-275 (Department of Justice, Washington, D.C.).

US Immigration and Naturalization Service, 1997, Statistical yearbook of the Immigration and Naturalization Service: 1996, November. (US Government Printing Office, Washington, D.C.).

US Office of Management and Budget, 1993, The budget for fiscal year 1993, Appendix one for the Immigration and Naturalization Service, Washington, D.C.

Van Arsdol, M., J. W. Moore, D. Heer and S. P. Haynie, 1979, Non-apprehended and apprehended undocumented residents in the Los Angeles labor market: An exploratory study, Population Research Lab, University of Southern California.

Venturini, A., 1999, Do immigrants working illegally reduce the natives' legal employment? Evidence from Italy, Journal of Population Economics 12, 135-154.

Vianna, P., Restricted entry, The Unesco Courier, Oct 1996.

Wachter, M. L., 1980, The labor market and illegal immigration: The outlook for the 1980s, Industrial and Labor Relations Review 33, 342-354.

Wadhwani, S., 1988, Profit-sharing as a cure for unemployment: Some doubts, International Journal of Industrial Organization 6, 59-68.

Warren, Y., 1994, Personal communication, US Immigration and Naturalization Service, Statistics Division 9.

Warren, R. and J. S. Passel, 1987, A count of the uncountable: Estimates of undocumented aliens counted in the 1980 United States census, Demography 24, 375-393.

Weiss, L., 1987, Explaining the underground economy: State and social structure, The British Journal of Sociology 38, 216-233.

Weitzman, M. L., 1983, Some macroeconomic implications of alternative compensation systems, Economic Journal 93, 763-783.

Weitzman, M. L., 1985, The simple macroeconomics of profit-sharing, American Economic Review 75, 937-953.

Weitzman, M. L., 1987, Steady state unemployment under profit-sharing, Economic Journal 97, 86-105.

White, M. J., F. D. Bean and T. J. Espenshade, 1990, The US 1986 Immigration Reform and Control Act and undocumented migration to the United States, Population Research and Policy Review 9, 93-116.

Winegarden, C. R. and L. B. Khor, 1991, Undocumented immigration and unemployment of US youth and minority workers: Econometric evidence, The Review of Economics and Statistics 73, 105-112.

Winegarden, C. R. and L. B. Khor, 1993, Undocumented immigration and income inequality in the native-born population of the US: econometric evidence, Applied Economics 25, 157-163.

Wong, Kar-Yiu, 1995, International Trade in Goods and Factor Mobility (The MIT press, Cambridge, MA).

Woodrow, K. A., 1990, Using census and survey data to measure undocumented immigration and emigration for the United States, Statistical Journal of the United Nations ECE 7, 241-251.

Woodrow, K. A., 1992, A consideration of the effect of immigration reform on the number of undocumented residents in the United States, Population Research and Policy Review 11, 117-144.

Woodrow, K. A. and J. S. Passel, 1990, Post-IRCA undocumented immigration to the United States: An assessment based on the June 1988 CPS, in F. D. Bean, B. Edmonston and J. S. Passel eds., Undocumented migration to the United States: IRCA and the experience of the 1980s (The Urban Institute Press, Washington, D.C.), 33-75.

Yanaihara, K. and T. Yamagata, 1992, International labour migration in Asia (in Japanese) (The Institute of Developing Economies, Tokyo).

Yoshida, C., 1993, The global welfare of illegal immigration: A note, Indian Economic Review 28, 111-115.

Yoshida, C. and H. Ohta, 1994, Unemployment, international migration and profit-sharing, Discussion Paper no. I-22 (Okayama University, Okayama, Japan).

Yoshida, C., 1996, The global welfare of illegal immigration in the presence of capital mobility, Journal of Economic Integration 11, 554-565.

Yoshida, C., 1998, The effects of border patrol on illegal Immigration, Seoul Journal of Economics 11, No. 1, 61-74.

Yoshida, C., 1999, The optimal enforcement of immigration law, in Demetri, Kantarelis ed., 'Business & Economics for the 21st Century – Volume III', ISBN #: 0-9659831-2-9, Library of Congress Catalog Card #: 99-097613, Worcester, MA, USA, 481-492.

Yoshida, C., 2000a, Can a profit-sharing scheme remedy large scale unemployment in a less developed country?, Indian Journal of Applied Economics 8, 161-172.

Yoshida, C., 2000b, Illegal immigration and economic welfare (Physica-Verlag, Heidelberg and New York).

Yoshida, C., 2004, The optimal enforcement of a finance-constrained immigration law, Open Economies Review 15, No. 1, 57-62.

Zhan, E. S., Navigating regional trade agreements, World Trade, September 1999.

Index